Democratising Development

Nijhoff Law Specials

Volume 64

The titles published in this series are listed at the end of this volume.

Democratising Development

The Politics of Socio-Economic Rights in South Africa

Edited by
Peris Jones and Kristian Stokke

MARTINUS NIJHOFF PUBLISHERS
LEIDEN • BOSTON

A C.I.P. Catalogue record for this book is available from the Library of Congress.

Printed on acid-free paper.

ISBN 90 04 14821 3

Koninklijke Brill NV incorporates the imprints Brill Academic Publishers, Martinus Nijhoff Publishers and VSP.

http://www.brill.nl

Typeset by *jules guldenmund layout & text*, The Hague.

Printed and bound in The Netherlands.

Table of Contents

Preface

This book originated as a conference in June 2004 entitled "The Politics of Socio-Economic Rights in South Africa", co-arranged by the South Africa Programme at the Norwegian Centre for Human Rights and the Network on Local Politics in Developing Countries (LPD), both at the University of Oslo. Many of the presenters are, in one way or another, collaborating partners of the South Africa Programme. The Programme would like to extend its gratitude to the Norwegian Agency for Development Co-operation for funding the Programme, especially concerning the fruitful collaboration with the Royal Norwegian Embassy in Pretoria. Other participants are from existing research collaboration projects between Norwegian and South African researchers. The latter and the LPD network itself were made possible by the Norwegian Research Council funding, which is warmly acknowledged.

In addition to the contributors to the book, the conference also benefited from the participation of the following: Charlotte McClain, Sibonile Khoza, Tor Arve Benjaminsen and Einar Braathen. Furthermore, Lalaine Stormorken and David Christoffer Lier provided indispensable logistical support to the conference. We thank you all.

Concerning the production of the book we would like to thank Jules Guldenmund, and at Martinus Nijhoff Publishers, Lindy Melman. The valuable input of Sophie Oldfield, Jonathan Klaaren and other colleagues in South Africa is also acknowledged.

The chapter by Albie Sachs is based on "The Judicial Enforcement of Socio-Economic Rights: The Grootboom Case", in *Current Legal Problems* 2003, Volume 56 pp. 579-601, Oxford University Press. Adam Habib's chapter was first published as "The Politics of Economic Policy-making", *Transformation,* no. 56. We are very grateful to the publishers for permission to reproduce these articles.

Peris Jones and Kristian Stokke.

1. Introduction
Democratising Development: The Politics of Socio-Economic Rights

Peris Jones and Kristian Stokke

Human rights discourse increasingly enframes contemporary approaches to development. Previously, "human rights" and "development" lay as if two distinct islands in mutually unchartered waters. Socio-economic issues comprised a vast channel that put great distance between human rights and development. Only vaguely registering on the other's radar, each "community" lacked the intrepidness required to explore unknown territory. In recent years, however, wherever we turn in development policy, be it at the level of United Nations agencies, bi-lateral donor agendas, international non-governmental organisations, and even state-civil society relations, the situation is changing. Even if they are not exactly integrated fields, then at least bridge-building between these "islands" appears to flourish. The "turn" to human rights and its deployment in the cause of development gives effect to a range of profound discursive, legal and institutional shifts, especially in regard to socio-economic rights. For the best part of half a century, and with only a handful of exceptions, the human rights "community" has ignored socio-economic rights.[1] One of the major outcomes of the growing dialogue therefore has been to place socio-economic rights firmly on both human rights and international development agendas.

Against this background, our point of departure is two-fold. First, we take a starting position in the debates on human rights that accepts that socio-economic rights are as legally and normatively valid as civil and political rights. Second, although socio-economic rights are there-

1 Uvin (2004) makes the observation, for example, that no major human rights watchdog organisations exist for Economic, Social and Cultural Rights. In recent years, however, there is a detectable gravitation in the advocacy and monitoring work of international human rights organisations towards socio-economic rights.

Peris Jones and Kristian Stokke (eds.), Democratising Development, *ISBN 90 04 14821 3, pp. 1-38.*

fore justiciable[2] and integral to a more holistic conception of human dignity, we also recognise that the fulfilment of these rights encounters political obstacles. The development process is prone to contradictory tendencies towards depoliticisation and politicisation. We believe that the former characterises much of the current international and national development agenda. If we are to undo this political deficit in development policy into which so many concepts such as "participation", "empowerment", "pro-poor" and, now, "rights-based development" fall and lose their radical edge, then we need to encourage a democratic politics of rights. This is the key concern in this introductory chapter and the book as a whole: the prospects and means of democratising development through a democratic politics of socio-economic rights.

State obligations to respect, protect and promote socio-economic rights are not only concerned with constitutional, legal and institutional frameworks, as important as these can be "for, at the very least, holding government accountable to constitutional commitments imposed upon it" (Davis 2004:6). What also appears to be critical is that upholding state obligations requires that citizens, and their organisational representatives, be considered legitimate participants and active agents in the process. In essence, the real potential lies in the way in which human rights interrogates, and consequently alters, the relationship between citizens and government.

The point, as we shall see in the various chapters, is not only that formal rights are guaranteed and institutionalised in South Africa but that a politics of acquiring and transforming such rights is enabled. The missing link for this transformative potential for human rights in development is not so much about asserting legal claims, again, as catalytic as they sometimes can be. Rather, it lies in "political struggles, in which human rights are tools that crystallize the moral imagination and provide power in the political struggles, but do not substitute for either." (Uvin 2004:176). Understanding the transformative potential for human rights in this way provides greater nuance to readings of rights-based approaches to development by foregrounding local and national struggles and power dynamics. It also has the potential to substitute the formalised and technocratic approach characterised by minimalist institutional and judicial reform in current donor driven understandings of rights-based development. Instead there is potential for a more dynamic approach that also "at the end of the day forces donors to modify their own struc-

2 That is, these rights can be invoked in a court of law.

tures, attitudes, behaviours, and incentive systems" (Uvin 2004:178).

In this chapter we continue by providing an overview of the meaning and position of human rights in international discourses on development. We place emphasis on the concept of rights-based development (RBD) because it represents a particularly prominent intersection between human rights and development discourse, not least in its potential for greater political accountability in development. This is then followed by a conceptual discussion of the significance of the relationship between democracy and socio-economic rights, before a general introduction to the post-apartheid politics of socio-economic rights in South Africa and the contributions to the book that follow.

1. "Placing" Human Rights in Development

After decades of splendid isolation, it is seemingly necessary to explore why there have been increasing bridge-building exercises between the human rights and development "communities" in recent years. Not least because addressing this issue also reveals the significant evolution that has taken place in thinking and practice not just between human rights and development actors but also within their respective "communities". A starting point is to chart the contours of the separation in thought and practice of both our "islands".

Whereas the Preamble to the International Covenant on Economic, Social and Cultural Rights (see in UN CESCR 2000), also following the Universal Declaration of Human Rights, accords socio-economic rights equal consideration to civil and political rights, it is undeniable that a bias has existed towards championing civil and political freedoms. The outcome has been to construct a "liberal consensus" which relegates socio-economic rights to the status of mere "aspirations" (Evans 2002). The emphasis upon civil and political rights therefore served to alienate many developmentalists concerned with material improvement, especially economic growth, associated with the project of development. The distinction between so-called "first" generation civil and political rights and "second" generation socio-economic rights is often attributed to issues of resource availability and the need to avoid interference in government decision-making over policy and budgetary allocation. To simplify, the first generation were often regarded as somehow "cheaper" to implement and also less problematic legally because states are obliged to *refrain* from actions that violate civil and political rights. Alternatively, socio-economic rights require positive actions and, hence, resources, in order to fulfil and promote these rights. Whilst we reject this dichotomy in rights as false, and, indeed, a range of human rights declarations foreground the interdependence of both sets of rights, first generation rights nonetheless became the standard bearer of international human rights.

The Cold War era served to ice over these distinctions and solidified them. Whereas "civil" and "political" freedoms were the domain of human rights, "development" focused upon its post-World War Two mission to eradicate poverty, principally through industrialisation and economic growth. A recipient regime's promotion of capitalist development often took greater precedence in determining development aid allocations and preferential treatment by donors, than whether it actually respected civil and political rights. An important historical opportunity to fuse the material concerns of development with the democratic content of political and civil rights was lost, with, we would maintain, detrimental effects for both.

When we historicise human rights, a potent reminder of the powerful role played by the geopolitical location of the different ideas and actors in influencing the human rights and development agendas is evident (Cornwall and Nyamu-Musembi, 2004). We can see at least two key examples wherein struggles in the global South challenged prevailing (Western) understanding and codification of human rights discourse. First, struggles for social justice against oppression that so defined the African anti-colonial liberation movements provided an important corrective to prevailing understandings of human rights:

> The concept of rights was not something that was 'God-given' in its universality, but forged in the fires of anti-imperialist struggles. It was informed by the need to overthrow all forms (not just colonial) of oppression and exploitation, not by constructs that had either been embodied in the UDHR or imported into Africa by those nationalist leaders who had spent periods in exile or study in the imperial homeland. (Manji 1998, no page number).

It was this popular spirit of struggle for social justice that rapidly became dissipated and eclipsed by the prevailing discourse of development and politics of the post-colonial state in post-liberation Africa. This same spirit of struggle also imbued the liberation of South Africa, and, arguably, similarly threatens to be superseded unless a democratic politics of socio-economic rights can be entrenched.

Second, by the 1970s, actors from the global South again sought to give additional meaning and content to the human rights discourse. The focus was the disenchantment with the New International Economic Order (NIEO). The NIEO was associated with the perception held by many countries in the South that benefits were unequally skewed towards the West. One early attempt to link the human rights and development agendas was found in efforts to realign the meaning of development as something other than economic growth and global inequality. In 1986, even before the end of the Cold War, the UN Declaration on the Right to Development, Article, 1, 1 (Office of UN Commissioner for Human Rights, 1986) proclaimed that this right was an "inalienable human right by virtue of which every person and all peoples are entitled to participate in, contribute to, and enjoy economic, social, cultural and political development". Proponents of the "right to development" projected a human rights preoccupation with dignity and justice upon the inequalities of global development as a means towards achieving a fairer development process. Rather than offering a theoretical approach to a process of change, a "right to development" implies everyone has a right to a process of change which is compatible with the human rights norms listed in international human rights treaties. For all its rhetoric, Marks (2003:15) suggests that "[I]t is unfortunate indeed that after 30 years of scholarly writing and diplomatic efforts to understand the right to development, and 15 years after the Declaration was adopted, the debate remains polarised and confused". We might ask, why? There was certainly legal ambiguity. But we could also inquire as to whether Western countries perhaps used this ambiguity as a smokescreen to obscure political implications. Article 3, 3, for example, includes "States have the duty to co-operate with each other in ensuring development and eliminating obstacles to development. States should realize their rights and fulfil their duties in such a manner as to promote a new international economic order based on sovereign equality, interdependence, mutual interest and co-operation among all States, as well as to encourage the observance and realization of human rights". The emphasis upon global inequity and commensurate donor obligations was probably much too political for Western states. This would explain why bilateral donors tend to avoid reference to the Right to Development in contemporary debates.[3]

3 According to Cornwall and Nyamu-Musembi (2004), proponents of a rights-based approach within the United Kingdom's Department of International Development, for example, were actually advised by their Foreign Office to exclude reference to the Right to Development.

Nonetheless, proponents did contribute to foregrounding human rights within the development process through the principle that all human rights must be respected in development planning and implementation (Marks 2003:15). By implication, proponents of the right to development also contributed to inserting socio-economic rights more prominently into the landscape of human rights itself. By advocating along the lines that the well-being of an entire population can only be improved through "the expansion of opportunities and capabilities to enjoy those opportunities" (Sengupta 2000:566), a significant opening was created for humans rights and development to overlap. However, the era of IMF and World Bank initiated Structural Adjustment Programmes (SAPs), for Sub-Saharan Africa in particular, led to erosion of the kind of social and health infrastructure required in creating and enjoying the "opportunities" so conducive to greater well-being.

At the time that criticism against the SAPs heightened, the Cold War was also coming to an end. The apparent collapse of a viable ideological alternative to liberal capitalist development also led to the upsurge of interest by development donors in promoting the "victorious" model of liberal democracy within the developing world. Criticism of SAPs, not least from economists within those multilateral institutions associated with the SAPs who sought explanations for why they had not been as effective as anticipated, overlapped with the triumphalist mood of Western donors to find common focus in the promotion of "good governance" in development cooperation. Although in its narrowest guise concerned with minimalist institutional reform, the rule of law and multi-party elections, the good governance agenda and the associated use of political conditionality was at least extremely influential in reinserting the role of democratisation in the development process. Development aid and preferential trade agreements were linked to the burgeoning agenda of encouraging recipient political and administrative reform. Donors would decrease, or, even cease, development aid to a recipient if it perceived human rights abuses had taken place, or, that democratisation was being openly opposed by the regime. There is not the space here to detail the problematic nature of this agenda, especially in terms of its dubious ethics, double standards, and doubts over its effectiveness (Lumina 2004).

In view of the problems with the donor imposed agenda there was a shift to a more incentive-oriented promotion rather than punitive model of good governance. Human rights also entered development therefore through so-called "positive conditionality". Specific targeted funds were provided for administrative reforms and projects promoting the rule of law in particular, such as training for judges, legal reforms, police training, Human Rights Commissions and so on. Furthermore, more and more development aid was being delivered directly as budget support to recipient governments. As a result, donors are promoting the rights-based discourse possibly as a means to encourage accountability over the way this money is spent (Cornwall and Nyamu-Musembi 2004). But whilst development was increasingly associated with human rights and democracy, there was nonetheless a continuing absence of social and economic rights on the good governance agenda, which even downgraded the significance of these rights (Sano and Alfredsson 2002). In view of the deepening poverty globally and growing discontent directed at the model of development promoted by the IMF and the World Bank (Stiglitz 2002),[4] these institutions and bilateral development agencies (DFID 1997, 2000; Norad 2002) embraced the discursive shift towards "poverty" and "participation". These shifts were not necessarily benevolent but rather related to the important political pressure generated by NGO lobbying and activism. These NGOs had been influential in promoting social and economic justice at the World Social Development Summit in Copenhagen in 1995. Furthermore, the Vienna Conference on Human Rights in 1993 declared the interdependence of human rights and helped to demarcate something of a sea change in relations between "human rights" and "development".

One tangible outcome of these shifts was multi-lateral agency promotion of the Poverty Reduction Strategy Papers (PRSP), which combined a focus upon both poverty and a new participatory-oriented discourse. The PRSPs became the new template for future assistance and negotiations over the Heavily Indebted Poor Countries debt relief initiative. The World Development Report for 2006 continues to locate concerns over "equity" in development and human rights further into the World Bank's historical mission to promote capitalist economic growth. Whilst significant differences undoubtedly continue to separate the Bretton Woods institutions from the UN agencies, there is apparent convergence around and reorientation towards placing human rights more centrally within the development process. It is perhaps Amartya

4 In discussing the policies associated with the so-called Washington Consensus of the IMF and World Bank, Stiglitz (2002:20) suggests that '[I]n many cases commercial interests and values have superseded concern for the environment, democracy, human rights and social justice'.

Sen's analysis, which contributed to the UNDP Human Development Report 2000, that best captures the contemporary *leitmotif* of international development in its convergence, rapprochement, even, between neo-liberal economics and rights-inspired institutional architecture:

> What is needed is not a rejection of the positive role of the market mechanism in generating income and wealth, but the important recognition that the market mechanism has to work in a world of many institutions. We need the power and the protection of these institutions, provided by democratic practice, civil and human rights, a free and open media, facilities for basic education and health care, economic safety nets, and of course, provisions for women's freedom and rights. ... The real debate associated with globalisation is, ultimately, not about the efficiency of markets, nor about the importance of modern technology. The debate, rather, is about inequality of power, for which there is much less tolerance now than in the world that emerged at the end of the Second World War. (Sen 2000)

No longer regarded as the outcome of development but rather as the critical means to achieving it (UNDP 2000), human rights march ever deeper into the development terrain. The outcome is an elevated focus upon political, economic, social and cultural rights understood as "claims to a set of social arrangements – norms, institutions, laws, an enabling economic environment – that can best secure the enjoyment of these rights" (UNDP 2000:73). The UNDP report (UNDP 2000:73) goes on to say that "[i]t is thus the obligation of governments and others to implement policies to put these arrangements in place". Reciprocally, the human rights treaty bodies of the UN, such as the UN Committee on Economic, Social and Cultural Rights, and the United Nations Office of the High Commissioner for Human Rights, have taken an increasing interest in the PRSP process, and in regarding poverty as inhibiting the enjoyment of human rights (see Nowak 2005 for an overview).

This brief summary of how bridge-building evolved also says as much about how each "community" has sought to respond to intellectual and political critique and challenge. It should therefore perhaps be expected that there will be different gradations of integration and commitment to a human rights based approach to development. Uvin (2004) evokes this as the uneven movement of actors along a spectrum encompassing the human rights approach to development. At one end of the spectrum are the rhetorical positions of some development cooperation actors, still unconvinced, yet, dedicated followers of fashion who cloak their work in the guise of "human rights". Then there are intermediate positions, as discussed above, where human rights are introduced into development via the donor driven, good governance agenda. At the other end of Uvin's spectrum, however, is a more integrated and committed relationship termed the "human rights-based approach to development" (RBD).

2. Rights-based Development

Characterised as iterative and evolutionary, RBD draws on and learns from a broad range of intellectual ideas and policy frameworks (for some of the overlaps and differences with other related approaches, see Marks 2003; Mohan and Holland 2001). It is, however, not merely an add-on to development but rather a fundamental shift in values:

> [T]he rights-based approach to development changes the nature of the game not because it edicts rights as fixed properties or legal certainties or because it somehow leads us to discover brand-new actions or services we would never have thought of beforehand. Rather, there are two basic ways in which the rights-based approach to development differs from its predecessors, and they permeate all we do when we "do" development. First, an RBA creates claims and not charity (the *end* of development aid differs, and consequently the whole process of thinking about it, of defining the nature of the problem, changes as well - a new vision emerges). Second, an RBA affects the way development actions are implemented (the *means*, the processes, are different, even if many goals remain the same. (Uvin 2004:129)

"A rights-based approach to development", according to Frankovits (2005:4-5), "integrates the norms, standards and principles of the international human rights framework into the plans, policies and processes of development." The approach therefore impacts on national planning priorities by having the ability to redirect resources and to militate against policies that undermine the realisation of economic, social and cultural rights. RBD therefore has unavoidable consequences for development processes. An integral feature of RBD, therefore, is that it provides a cohesive, or, "interdependent" in human rights parlance, normative and legal framework derived from internationally negotiated norms and legal standards (Andreassen 2003). As the main duty-holder, these standards are binding on states and enable scrutiny of state obligations to respect, protect and fulfil each right. Rights-based approaches utilise the principles embodied through the "right to development" as a "complementary perspective that offers a grid of development norms and goals" (Andreassen 2003:32). The difference between the two might be better understood as relating to the scale of implementation. Whilst the right to development does not preclude national implementation, which is more closely related to RBD, it is more preoccupied with the development process per se, and international development co-operation (Marks 2003). The implication, nonetheless, is that rights are indicators of change, standards for planning and assessment that development actors can use to establish clear objectives, ensure meaningful participation and set appropriate benchmarks and indicators (Frankovits 2003; Andreassen 2003).

There are considerable implications of the growing emphasis upon social, economic and cultural rights – such as the right to work, health, education, and so on, for legitimising human rights approaches in policy dialogues (Frankovits 2003; and see Jones 2003). RBD is particularly relevant when addressing a specific sectoral issue. Talking about health, for example, Yamin succinctly captures some of the key elements of RBD and the implications for state duties:

> [A]sserting a right to health means that not only has a government moral or humanitarian responsibilities to attend to the health needs of the most vulnerable and economically disenfranchised of the population, but it also has legal obligations that, at minimum, require it to establish a normative framework consistent with international law, to reflect health as a priority in its budget, and to devise a plan to take deliberate steps to move toward the progressive realization of the right to health. (Yamin 2002:38-39)

A human rights perspective therefore provides normative and legal protection to vulnerable groups in particular, which is further reflected in the principles of "minimum core" and "adequate realisation". Here, in view of resource constraints placed particularly upon poorer countries, we are concerned with the steps that states take toward the progressive realisation of the right in question to the "maximum available extent of its resources". Minimum core obligations, are regardless of resources "to ensure the satisfaction of, at the very least, minimum essential levels of each of the rights" (UN CESCR 2000). The approach therefore embraces those most in need as it identifies those whose rights are most denied. The empowerment of the neediest based on the recognition of state obligations supposedly results in increased participation and, hence, ownership and sustainability. According to Frankovits (2003), RBD should support governments to ensure that they satisfy their minimum obligations relating to each right in the International Bill of Rights; plan strategies and programmes for the eventual fulfilment of all their obligations; monitor both the fulfilment and the obstacles to the fulfilment of these obligations over time. RBD therefore asks politicised questions of legal and policy reforms wherein these rights can be enjoyed.

Due to its emergence within a regime of international donor conditionality, caution is warranted concerning RBD's "state-centrism" at a time of rampant ideologically driven neo-liberalism which is undermining state capacity in Sub-Saharan Africa (Stokke 2005; Manzo 2003; Mohan and Holland 2001). Elsewhere, more generally, the failure to extend "rights" is compounded by, and in turn compounds, the crisis of legitimacy that many states face. The fragile nature of democratic transition in many African countries encounters additional challenges of pronounced economic exclusion and with this also "the shifting alliances characteristic of the post-Cold War world, the fluidity of global capitalism, and the pressures from donors for privatisation, 'good governance' and the opening of economies" (Barnett and Whiteside 2002:296). Mohan and Holland (2001:178-179; and see Manzo 2003) therefore ask "whether the emerging human rights-based approach to development, honed in the period of revisionist neo-liberalism, can deliver meaningful improvements to the African crisis?" Furthermore, according to Cornwall and Nyamu-Musembi (2004:1433), "[P]erhaps it is the lack of clarity on corresponding duties [of donors themselves] that makes the corresponding language of rights in development less threatening to the governments of rich countries than the Right to Development?" Perhaps the rejoinder is that a more politicised application of RBD, in other words, that which shows up the root causes of the exclusion that leads to violation of rights, is conducive to "meaningful improvements to the African crisis". Inevitably, by implication, greater dialogue between human rights and economic globalisation is required, but, arguably, there are already nascent signs of concrete impact.[5]

5 We are thinking here, for example, about the role of an activist driven rights-based discourse in debates concerning intellectual property rights and the pricing of medication for HIV/AIDS, in particular (see Heywood 2002).

In terms of implementing RBD the obstacles to entrenching human rights legislation internationally and in national political and judicial structures in Africa, for example, are considerable and systemic. A key tension in rights debates in an African context concerns whether political rights or socio-economic rights should be prioritised and what the appropriate political arrangements should be to implement them. Not least, the discrepancy between the failure of many African states to protect social, economic and cultural rights, for whatever reasons, as well as being perpetrators of human rights abuses, at the same time as they are also considered in international law as the defenders and implementers of "rights", therefore casts doubt on the role of the African state and constitutionalism to deliver rights (An Na'im, in Mohan and Holland 2001). However, in reply to these difficulties posed concerning implementation, we should point out that a rights-based approach is anchored within claims, rather than charity. Because of this RBD is inherently also about mechanisms of accountability directed at those violating claims. At times, judicial reform and legal mechanisms will be suitable remedies. At others, more traditional human rights tactics of the confrontational "naming and shaming" approach towards states not conforming to these normative principles may be more appropriate. However, such strategies should go beyond a legal approach and should also work on many non-legal, social and political paths for ensuring enforcement of rights claims. Uvin (2004:176), for example, mentions some of these as the dissemination and internalisation of new social norms, the mobilisation of grassroots and citizen power in favour of certain rights, and the creation of ombudsmen, whistle blowers and other administrative complaint mechanisms. All these approaches contribute to a climate of accountability, not only of states, but, arguably, all development actors.

There is also the need for the cultural norms, symbols and traditions of non-Western societies to enter into international human rights discourses unless these continue to be seen in the "Third World" as "invasive of sovereignty, a result of imbalances of power and ethnocentric" (Penna and Campbell 1998:7). Whilst it is of course recognised that sensitivity to cultural context is required, and that the local and universal should be considered simultaneously, that said, the often difficult intersection of human rights with customary law, for example, should not at the same time legitimise traditions which violate fundamental human rights (female genital mutilation, for example, and also inheritance rights of women, and so on). Interestingly, some of these controversial issues have been deliberately avoided by development actors, whether in their apolitical donor-driven or more progressive guises. Again, the point here is that human rights approaches attempt to expose the discriminatory and exclusionary behaviours responsible for violating rights. It is an area of mutual benefit to both human rights and development. The latter often shies away from political controversy, whereas the former have a different approach in identifying violators of the right in question but may not be as connected "on the ground" as their developmental counterparts.

Another area of mutual benefit in overlap and intersection concerns "participation". RBD has great potential in conjoining two strands of "participation" hitherto generally kept apart. On the one hand, there is "community-based participation", regarded for a number of years by development practitioners as a vehicle for meeting the needs of local people more directly through their own involvement. Results have been uneven, in part due to the many different interpretations of "what" participation is and does, and "why" it is done (Cooke and Kothari 2001). Above all, from a rights-based perspective the issue of "who" does it and how to ensure participation of the weakest and most marginal in any society is a prime consideration. However, whether localised participation can alter inequality in communities is also unclear. The tremendous obstacles to "participation" include its own often-uncritical orthodox discourse, with similar dilemmas also associated with "empowerment" (for example, Mercer 2002). These topics are receiving critical reflection in contemporary development theory that should be of particular relevance in contrast to the rather rhetorical and unanalytical deployment of these same concepts in human rights circles. Reciprocally, progressive readings of RBD have the ability to provide a political channel to more formal political participation and engagement with the state by excluded individuals and groups, through social mobilisation and rights-based argumentation, such as non-discrimination, for example. Gender inequality is a case in point, with women encountering discriminatory exclusion from local decision-making structures governing access to services and resources. Rights-based approaches might therefore be a useful bridge between local participation and broader discourses of state and policy making, hence reconnecting citizens to state duties and obligations, and, as stated earlier, redefining and challenging state and citizen relations.

In summary, it is therefore suggested that RBD and its commensurate set of human rights principles and standards – or, "grid" – may, under certain conditions, offer a useful tool in strategic struggles over development processes. More progressive readings of RBD can potentially alter governance decision-making processes to enhance political space *between* citizens and the state. This influence is not least in manufacturing accountability of state and also non-state actors. Critically, and as the crux of RBD, shifting attention away from consideration of mere *de jure* rights towards actual fulfilment of these rights, *de facto*, surely involves a process of exercising and claiming rights. For RBD to be regarded as useful and relevant, arguably, then debates can and should be informed by considering actual political struggles over rights in specific contexts. Ultimately, whether RBD is merely new wine in old leaky "development" bottles, or holds out new and different possibilities to re-politicise development discourse and practices depends on our understanding of the relationship between human rights and democracy.

3. Democratic Politics of Socio-Economic Rights

What is the relationship between human rights and democracy? Beetham (1999) observes that the answer to this question depends on how we conceptualise democracy and whether we extend the conception of human rights beyond civil and political rights. While there is a growing attention to socio-economic rights and popular democratic participation, contemporary debates tend to revolve around narrow conceptions of both democracy (as a matter of liberal democratic institutions) and of human rights (as being identical to civil and political liberties).

The last three decades have seen a global expansion of liberal democracy that has been famously labelled as a "third wave of democratisation"[6] and celebrated as a global triumph of Western economic and

6 The 'third wave' refers to a series of democratic transitions in Southern Europe in the 1970s, in Latin America in the 1980s, in East and Central Europe and the former Soviet Union from the late 1980s, and in parts of Africa in the 1990s. This followed after a 'first wave' of democratic expansion in Western Europe, the United States and some British settler colonies (Canada, Australia and New Zealand) in the 19th and early 20th centuries, and a 'second wave' of democratisation after the Second World War in the defeated Axis powers (West Germany, Italy, Japan) and some former colonies up to the early 1960s. Each wave was followed by a reverse wave, when some countries turned to fascism in the period between the two world wars and when many African and Latin American countries returned to authoritarian forms of rule in the 1960s and 70s.

political liberalism (Huntington 1991). Less triumphalist scholars have problematised the dynamics and substance of these new democracies, describing them as elitist and formal rather than popular and substantive, thereby questioning their political and socio-economic relevance to ordinary people (Grugel 2002).

The transitions of the "third wave" and the associated academic discourses have revolved around the formal rules, procedures and institutions of liberal democracy, most notably the repeated conduct of relatively free and fair elections with competition between at least two political parties (Harriss, Stokke and Törnquist 2004; Whitehead 2002). Special emphasis is placed on negotiations and pacts within the political elite, and especially between reformers within an authoritarian regime and moderate dissidents. Democratic transitions are conceived in a narrow manner, excluding popular forces from the process of bringing about, consolidating and deepening democracy:

> Democracy is visualised as a set of procedures for government negotiated by and between political leaders. Thus the transition approach separates democracy from its essential meaning as rule by the people and conceptualizes it principally as the establishment of a set of governing institutions. (Grugel 2002:61)

Beetham (1999) describes this as a tendency to elevate a means to an end, to mistake institutional instruments with their democratic purpose. He proposes that democracy should be defined in terms of its core principles rather than through the institutions that uphold them:

> The core idea of democracy is that of popular rule or popular control over collective decision-making. Its starting point is with the citizen rather than with the institutions of government. Its defining principles are that all citizens are entitled to a say in public affairs, both through the associations of civil society and through participation in government, and that this entitlement should be available on terms of equality to all. Control *by* citizens over their collective affairs and equality *between* citizens in the exercise of that control are the basic democratic principles. (Beetham 1999:90-91, italics in original)

This means that a system of decision-making is democratic to the extent that it embodies the principles of popular control and political equality, and that institutions are democratic to the extent that they help realise these principles.

Beetham argues that the realisation of democracy is contingent on two general conditions: judicial and political guarantees for civil and political rights and institutional arrangements that promote popular control and political equality. Herein lies an answer to the question about the general relationship between democracy and human rights. Democracy and human rights have often been seen as separate phenomena, where democracy is conceived as the institutional arrangement of government, and human rights as a matter of individual freedoms. Beetham's position, however, means that the relationship between democracy and human rights (understood as civil and political rights) "is an intrinsic rather than extrinsic one; human rights constitute a necessary *part* of democracy" (Beetham 1999:92, italics in original). Without fundamental civil and political rights there can be no guarantee for popular control over government.

What about the relationship between socio-economic rights and democracy? Are socio-economic rights a requirement for democracy and is democracy a precondition for socio-economic rights? There are many concerned scholars who argue that democracy will remain a formality unless it also includes substantive social and economic equality. Törnquist rejects this position as one that is "closing our eyes to the possible importance of political democracy *in the promotion of* social and economic equality" (Törnquist 2004:201, italics in original). Democracy is severely compromised if the privileged can use wealth or status to purchase undue political influence or if the poor are so deprived that they are incapable of exercising their basic civil or political rights. However, civil and political equality does not require complete economic levelling.

This may be exemplified by South Africa's record of democratic elections in the post-apartheid period. Despite persistent problems of poverty and inequality, South Africa has successfully conducted repeated free and fair local and national elections. Likewise, it can be observed that consultation forums have been established to ensure that people can voice an opinion, even amidst severe resource deprivation and inequality. This means that the redistribution of political power has entailed a transformation of the political spaces for popular participation. The question then regards the prospect for utilising these political spaces to promote socio-economic rights.

Is democracy then a precondition for socio-economic rights? Diametrically opposed positions exist regarding the developmental outcomes of liberal democracy. On the one hand is the assumption that civil and political rights play an instrumental role in promoting socio-economic rights. This is most famously expressed by Sen (1994, 1999) in his argument that democratic institutions are guarantors for public deliberation and effective responses to poverty and deprivation. Radical critics, on the other hand, argue that democracy in capitalist societies is no more than a capitalist democracy in which public policy is subject to the economic and ideological influence of powerful economic interests. This means that the socio-economic rights for the many will be subordinated to the requirements of profitability for the few and that discourses on human rights are void of substance for ordinary people and may even serve to depoliticise popular forces. We subscribe to a more open-ended position, acknowledging that democracy introduces mechanisms of accountability through which government policies have to be publicly justified: "The systemic features of democracy – openness, accountability, the distribution of power – make it likely, therefore, that democratic governments will pay attention to the protection of economic and social rights" (Beetham 1999:107). This is not to say that liberal democracy will automatically lead to social justice. Rather, democracy (democratic institutions and civil/political rights) is a necessary but not sufficient condition for a democratic politics of socio-economic rights and a realisation of the right to development.

To return to the overall question about the relationship between human rights and democracy, it can now be concluded that these are intimately linked but also that there are important differences in how different "generations" of rights relate to democracy. Civil and political rights are, on the one hand, an integral part of democracy: "Democracy without them would be a contradiction in terms, since the absence of freedoms of speech, of association, of assembly, of movement, or of guaranteed security of the person and due process would make elections a façade and render any popular control over government impossible" (Beetham 1999:114). Socio-economic rights, on the other hand, are in a relation of mutual dependency with democracy: "The widespread absence of such rights compromises civil and political equality, the quality of public life and the long-term viability of democratic institutions themselves; democracy, on the other hand, constitutes a necessary if not sufficient condition for the protection of economic and social rights" (Beetham 1999:114). There is no guarantee that democracy will deliver development of a certain kind or extent, but democracy may provide vital means for asserting interests and rights in regard to development. Thus, it remains an important task to examine the politics of socio-economic rights within formal democracies, or in other words, the ways in which socio-economic rights are politicised and political representatives are held accountable to these rights.

How do we examine this democratic politics of socio-economic rights? One entry point is to recognise that real world democracies, as opposed to the normative ideal of liberal democracy, contain a complex mix of democratic and non-democratic institutions and practices. This coexistence of democratic spaces and deficits creates both opportunities and obstacles for democratic politics of socio-economic rights. Luckham, Goetz and Kaldor (2003) offer a useful analytical framework for disaggregated assessments of such real world democracies. Their approach is, first, based on a distinction between the deficits of formal democratic institutions and those emanating from the lack of democratic politics:

> In some cases democracy is diminished by the absence of one or another of its formal attributes, such as full political contestation or civil liberties. In others the formal attributes are in place but there is a lack of substantive democracy, due for instance to political corruption, clientelism or the absence of a culture of participation. (Luckham, Goertz and Kaldor 2003:22)

The democratic transitions of the "third wave" have often produced minimalist democratic institutions in coexistence with a combination of democratic and non-democratic politics. Collier and Levitsky (1997) describe these as "democracies with adjectives", referring to formally democratic regimes that in reality are more accurately described as illiberal, patrimonial, semi-authoritarian, low-intensity, guided or choiceless.

A second distinction is made between the different levels of government accountability where democracy deficits may appear. Government accountability is commonly understood as the mechanisms through which rulers are made to explain and justify public actions to those who are being ruled. While the term has been appropriated by diverse development actors for quite different purposes, its conceptual core revolves around notions of answerability and enforceability (Goetz and Jenkings 2001). Contemporary debates about accountability revolve around two analytically distinct mechanisms, commonly described as horizontal and vertical accountability (Newell and Bellour 2002). Horizontal accountability refers to ways in which different institutions within the state machinery control and check each other. These are first and foremost the balances of power between judiciary, executive and legislature branches of government. Modern democratic regimes also include a range of additional institutions, which are granted the task of ensuring economic accountability (e.g. auditor general, anti-corruption commissions), accountability to rights (e.g. human rights commissions, ombudsman,) and securing the integrity of the political institutions (e.g. electoral commissions, media boards, judicial councils) (Gloppen and Rakner 2005).

To be effective, horizontal accountability is contingent on vertical accountability, i.e. ways in which public officials and government practice are scrutinised and sanctioned by "the people". Government, first and foremost, rests on and may be held accountable to systems of citizens' rights and claims to citizenship. Beyond this foundation, the predominant mechanism of vertical accountability is free and fair elections in a competitive party system that allows people to select and sanction political representatives and thereby determine the composition of the legislature and the government. However, public officials may also be held more directly accountable to popular demands through public deliberations or through corporatist arrangements. While the systems of participatory budgeting in the Brazilian city of Porto Alegre and popular planning in the Indian state of Kerala are often mentioned as successful examples of democratic participation through public deliberation (Fung and Wright 2003), Scandinavian social democracies provide illustrative examples of political inclusion through corporatism.

These two distinctions, between democratic institutions and democratic politics and between different mechanisms of government accountability, provide a basis for assessing the quality of real-world democracy. Luckham, Goertz and Kaldor (2003) offer a set of general observations about the types and location of democracy deficits in real world democracies. These can be briefly summarised in three points.

First, at the level of citizenship, democracy has limited meaning if people cannot enjoy equal citizens' rights. This happens when the legal and constitutional arrangements fail to guarantee civil/political and social/economic rights. This can occur because rights are narrowly defined, citizenship is socially and ethnically exclusive or access to the legal system is systematically biased against minorities and those who are poor and unorganised. Democracy deficits at this level may also be of political rather than constitutional nature. This happens for instance when major social inequities based on class, gender, region, religion, ethnicity yield a systematic exclusion from the public sphere, when poor people are *de facto* disenfranchised due to lack of resources and organisation, or when cultures of intolerance yield an uncivil rather than a democratic society.

Second, at the level of vertical accountability, citizens may be unable to hold government and political delegates accountable due to formal procedural defects. For instance, if electoral systems distort outcomes or disenfranchise minorities, if the constitution and structures of governance are over-centralised, or if there is a lack of formal contact points between civil society and political/administrative structures, accountability is impaired. Beyond such formal structures, vertical accountability problems may also originate in politics, for instance when voters have little effective choice between alternative political programmes, when there is weak interest aggregation by political parties and especially in regard to the interests of the poor and marginalised or when there are few effective civil society associations.

Third, democracy deficits may also originate in weak mechanisms for horizontal accountability. This may be due to weak constitutional checks and balances on powerful executives *vis-à-vis* the legislature or judiciary. Absent or weak "watchdog" institutions to ensure accountability of the political institutions, weak or absent rule of law, or weak control of military, police and intelligence bodies are additional deficits. It may also originate in the field of politics if this is dominated by patrimonial practices whereby government is subordinated to narrow self-interest and patronage. Perhaps the judiciary is weak or co-opted, opposition parties are weak or there is a legacy of authoritarian governance.

Such democracy deficits limit the possibilities of a democratic politics of socio-economic rights. However, the formal arrangements and practical politics of real-world democracies also contain diverse spaces for democratic politics. Such spaces may originate in collective action that constitutes individuals as equal citizens. This may be manifested as class and social movements mobilising for the implementation of citizens' rights, but in the process also challenging and transforming the meaning of citizenship. Civil society is shaped by and may transform the opportunities offered by the public sphere. Thus, government accountability is structured by the formal arrangements of the democratic state, but also the way in which active citizens understand and make use of democratic political spaces (Harriss, Törnquist and Stokke 2004):

> Government accountability not only depends on the organisation of the public sphere itself – how far there is open government, whether power is decentralised, and so on. Even more, it depends on the ability of citizens to insist upon accountability when governments resist it. This is normally facilitated by factors such as the existence of civil society groups, organised and internally democratic political parties, and robust traditions of local democracy. (Luckham, Goetz and Kaldor 2003:28).

Finally, international human rights covenants, discourses and conditionality also frame spaces for democratic politics of rights (Jones 2004; Donnelly 1997). And, as we saw in the earlier section, rights-based development has at its core issues of accountability of duty-bearers in relation to citizens.

This brief discussion leads us to the conclusion that there are close but differentiated links between different "generations" of human rights and democracy. It also shows that democratic institutions and politics offer both obstacles and opportunities for socio-economic rights. The pursuit of development through democracy is framed by the complex coexistence of democratic and non-democratic institutions and politics. Few cases are better suited to illustrate the complexities and tensions of such democratic politics of socio-economic rights than post-apartheid South Africa.

4. The Politics of Socio-Economic Rights in South Africa

South Africa's political transition in the early 1990s has been widely celebrated as a "miracle" (Sparks 1995, 2003). Through the transition, the apartheid kind of 'democracy' based on the political exclusion of the majority on grounds of alleged racial differences, gave way to a post-apartheid inclusive liberal democracy based on the assumed equality of all citizens. What makes it especially miraculous, according to standard accounts, is that it happened in a relatively peaceful manner and that it had a transformative character (Alexander 2002). South Africa's transition to liberal democracy is, thus, seen as a social revolution by peaceful means with the popular masses being the real beneficiaries. This "negotiated revolution" is both typical and distinct in comparison with other "third wave" transitions.

The South African transition is typical in the sense that many of the recent transitions to democracy have come about through negotiations between "softliners" within the outgoing regime and moderate forces within the emerging one. In fact, the "third wave" of democratisation has been characterised by elite negotiations rather than popular mass struggles. Such transitions have come as a surprise to many observers as they contradict the predominant understanding of democratisation dynamics, which holds that democracy is brought about by structural changes towards capitalist modernisation and associated changes in class structures and politics. These social conditions and changes have generally not been key factors in the "third wave" and may even have been weakened by neo-liberal globalisation (Harriss, Stokke and Törnquist 2004). This apparent absence of structural transformation and popular mobilisation for democracy has given rise to a school of transition studies that argues that democracy can be "crafted" by visionary and committed actors within the political elite, shored up by support or pressure from international actors (Linz and Stepan 1996; Schmitter, O'Donnell and Whitehead 1986; Whitehead 2002). Popular forces are rendered a marginal role in democratic transitions and may even be considered an obstacle to fruitful negotiations: "Indeed, transition theory cautions against popular pressure for more radical change which could induce conservatives to abort democratization in its entirety" (Adler and Webster 2000:6).

While many analyses of the South African transition have been inspired by this approach, this seems like a narrow interpretation of the process towards post-apartheid liberal democracy. There is no denying the critical role played by individual actors in the South African transition, most notably that of Nelson Mandela (the "Madiba factor"). But a one-sided emphasis on individuals unjustly downplays the critical impact of mass struggles and structural conditions in creating conjunctures and defining parameters for political negotiations. Whereas the democratic transition itself was a negotiated settlement between the old and the new political elites, the political conjuncture for these negotiations came about through a prolonged and extensive mass mobilisation. This makes the South African "miracle" distinct from many recent democratic transitions in Africa, but not necessarily when compared to simultaneous democratisation processes in South America and Eastern Europe.

South Africa's recent political history is entwined with popular mass struggles. The final decade and a half of the apartheid era brought together a broad anti-apartheid movement consisting of diverse civil society associations and umbrella organisations such as the United Democratic Front (UDF), trade unions within the Congress of South African Trade Unions (COSATU), exiled political parties such as the African National Congress (ANC) and the South African Communist Party (SACP), and international solidarity movements (Adler and Webster 2000; McKinley 1997; Seekings 2000). The anti-apartheid movement combined local struggles around everyday experiences of state repression and social injustice with an ideological program of overthrowing the apartheid regime (Bozzoli 2004). It contained a great diversity of ideological positions and strategies, spanning conventional divides between reformism and revolution, and between non-violent mass resistance and armed guerrilla struggle. Gradually the ANC assumed a hegemonic position within this movement, calling for a people's war to render South Africa ungovernable and, after assuming state power, bringing trade unions, civil society associations and political parties into collaborative and consultative arrangements as well as into the governing alliance itself. This complex political history cannot be addressed here, but our point is simply that the dynamics and character of South Africa's negotiated transition cannot be separated from the movement politics of the preceding decades. On the contrary, popular mass struggles played a vital role in bringing about and defining the terms of the transition to democracy, and thereby also the post-apartheid politics of socio-economic rights.

As much as the negotiated transition was conditioned by mass mobilisation, the anti-apartheid movement itself reflected a structural context of mutually constitutive racial and class oppression. South Africa's democratic transition may not be the outcome of capitalist modernisation per se – as hypothesised by conventional theories of democratisation – but it was certainly conditioned by structural changes, and especially the multifaceted crises of accumulation within apartheid capitalism. Along these lines, Marais argues that the transition must be understood as the outcome of the apartheid state's inability to resolve complex economic, social and political crises that had grown steadily since the 1970s:

> In South Africa's case, severe contradictions were engendered within an accumulation strategy that depended on cheap, expendable African labour, but also rested on an import-substitution (and capital-intensive) industrialization strategy which required an ever-expanding market for

> its products. Simultaneously, the expulsion of the vast majority of the population from the enclave of (even comparative) privilege generated a variety of social and political responses which ranged from low productivity to forms of resistance that threatened the legitimacy and authority of the capitalist state. The result was a burgeoning, multi-dimensional crisis. (Marais 2001:37)

Thus, there was both a popular demand for democracy and social justice as well as a structural imperative for political reforms to overcome the contradictions and crises of the apartheid accumulation regime. This yielded various attempts at state reform in the 1980s but these were far from sufficient to overcome structural crises and popular resistance.

This brief account leads to two main observations regarding the South African "miracle". First, the South African transition was clearly a negotiated settlement, but this must be understood in the context of popular mass resistance and multiple crises of the apartheid regime. Second, the apartheid legacy of class and racial oppression and the popular mobilisation for democracy and social justice gave the South African transition a distinctly transformative character based on equal citizenship with extensive civil/political freedoms and justiciable socio-economic rights. However, this transformation has been circumscribed by the continuation of a highly uneven social economy and a shift in macro-economic policy away from social redistribution to a neo-liberal market economy. This leads Alexander (2002) to the conclusion that the South African "miracle" has produced a "normal" bourgeois democratic social formation with universal liberal rights but where the meaning of these are called into question by the continuation of widespread poverty and inequality:

> The stark reality is that the political settlement of 1993-94 was based on the retention of the *status quo ante* in respect of the fundamental economic relations and on the assumption of a more or less rapid trickle-down effect deriving from the 'miraculous' increase in the rate of growth of the GDP which most commentators and analysts foresaw as one of the main consequences of the end of the apartheid regime. ... The real situation is that hardly any change has taken place in the relations of economic power and control. Moreover, in the foreseeable future and in terms of the prevailing system, no such fundamental change is to be expected. With hardly any exceptions, the sources of economic power remain in the hands

> that controlled them under apartheid. (Alexander 2002:144, 146, italics in original)

The post-apartheid context is therefore replete with ambiguity. On the one hand is the considerable democratic and institutional "space" created in the post-apartheid era. Underpinned by strong oversight institutions, and a Constitution considered by many to be one of the most progressive in the world, these spaces give broad scope for the extension of socio-economic rights to the majority. Alternatively these progressive spaces for manoeuvre are surely circumscribed, on the other hand, by the legacy of class and race inequalities, the character of the negotiated transitions, and the contemporary context of neo-liberal globalisation. The general question that underpins the following chapters, addressing different dimensions of post-apartheid politics of socio-economic rights, is to what extent and by which means the liberal democratic dispensation of post-apartheid South Africa can function as a basis for a transformative politics of socio-economic rights?

5. Overview of Chapters

Our point of entry into this field is the current debate about policy-making, accountability and transformation under the ANC-led governing alliance. It is commonly observed that South Africa's first democratic decade has been a good start towards socio-economic transformation, not the least in terms of progressive legislation and constitutional reform. Yet Adam Habib reminds us that the statistics regarding poverty and inequality remain horrifying and that the government's macro-economic policy has taken a remarkably conservative turn. This may lead to a deracialisation of the upper strata of the class structure but is not likely to transform the large class of working poor, which remains economically marginalised and overwhelmingly black. Habib locates the explanation for this in the balance of power within South Africa and in the larger international context, generating policies that are favourable to foreign investors and the domestic business community, but work against redistribution and the social expenditure components of the budget. In a situation with a weak and racialised political opposition and an overwhelming electoral support for ANC, the vertical accountability between the state elite and the citizenry has eroded in the sense that the citizenry does not have the leverage to ensure substantial government concessions towards socio-economic transformation. This leads Habib to call for a reintroduction of substantive uncertainty into the political system and especially into economic policy-making. Without such substantive uncertainty, he argues, the realisation of socio-economic rights for the broad citizenry will elude South Africa's democratic transition.

Where may the sources of substantive uncertainty lie in South African politics? Given the absence of a viable political opposition, one source may be found in the large, well-organised and highly politicised labour movement. Thus, Liv Tørres examines the current political role of labour with a special focus on the dynamics and tensions within the governing alliance between the African National Congress (ANC), the South African Communist Party (SACP) and the Congress of South African Trade Unions (COSATU). This tripartite alliance was initially based on the shared Reconstruction and Development Programme (RDP), but Tørres observes that this class compromise has been undermined and replaced by the neo-liberal Growth, Employment and Redistribution (GEAR) strategy, shifting the balance of power within the alliance and producing policies that are at odds with the interests of labour. This has produced tension within the alliance over policy issues such as privatisation, trade liberalisation and public sector retrenchments, but has also raised more fundamental questions about the nature of the alliance and whether it serves the interest of labour to remain loyal to it. As a representative of the working class and the political left, labour is performing a balancing act between cooperation and opposition within the alliance. In the long run, this may yield a break-away left-wing opposition party, but the immediate future is most likely to see the continuation of alliance politics, providing certain opportunities for political participation by labour but also remaining heavily dominated by conservative economic and social policies. In this situation, Tørres concludes that the power and gains of labour within the alliance will depend largely on its strength outside the formal political sphere. As much as general socio-economic rights and specific labour rights served as a basis for mass mobilisation of workers in the 1980s, labour's ability to mobilise its constituency on the basis of the same rights will largely determine its political influence and the realisation of these rights in the future.

Another source of political contestation is found in civil society. Richard Ballard observes that South Africa's transition to democracy has radically altered the political spaces for social movements. Such movements, which were instrumental in the struggle against apartheid, were largely absorbed into government in the 1990s. In the context of regime change and collaborative state/society-relations, the political opportunity structures for these movements have significantly improved, especially for those who have transformed themselves into professional NGOs and work with the government in a subordinate role to deliver social welfare. Ballard points out that these congenial state/society relations changed towards the end of the 1990s. Born out of entrenched problems of poverty and inequality and catalysed by the shift to neo-liberalism, a range of new social movements emerged around diverse socio-economic issues and rights in the late 1990s. The political strategies of these new movements are highly varied, but many are characterised by creative combinations of strategies of engagement and disengagement with the state. In the same way as people were often mobilised into the anti-apartheid struggle around local everyday experiences of state repression and social injustice, the post-apartheid movements also emerge from everyday "bread and butter" issues with the material living conditions for poor people being the main common point of identification (Bozzoli 2004). Whereas the anti-apartheid struggle combined local struggles with a coordinated and ideological program of overthrowing the apartheid regime, the new movements have so far been issue-based and fragmented with limited capacity to merge diverse issues and build a coherent movement that can effectively challenge national policy-making processes. As fragmented, under-resourced and issue-based as many of the new movements are, their presence and activities nevertheless challenge the government and reinforce its accountability to marginalised social groups and their socio-economic and political struggles.

The chapters by Habib, Tørres and Ballard support the view that South Africa's post-apartheid political system is marked by limited substantive uncertainty, despite well-functioning institutions of liberal democracy. One outcome of this, according to Habib, is a set of policy concessions to domestic and international capital, which add to rather than resolve the problems of poverty and inequality. The exact character and extent of poverty and inequality is, however, a matter of academic and political debate. Julian May and Nina Hunter provide a critical review of poverty analyses and use this as a basis for examining the composition and impacts of government expenditures on the "social wage". The authors cautiously observe that the incidence and severity of income poverty continued to increase in the early post-apartheid period. This reflects the sluggish growth of the South African economy throughout the 1990s and the persistent and high unemployment rates, with unskilled workers and poor households carrying the adjustment costs of economic liberalisation. To what extent is this compensated by government social spending? Although May and Hunter find that existing programmes may be patchy in terms of coverage and quality, they also observe that the first years after the transition saw a significant increase in government social spending and that this has been redistributive and relatively well targeted. Nevertheless, this must be seen against the macro-economic policies of neo-liberalism that are found to be fundamentally poor unfriendly. It is in this situation that a new government discourse on the "social wage" has appeared, apparently as an attempt to counter critical analyses of South Africa's progress in its first decade of democracy. May and Hunter's discussion amply demonstrates that poverty analysis is both methodologically difficult and highly political in the post-apartheid context.

The detailed analysis of May and Hunter expertly confirms the deepening of poverty after 1994. If, then, as argued by the United Nations Office of the High Commissioner for Human Rights, poverty is a major inhibitor of the enjoyment of socio-economic rights, the worsening situation concerning poverty in South Africa would appear to greatly outweigh the modest gains of a rights-based approach. There is even the spectre that failure to remedy this distress threatens to unravel the constitutional project per se (Davis 2004). It is apparent that any attempt to improve the situation for socio-economic rights runs up against the broader challenges of economic policy-setting in its neo-liberal interpretation.

A rights-based approach, as indicated earlier, should impact upon policy-making in terms of human rights guiding policy development, in holding governments accountable through monitoring and in enabling advocacy. Arguably, however, it should also display provision of structural relief in terms of fulfilment of socio-economic rights. On paper, at least, South Africa would appear well-equipped to meet these endeavours. There is a post-liberation movement government, with a highly progressive Constitution cast in the imagery of correcting the social injustices of the past. The judiciary is also imbued with an ethos of redistribution, and a culture of socio-economic rights, equality and non-discrimination. There are additional favourable features to do with effective oversight institutions and strong civil society organisations. On the plus side, indeed, a range of key judgements of the Constitutional Court of South Africa appear to affirm how a strong legal commitment to human rights does appear to be influencing and shaping social policy and legislation (Liebenberg 2003).

To what extent then does the judicial system provide leverage on policy-making and development? Due to its highly innovative and progressive Constitution and Bill of Rights, South Africa is often hailed as an "exceptional" example of making socio-economic rights justiciable (Sunstein 2001). The socio-economic rights entrenched in the Bill of Rights are:

> The right to equitable access to land (s 25(5)); the right to access to adequate housing (s 26(1)); the right not to be arbitrarily evicted (s 26(3)); the right to access to health care service. To sufficient food and water and to social security and assistance (s 27(1)) and the right not to be refused emergency medical treatment (s 27(3)); the right of children to shelter, basic nutrition, health care services and social services (s 28(1)(c)) and their right to parental or alternative care (s 28(1)(b)); the right to basic education and to further education (s 29(1)); and, finally, the right of detained persons to the provision, at state cost, of adequate accommodation, nutrition, reading material and medical treatment (s 35(2)(e)). (Heyns and Brand 2004:28)

The Constitutional Court has considered claims for the enforcement of socio-economic rights on an increasing number of occasions and the courts have recognised that the state is under constitutional duty to comply with its positive obligations imposed on it.

Albie Sachs reviews the process whereby these rights were included in the Constitution as fundamental rights. Acknowledging the political controversies around the justiciability of socio-economic rights and the blurring of the boundary between law and politics, Sachs argues nonetheless that the main function of courts is to ensure respect for the dignity of every person at all times. The key constitutional test regards the reasonableness of state programmes to meet socio-economic rights, as the Constitution requires that "the state should take reasonable legislative and other measures within its available resources, for the progressive realisation of each of these rights" (Constitution of the Republic of South Africa, Section 27 (2)). The *Grootboom* case significantly declared the state housing programme to be unreasonable but also left it to the state to address the practical side of remedying this policy failure.[7] This

7 *Government of the Republic of South Africa v Grootboom* 2001 1 SA 46 (CC).

leads some to observe that the court order was not binding enough and is therefore, perhaps, "not exceptional enough" in terms of instigating actual policy changes on the ground for homeless people (Roux 2002). In another key case, regarding the right of pregnant women living with HIV to receive the drug Nevirapine (*Treatment Action Campaign* case), it can similarly be noted that the judgment did not require government to report back to the courts on the progress on meeting its constitutional obligations.[8] Citing technical and political factors, Sachs maintains, however, that it is not necessarily appropriate for judges to take positions on often highly controversial policy related issues. Although clearly rejecting the idea that the relationship between the judiciary and executive is somehow "deferent", Sachs does allude to the careful balancing act required of the courts. For Sachs, "it is a question of giving full acknowledgement to the functional and institutional roles given by the Constitution to the different branches of government".

But to have a transformative impact successful socio-economic rights litigation is contingent on a range of institutional and societal factors. Siri Gloppen unpacks the litigation process in order to identify and assess the factors that are critical in determining whether social rights litigation succeeds or fails. This leads her to the general observation that:

> The success or failure of social rights litigation depend on (a) the ability of groups whose rights are violated to articulate their claims and *voice* them into the legal system – or have the rights claimed on their behalf; (b) the *responsiveness* of the courts at various levels towards the social claims that are voiced; (c) the *capability* of the judges – that is, their ability to find adequate means to give legal effect to social rights; and (d) whether the social rights judgments that are handed down have authority in the sense that they are accepted, *complied* with and implemented through legislation and policy.

It has already been noted that the South African Constitution and legal system are quite favourable to socio-economic rights litigation. Yet, Gloppen also points out that there are numerous – and socially uneven – practical barriers for victims of social rights violations to voice their claims in the legal system. These barriers imply that the differing and uneven capabilities of civil society organisations and social movements

8 *Minister of Health v Treatment Action Campaign* 2002 5 SA 721 (CC).

have a critical bearing on the outcome of litigation. At the same time, the Constitutional Court has demonstrated that it takes a lot to succeed with such claims, thus "stemming the tide" of social rights cases despite the harsh socio-economic realities for the majority of South Africans. In those cases where courts have ruled in favour of victims of social rights violations, Gloppen observes that the government has accepted the judgments but that there has been noticeable foot-dragging in changing and implementing relevant policies. This leads to the conclusion that litigation cannot be seen in isolation from the wider politics of socio-economic rights. In the aforementioned *Treatment Action Campaign* case it was especially important that the legal case was part of a larger process of social mobilisation by the Treatment Action Campaign, where socio-economic rights provided a focal point and platform for struggle.

The Treatment Action Campaign is often lauded as an example of how civil society may use justiciable socio-economic rights to influence government policy. Focusing on the campaign for a National HIV/AIDS treatment plan, Mark Heywood examines how the Treatment Action Campaign has grounded political mobilisation and advocacy in moral and legal questions of human rights. By invoking the constitutional right to health care TAC has established HIV/AIDS treatment as a human right, thereby gaining moral legitimacy for their political advocacy and for mobilising popular support. This platform was used initially to challenge pharmaceutical companies for profiteering instead of responding to health needs and, thus, curtailing the right to health care for people living with HIV/AIDS. Thereafter the target for HIV/AIDS advocacy shifted to the government. Heywood's account of the campaign for a National Treatment Plan emphasises the strategic combination of political negotiations and confrontational mass struggle. While TAC has gained recognition for its skilful use of the court system in the *Treatment Action Campaign* case, the author shows that this is merely one way of engaging with the law. In the case of the National HIV/AIDS treatment plan, TAC pursued a negotiated agreement through the channels of the democratic state and only turned to more confrontational tactics of civil disobedience and threats of legal action when it became clear that the negotiations would fail to fulfil the right to health care. Heywood concludes that the Treatment Action Campaign demonstrates that human rights can be invoked to provide a moral legitimacy for advocacy and that strategic and political use of the Bill of Rights opens up a space for contesting policies and practices of both government and the private sector. This moral and legal basis for advocacy, the willingness to engage government in political negotiations, and the ability to mobilise popular support for rights-based struggles, lie at the core of TAC's relatively successful campaign for health care for people living with HIV/AIDS.

While Ballard and Heywood document the emergence of new social movements in the post-apartheid context of entrenched socio-economic grievances and democratic political spaces, Mandisa Mbali points to the need to place these new movements within a longer trajectory of civil society activism. Adding to Heywood's analysis she demonstrates that there are historical antecedents for contemporary HIV/AIDS activism to be found in the anti-apartheid, gay rights activism in the 1980s and early 1990s. Mbali characterises TAC as "patient-driven activism", mobilising activists and members from the large number of young, relatively fit and active individuals who are living with HIV/AIDS, some of whom were active in the gay rights and anti-apartheid movements. In addition to being "patient-driven", Mbali emphasises that both struggles have been marked by the centrality of openness and a struggle against stigma and discrimination. Most notably, HIV/AIDS has been transformed from an unspeakable and invisible epidemic in the early 1990s to a prominent political issue with a highly vocal and visible constituency in the early 2000s. Such courageous openness has been as important for the success of post-apartheid HIV/AIDS activism as it was for anti-apartheid gay rights activism earlier. Both struggles have been marked by combined strategies of civil and political society activism aimed at contesting and transforming both discourses and political decision-making. Mbali argues that these two struggles, while being issue-based and patient-driven, have also used and sustained the public sphere and thereby given meaning and substance to first generation civil and political rights.

Whilst land remains a highly charged symbolic and material issue in South Africa, discussions of the concrete role of land rights in democratising development have received relatively scant debate. The contribution by Ben Cousins and Aninka Claassens is therefore an important corrective to this deficit. Their analysis of the controversy surrounding the recent Communal Land Rights Bill illustrates competing meanings of the conceptualisation and implementation of land rights in post-apartheid South Africa's rural periphery. Two particularly controversial issues in the Communal Land Rights Act of 2004 are identified: first, whether or not titling is necessary to ensure security of tenure, and; second, what should be the role of local land administration bodies in the realisation of such rights. In relation to land rights, the predominant view has been that land titling (*i.e.* private ownership) is a prerequisite for adequate tenure security, but the authors note an increasing acceptance of communal tenure. Regarding land administration, Cousins and Claassens point to a convergence around the centrality of local institutions, but also highly divergent views on the future role of traditional authorities and the need to make local land administration accountable and responsive to people's needs. In doing so, however, prevailing understandings of "constitutional rights" encounter a challenge associated with the politics of ethno-identity, *i.e.* custom and tradition, in rural areas. Although problematic, significantly, the authors suggest that these competing understandings are not necessarily incompatible. As active participants in the process surrounding the Bill the authors are well placed to observe that the new Constitution has carved out political space to increase awareness and debate surrounding land rights. But a fundamental point the authors also make is that the specific structural and political characteristics of rural areas require special efforts to enhance citizen capacity through organisation, which for the moment appears limited. A strong state is also necessary for intervening locally to uphold both legal rights and to maintain local accountability. In all this, however, Cousins and Claassens raise doubts as to the extent to which the state presently is willing to hear the "voice of the people".

Following these and other analyses of the complex and dynamic politics of socio-economic rights in South Africa, the final chapter returns to the overall question about the relationship between socio-economic rights and democracy. While rejecting the conventional view that democracy can only come about and be sustained once a certain level of development has been reached, and also expressing scepticism towards the claim that democracy will automatically lead to economic development, Paul Graham argues that there is a strong positive relationship between democracy and socio-economic rights. With inspiration from Sen, he maintains that various freedoms are not only indivisible but have a virtuous effect on each other. Ten years of democracy in South Africa has demonstrated that civil and political rights in themselves are not a guarantee for the rapid elimination of poverty and inequality, but the democratic dispensation constitutes a structure that can be used to address past and present injustices. The state of poverty and inequality in South Africa shows, furthermore, that it is not sufficient merely to codify socio-economic rights. Such rights, says Graham, come about as a result of struggle and their exercise and extension require continuing struggle of diverse kinds and in multiple arenas. South African experiences demonstrate both that there is no realisation of socio-economic rights without politics and that democratic politics of socio-economic rights deepens democracy itself. To put it programmatically, democratic politics of socio-economic rights democratises development while also developing democracy.

References

Adler, G. and Webster, E. (eds.) (2000). *Trade Unions and Democratization in South Africa, 1985-1997*. Witwatersrand University Press, Johannesburg.

Alexander, N. (2002). *An Ordinary Country. Issues in the Transition from Apartheid to Democracy in South Africa*. University of Natal. Press, Pietermaritsburg.

Andreassen, B. A. (2003). "Shifting notions of development: Implications for the right to development?" In, Franciscans International (eds.) *The Right to Development*. Franciscans International, Geneva, 24-33.

Barnett, T. and Whiteside, A. (2002). *AIDS in the Twenty-first Century*. Palgrave Macmillan, Houndmills.

Beetham, D. (1999). *Democracy and Human Rights*. Polity Press, Oxford.

Bozzoli, B. (2004). *Theatres of Struggle and the End of Apartheid*. Witwatersrand University Press, Johannesburg.

Collier, D. and Levitsky, S. (1997). "Democracy with adjectives: Conceptual innovation in comparative research." *World Politics* 49(3):430-451.

Cooke, B. and Kothari, U. (2001). *Participation: The New Tyranny?* Zed Books, London.

Cornwall, A. and Nyamu-Musembi, C. (2004). "Putting the 'rights-based approach' to development into perspective." *Third World Quarterly*, 25(8): 1415-1437.

Davis, D. (2004). "Socio-Economic rights in South Africa: The record of the Constitutional Court after ten years." *ESR Review*, 5(5): 3-5. Community Law Centre, University of the Western Cape.

DFID (1997). *Eliminating World Poverty: A Challenge for the Twenty-first Century*. DFID, London.

DFID (2000). *Eliminating World Poverty: Making Globalisation Work for the Poor*. DFID, London.

Donnelly, J. (1997) *International Human Rights (Dilemmas in World Politics).* Westview Press, Colorado.

Evans, T. (2002). "A human right to health?" *Third World Quarterly* 23(2): 197-215.

Frankovits, A. (2003). "Human Rights Approach to Development." In, Jones, P.S. (ed.), *Learning Together: The Right to Education, Lessons and Experiences from Zambia.* Published report from the Lusaka workshop, Norwegian Centre for Human Rights, Oslo.

Frankovits, A. (2005). "Introduction." In, *Empowerment, Participation, Accountability and Non-Discrimination: Operationalising a Human Rights-Based Approach to Development, Human Rights in Development Yearbook 2002*, Martinus Nijhoff Publishers, Leiden, 3-14.

Fung, A. and Wright, E. O. (eds.) (2003). *Deepening Democracy: Institutional Innovations in Empowered Participatory Governance.* Verso, London.

Gloppen, S. and Rakner, L. (2005). *Checking the State; Exploring Accountability Institutions in New Democracies*, Christian Michelsen Institute, Bergen, Working Paper 2005:5.

Goetz, A. M. and Jenkings, R. (2001). "Hybrid forms of accountability: Citizen engagement in institutions of public sector oversight in India." *Public Management Review* 3(3): 363-383.

Grugel, J. (2002). *Democratization: A Critical Introduction.* Palgrave Macmillan, Houndmills.

Harriss, J., Stokke, K. and Törnquist, O. (2004). *Politicising Democracy: The New Local Politics of Democratisation.* Palgrave Macmillan, Houndmills.

Heyns, C. and Brand, D. (2004). "Socio-economic Rights and the Transition." In, Manganyi, C. (ed.), *On Becoming a Democracy.* University of South Africa Press, Pretoria.

Heywood, M. (2002). "Drug access, patents and global health: 'Chaffed and waxed sufficient'". *Third World Quarterly* 23(2): 217-231.

Huntington, S. P. (1991). *The Third Wave: Democratization in the Late Twentieth Century.* University of Oklahoma Press, Norman.

Jones, P. S. (ed.) (2003). *Learning Together: The Right to Education, Lessons and Experiences from Zambia.* Published report from the Lusaka workshop, Norwegian Centre for Human Rights, Oslo.

Jones, P. S. (2004) "When 'development' devastates: Donor discourses, access to HIV/AIDS treatment in Africa and rethinking landscapes of development", *Third World Quarterly,* 25, (2): 385-404.

Liebenberg, S. (2003). *Making a Difference: Human Rights and Development-Reflecting the South African Experience.* Paper to the Nobel Symposium on the Right to Development, Human Rights in Development, Holmenkollen Hotel, Oslo, October.

Linz, J. J. and Stepan, A. (1996). *Problems of Democratic Transition and Consolidation: Southern Europe, South America, and Post-Communist Europe.* Johns Hopkins University Press, Baltimore.

Luckham, R., Goetz, A. M., and Kaldor, M. (2003). "Democratic Institutions and Democratic Politics." In, Bastian, S. and Luckham, R. (eds.), *Can Democracy Be Designed? The Politics of Institutional Choice in Conflict-torn Societies.* Zed Books, London.

Lumina, Cephas, K. (2004). "Political Conditionality and its Implications for Human Rights: the Case of Zambia." In, Nhema, A.G. (ed.), *The Quest for Peace in Africa: Transformations, Democracy and Public Policy.* International Books.

Manji, F. (1998). "Depoliticisation of poverty." In, Eade, D. (ed.) *Development and Rights,* Development Practice Readers. Oxfam, Oxford. http://www.developmentinpractice.org/readers/rights/intro.htm

Manzo, K. (2003). "Africa in the rise of rights-based development." *Geoforum* 34, 437-456.

Marais, H. (2001). *South Africa. Limits to Change: The Political Economy of Transition* (2 ed.). Zed Books, London.

Marks, S. P. (2003). *The Human Rights Framework for Development: Seven Approaches.* Working Paper number 18, François-Xavier Bagnoud Center for Health and Human Rights, University of Harvard.

McKinley, D. T. (1997). *The ANC and the Liberation Struggle: A Critical Political Biography.* Pluto, London.

Mercer, C. C. (2002). "The discourse of Maendeleo and the politics of women's participation on Mount Kilimanjaro." *Development and Change,* 33, 101-127.

Mohan, G., and Holland, J. (2001). "Human Rights and Development in Africa: Moral Intrusion or Empowering Opportunity." *Review of African Political Economy* 88, 177-196.

Newell, P. and Bellour, S. (2002). *Mapping Accountability: Origins, Contexts and Implications for Development.* Institute of Development Studies, Sussex.

NORAD (2002). *Fighting Poverty: the Norwegian Government's Action Plan for Combating Poverty in the South Towards 2015.* Ministry of Foreign Affairs, Oslo.

Nowak, M. (2005). "A Human Rights Approach to Poverty." In, *Empowerment, Participation, Accountability and Non-Discrimination: Operationalising a Human Rights-Based Approach to Development, Human Rights in Development Yearbook 2002*, Martinus Nijhoff Publishers, Leiden.

Office of the UN High Commissioner for Human Rights (1986). *Declaration on the Right to Development, Adopted by General Assembly resolution 41/128 of 4 December 1986.* UN, New York.

Penna, D. R. and P. J. Campbell (1998). "Human Rights and culture: beyond universality and relativism", *Third World Quarterly*, 19(1): 7-27.

Roux, T. (2002). "Understanding Grootboom - A response to Cass R. Sunstein." *Constitutional Forum*, 12, 112-122.

Sano, H. O. and Alfredsson, G. (eds.) (2002). *Human Rights and Good Governance.* Kluwer Law International, The Hague.

Schmitter, P., O'Donnell, G. and Whitehead, L. (1986). *Transitions from Authoritarian Rule.* Johns Hopkins University Press, Baltimore.

Seekings, J. (2000). *The UDF: A History of the United Democratic Front in South Africa, 1983-1991.* David Philips, Cape Town.

Sen, A. (1994). "Freedom and Needs: An Argument for the Primacy of Political Rights." *The New Republic* 210(2-3): 31-38.

Sen, A. (1999). "Democracy as a Universal Value." *Journal of Democracy*, 10(3): 3-17.

Sen, A. (2000). "Freedom's Market", June 25th, *Observer* newspaper, United Kingdom.

Sengupta, A. (2000). "Realising the Right to Development." *Development and Change*, 31, 553-578.

Stiglitz, J. (2002). *Globalization and its Discontents.* W.W Norton and Company, New York.

Sparks, A. (1995). *Tomorrow is Another Country.* Jonathan Ball, Johannesburg.

Sparks, A. (2003). *Beyond the Miracle. Inside the New South Africa.* Jonathan Ball, Johannesburg.

Stokke, H. (2005). "What is left of state responsibility?" In, *Empowerment, Participation, Accountability and Non-Discrimination: Operationalising a Human Rights-Based Approach to Development, Human Rights in Development Yearbook 2002*, Martinus Nijhoff Publishers, Leiden, 39-70.

Sunstein, C. R. (2001). *Social and Economic Rights? Lessons from South Africa.* University of Chicago, Public Law Working Paper No. 12; University of Chicago Law & Economics, Olin Working Paper No. 124.

Törnquist, O. (2004). "The Political Deficit of Substantial Democratisation." In, J. Harriss, K. Stokke and O. Törnquist (eds.). *Politicising Democracy: The New Local Politics of Democratisation.* Palgrave Macmillan, Houndmills.

United Nations CESCR General Comment 14 (2000). *Substantive Issues Arising in the Implementation of the International Covenant on Economic, Social and Cultural Rights* (E/C.12/2000/4).

United Nations Development Programme (2000). *Human Development Report 2000: Human Rights and Human Development.* United Nations Publications, New York.

Uvin, P. (2004). *Human Rights and Development.* Kumarian Press, Bloomfield.

Whitehead, L. (2002). *Democratization. Theory and Experience.* Oxford University Press, Oxford.

Yamin, A. E. (2002). "Challenges and Possibilities for Innovative Praxis in Health and Human Rights: Reflections from Peru." *Health and Human Rights,* 6(1): 35-62.

2. The Politics of Economic Policy-Making: Substantive Uncertainty, Political Leverage, and Human Development

Adam Habib *

There have been many assessments of the first ten years of post-apartheid South African democracy. And there will be many more to come. But perhaps the most notable one is the president's annual State of the Nation address, delivered in February 2004 at the opening of parliament, which focussed on and served as a self-review of the ANC government's performance. At one level, it was a magnificent speech in particular because the president resisted what would have been a natural inclination to electioneer. Instead, in true *statespersonlike* behaviour, he delivered a presidential rather than a party leader's speech, which reviewed government's performance over the decade and emphasized the importance of reconciliation and transformation as mechanisms to facilitate nation-building, peace and democracy. Of course the President did put a positive gloss on government's performance. This was not only expected, but was in many cases fair. The issue that raised eyebrows, however, was the president's claim that he did not see the necessity for any policy shifts. The failure of poverty alleviation and development, and the inadequacy of service delivery, was in his view, a result of poor implementation rather than policy failures as such (Mbeki 2004b).

The president is not alone in this view. It is essentially the message of government as a whole and is reflected in both the presidency's review of the first decade of South Africa's democracy (PCAS 2003), and the series of presentations of the synthesis report of this review, pre-

---

* Adam Habib is executive director of the Democracy and Governance Program at the Human Science Research Council (HSRC), and a Research Professor in the School of Development Studies (SODS) and Centre for Civil Society (CCS) at the University of Kwazulu-Natal.

Peris Jones and Kristian Stokke (eds.), Democratising Development, *ISBN 90 04 14821 3, pp. 39-53.*

sented by Joel Netshitenzhe to a variety of fora and stakeholders within society.[1] The review emphasizes the delivery record of government. It provides empirical evidence demonstrating that 1 985 545 housing subsidies have been approved to a value of R24, 22 billion (p. 25), new water connections benefit 9 million people (p. 24), electricity connections had been extended to 70 percent of households by 2001 (p. 25), 1.8 million hectares of land have been redistributed since 1994 (p. 26), and 1 600 633 new jobs have been created (p. 36). The review also maintains that if these social provisions are taken into account, then poverty rates have declined significantly in our society (p. 17-18). However, it also admits that unemployment has gone up in this period, a result of new entrants to the labour market exceeding the number of new jobs created. And it recognises that delivery has been most significant in arenas where the state has retained predominant control. But the overall message is that government has delivered as best as was possible. Its performance was phenomenal given the adverse conditions in the global economy. The tight fiscal reign was part of a far-sighted strategic manoeuvre to stabilise finances so that increased spending on social expenditure could be realised when this had been achieved (pp. 31-33). The first ten years, the review maintained, was a good start to transforming South Africa in the interests of all of its citizens.

Is this a fair assessment? The ANC government has without doubt passed a significant amount of legislation – the Labour Relations Act, the Equity legislation – that is progressive and addresses the inequities of South Africa's past. If one couples these with the country's rights based constitution, one is obliged to conclude that today South Africa is a far better place than it has ever been. But is apartheid an appropriate yardstick by which to judge South Africa's progress? After all, was not apartheid described as a crime against humanity? How can it then be described as a reference point for South Africa's democratic transformation? Are not the aspirations of the liberation movement, encapsulated in the *Freedom Charter*, the *Azanian Manifesto*, and the *Ten Point program*, or the comparative experience of other African countries in

1 This presentation, for instance, was made to diverse constituencies, from on the one hand the Board of Anglo-American, to on the other, academics, both from South Africa and the continent, through a conference hosted by the Africa Institute on March 24-26, 2004.

their first decade of decolonisation,[2] more legitimate reference points to assess South Africa's political and socio-economic progress?

When these programmatic collective aspirations of the liberation movement or the comparative experiences of other Sub-Saharan African countries are used as a political compass, then what is noteworthy is the conservative character of government's macro-economic programme, which is located at the heart of its policy ensemble. This program, known as the Growth Employment and Redistribution Strategy (GEAR), has, as has been argued elsewhere, not only had negative consequences for poor and marginalized people in South Africa, but it has also compromised the outcomes of the raft of other progressive legislation (Habib and Padayache, 2000; Daniel, Habib and Southall, 2003; UNDP, 2004). Government is correct to note that it has built 1.6 million houses, supplied water to 9 million people, sanitation to 6.4 million, and created 2 million jobs (Mbeki 2004). However, what it is neglecting to inform the citizenry of is the fact that as much as people have been connected to water, so have millions of people been cut off from water. As much as millions of people have been connected to electricity, so have millions of people been cut off from electricity.[3] As much as millions of people have been connected to telephony, so have millions of people been cut off from telephony. As much as jobs have been created, so too have millions of people been thrown onto the unemployment lines. The 2003-2004 edition of the *State of the Nation* concluded that the combination of progressive policy in some arenas and a conservative macro-economic policy on the other has led to the deracialisation of the apex of South Africa's class structure. Black professionals and entrepreneurs have particularly benefited, but poor and marginalized people are really struggling. President Mbeki has often spoken of two

2 Adebayo Olukoshi, the General Secretary of CODESRIA, the premier social science body on the continent, made this point explicitly at the Africa Institute conference in March 2004, suggesting that in terms of economic growth and the realisation of human indicators, South Africa's performance lagged far behind that of its neighbours at the end of the first ten years of their founding democratic elections.

3 David McDonald, for instance, estimates that water and electricity cut-offs have impacted on some ten million people respectively, while another two million people have suffered through being evicted from their homes (McDonald 2002; see also Coalition Against Water Provision, Anti-Privatisation Forum, Public Citizen, 2004). Note, however, that the Department of Water Affairs and the Presidency have contested these numbers.

nations and two economies in South Africa, and the need to transcend this dichotomy. But the editors' conclusion was that the policies of his government would not lead to this. Instead it will lead to the deracialisation of the first nation, while leaving the second exactly where it currently is: marginalized, poor and overwhelmingly black (Daniel, Habib and Southall 2003:20).

This is borne out by the figures. The United Nations Development Program (UNDP) reports in a recently released study that the country's poverty rate has reached a staggering 48 percent (UNDP 2004). The Presidency, of course, contested this conclusion in a harshly worded response. But most independent commentators were not surprised by the UNDP's conclusion. After all, the Taylor Commission for the Department of Social Welfare estimated the country's poverty rate at a staggering 45 to 55 percent. It suggested that 10 percent of African people are malnourished, and 25 percent of African children are born stunted (Report of the Committee of Inquiry into a Comprehensive System of Social Security for South Africa 2002:225-276). Statistics South Africa (SSA), through its most recent census, estimated the unemployment rate to be at 41.6 percent (Statistics South Africa 2003). Most independent studies suggest that while the inequality level between white and black has been decreasing, the gap is widening within the African population and the country as a whole.[4] These statistics are horrifying. If they had occurred in any country of the industrialised world, a state of economic emergency would have already been declared and governments would have fallen. In South Africa, however, not only has this not happened, but it is has been difficult to get public institutions to recognise the enormity of the problem. Note, for instance, the fact that the South African Reserve Bank has only the reduction of inflation as its explicit mandate. No mention is made of unemployment. Yet its counterpart in the United States, the Federal Reserve, has employment creation as its explicit aim stipulated within its charter even though the unemployment level in that country stands in the region of a mere five percent (Stiglitz 2003:82).

So why did government adopt such a conservative macro-economic stance? There are currently two broad explanations. The first, preferred

---

4 Note, for instance, that the *Sunday Times* (9 May 2004) reports that South Africa's super-rich – those with assets of more than $30 million – has jumped from 150 in 1994 to 600 in 2004. This, in a period when the share of national income of South Africa's more marginalized has decreased dramatically.

paradoxically by both the far left and right, focuses on state elites. For the left, they are believed to have sold out (Bond 2000). For the right, they are believed to have finally seen sense.[5] Both explanations are deficient because of their assumption of a homogeneity of thought and behaviour among political elites that simply cannot be there, especially in a transitional society where there has been such a significant turnover in public service representatives and state personnel. But perhaps an even more serious criticism that can be levelled at these explanations is a methodological one, namely their almost exclusive focus on agents and actors. Advocates of these explanations have not internalised, and as a result do not recognise, that individuals, parties and movements are constrained in their choices by their institutional locations and the balance of power. In the celebrated words of Karl Marx's maxim enunciated in *The Eighteenth Brumaire of Louis Bonaparte*: "Men make their own history, but they do not make it just as they please; they do not make it under circumstances chosen by themselves, but under circumstances directly found, given and transmitted from the past" (Marx 1972:437).

The second explanation, and the one I prefer, suggests that the balance of power in the global and national arenas was unfavourable to poor and marginalized citizens, and as a result it made sense for state elites to make the choices they did. According to this view Mbeki and other state elites confronted two diametrically opposed sets of interests with contrary policy choices. The first, foreign investors and the domestic business community, advocated neo-liberal economic policies – privatisation, deregulation, financial and trade liberalisation, and low budget deficits. Their leverage: investment (Habib and Padayachee 2000). The second, the broader citizenry demanded poverty alleviation, service delivery, and transformation. Their leverage: the vote. The latter, however, was compromised given the racial structure of party formation and the lack of a viable opposition (Habib and Taylor 2001). In this context, foreign investment served as a more real leverage with the result that Mbeki was prompted to make concessions to the investor community. This of course reflected itself in the adoption of GEAR.

The explanation here has been presented simplistically for explanatory effect. The point to note is that power configurations lay behind the state's adoption of GEAR (Alexander 2002; Habib and Padayachee 2000). Moreover, the shift to neo-liberal economics should not have

5 This has been the steady diet of any one of a number of business newspapers and magazines. For just one example, see Abedian 2004.

been surprising. After all, indications were there that this was going to happen at least since the early 1990s. Nationalisation, a cornerstone of ANC economic thinking since the mid-1950's, was abandoned within the first year of the organisation's return from exile. Terminology like 'growth through redistribution', which associated the ANC with a demand-led economic strategy, and suggestions of controls on investors (both foreign and domestic) disappeared in the organisation's policy discourse by 1993. This prompted American academic Martin Murray (1994:24), to observe the fact that the "twin objectives of restoring business confidence and attracting foreign investment seemed to swamp all other considerations" in the ANC's evaluation of its economic policies. Of course, for a year preceding the election, it seemed as if Keynesian arguments had won the day. But this was largely a result of the demands imposed by a looming election, and was abandoned within a couple of months in some areas, and within two years in others.

So where do we stand today? Some, both academics and political activists, have argued that government's economic stance has begun to change in the last three to five years (Padayachee and Valodia 2001). They point to a rise in social expenditure since 1999, and the increasingly progressive noises the president has been making in the last year. Some also note the role of South Africa in establishing the Group of 20, which was so instrumental in preventing an iniquitous settlement being imposed on the developing world at Cancun. Still others point to the president's speeches, which speak about the necessity of linking with social movements outside of the formal multinational forums. And, they contrast this with Minister Erwin's statement after the Seattle protests which was laced with disdain for activists outside of formal political structures. These voices collectively suggest that something new is afoot, even if it is unstated. And, it does seem as if some in the business community tend to concur. Tim Cohen (2004), in an opinion editorial published in *Business Day*, reflects a similar view when he argues that the ANC has loss faith in the business community and is now beginning to pursue a more interventionist state led economic strategy.

So is there change? The left in the ANC definitely believe so (Cronin 2004; COSATU 2004). They suggest that the government is reappraising its position.[6] It recognises that its gamble did not pay off.

6 This was the message of ANC Member of Parliament Rob Davies at an IDASA panel discussion in Cape Town in March 2004 where he presented the shift in economic thinking on the part of government, as a rational

Therefore there has been a significant shift in the last budget in spending priorities in favour of infrastructural investment, a public works program and increased social expenditure. But others are more cynical of these developments. They suggest that 2004 was an election year, and that state elites have always made progressive noises just before an election.[7] There is some truth in this of course. In both 1994 and 1999, similar things happened. COSATU and the SACP were appeased. The policy agenda took a slight shift to the left. The conservative flavour of South Africa's macro-economic stance, however, resurfaced as soon as a respectable time lapsed from the date of the elections.

But is this a fair reading of the situation? Is it not too cynical an interpretation of developments? My own view is somewhere in between the romantic optimism of the ANC left and the almost resigned pessimism of both liberal and more left-leaning commentators. I believe government is in reappraisal mode, and there is ample evidence for it. The most recent of these is of course President Mbeki's inaugural address to South Africa's third democratic parliament in which he acknowledged that not enough was done for South Africa's marginalized in our first decade of democracy. As a result he laid out a comprehensive set of policies and targets that would facilitate service delivery and address the poverty that so many of South Africa's people are mired in. But he did more. He announced plans that herald a far more state interventionist strategy to regulate the formal economy, and condition its evolution in a direction that would lead to higher levels of employment (Mbeki 2004a). Much, however, can be read by what was not said. The President remained silent on the rigid fiscal policy, on the commitment on financial and trade liberalisation, on the narrow focus of our monetary authorities on inflation, and even on privatisation. As a result he signalled a contradiction in the state's policy ensemble. Social expenditure will rise, as it has for a number of years, mainly to deal with the devastating consequences of poverty and inequality in what President Mbeki refers to as the 'second economy' (Mbeki 2004a; 2003). But much of the economic policy choices of post-1996 South Africa will remain.

---

process in which economic technocrats learnt the lessons from past implementation experiences.

7 This was the view of Steven Friedman, articulated in the question and answer session of a presentation he made to the Harold Wolpe Lecture series, hosted by the Centre for Civil Society, University of Natal, in November 2003.

Moreover, it is important to note that the entire analogy of two economies is itself misleading for it assumes the existence of a Chinese wall between the two; the one having nothing to do with the other. This then enables state elites to suggest that the formal economy is doing well and should be left untouched for it is modern, efficient, and internationally competitive. The second economy is seen to deficient, and requires both policy reform and social assistance for its inhabitants. But what if, to stick with the analogy, the policy reforms and interventions of the first economy is what creates the poverty and immiseration of the second? Apartheid of course established two economies; one white and privileged, the other black and disadvantaged. The ANC had as its explicit mandate the transcention of this racial economic divide. Instead, however, the economic and social policies it pursued in the first decade of its rule began the process of deracialising the first economy, while simultaneously increasing the size and aggravating the problems of the second. Current initiatives to increase the social expenditure components of the budget are unlikely to resolve the problem. For as Alec Erwin, South Africa's current Minister of Public Enterprises, and its Minister of Trade and Industry for much of the first two terms of ANC rule, pointed out in 1992, "the ... approach is likely to fail ... even on its own economic terms. It is not a sustainable growth option. It will certainly never meet the most basic aspirations of the broad majority of our country" (Erwin 1992:16). Simply put, so long as South Africa's industrial, trade, monetary and fiscal policies retain their neo-liberal flavour, they are likely to work against the social expenditure components of the budget. This contradiction at the heart of the ANC government's current policy ensemble is unlikely to be sustainably resolved so long as the political environment does not change.

How can it change? An answer to this question can be arrived at by reflecting on why democracies are seen as the best political system to achieve a human centred development program. The essence of democracy is political uncertainty, and it takes two distinct forms; institutional and substantive. Institutional uncertainty – the uncertainty about the rules of the game – implies the vulnerability of the democratic system to anti-democratic forces. Substantive uncertainty – the uncertainty of the outcomes of game – is about the perceptions of ruling political elites in a democratic system on whether they will be returned to office (Schedler 2001:19). The former – institutional uncertainty – is bad for democracy for it raises the prospect of the return to authoritarianism in the Third Wave of democracies. The latter – substantive uncertainty

– is good for democracy for it keeps politicians on their toes, and makes them responsive to their citizenry.

There has been much investigation into and reflection on institutional uncertainty. But there is surprisingly little work on substantive uncertainty. Perhaps this should not surprise one. After all much of the preoccupation of the democratisation researchers and activists has been about transcending authoritarian regimes and institutionalising democratic ones (O'Donnell and Schmitter 1986; Huntington 1991).[8] Prospects of reversions to authoritarianism – institutional uncertainties – then, would naturally occupy their immediate attention. But the lack of scholarly reflection on substantive uncertainty has significant political costs. Indeed, the weakness of much of the contemporary democracies lies precisely in this arena. Despite the presence of institutional mechanisms that are intended to promote substantive uncertainty – legislative elections, separation of powers, civil liberties, opposition political parties, independent press – this goal still eludes much of the Third Wave of democracies. Part of the reason for this is the shift in power from the legislature to the executive across the globe in the last two decades. Part of it emanates from the inclination of democratisers and democratisation scholars to not rock the boat in societies undergoing democratic transitions. Fearful of the very real danger of a reversion to authoritarianism, these actors have focussed on procedural aspects of democratisation and made significant political and institutional concessions to the state and economic elites of the authoritarian order.[9] And part of it is a result of the honeymoon phenomenon where citizens are reluctant to vote against liberation parties who were responsible for coordinating the popular rebellions that brought down authoritarian regimes.

These factors, coupled with the economic transformations of the last two decades – the rise of financial capital, the technological innovations that have permitted capital's mobility, the integration of production systems across the globe, the dominance of multi-national corporations – fundamentally transformed the political and socio-economic foundations of developing nations. In essence they transformed the relations of power between different constituents within these societies.

8 The most comprehensive study on Africa in this regard is Bratton and van de Walle 1997.

9 This was the recommendation of a diverse set of democratisation scholars. For just two examples from different parts of the ideological spectrum, see O'Donnell and Schmitter 1986, and Huntington 1991.

The economic transformations enhanced the leverage of the foreign investors by providing them with many different locations for their investment. The leverage of citizens (the vote) was relatively weakened as a result of the political institutional concessions made by democratisers, and the weakening of the legislatures *vis-à-vis* the executives. This state of affairs prompted governments in the Third Wave of democracies to make policy concessions to foreign investors and domestic capital, even when it went against the interests of their very own citizenry. The result has been the rise of neo-liberal economics, the increasing impoverishment of the majority of the citizenry of the developing nations, and the rise of what some have termed delegative or illiberal democracies (O'Donnell 1993).

South Africa is perhaps the best exemplar of this pattern of events as was indicated earlier. And, the systemic cause of this outcome is the lack of substantive uncertainty in the political system, largely as a result of some of the international developments discussed above, and peculiar contextual factors, such as the racialised (and or ethnic) character of South Africa's principal opposition parties – the Democratic Alliance (DA), Inkatha Freedom Party (IFP) and the New National Party (NNP) – who continue to fish in the shallow electoral pool of minority communities (Habib and Taylor 2001). These factors then ensure that the ANC is not seriously threatened at the polls, eroding thereby the implicit accountability relationship within democratic systems between state elites and their citizenry. The result: economic concessions to the investment community and the imposition of a neo-liberal economic paradigm. The outcome: increasing unemployment and economic inequality making it almost impossible for government to adequately deal with the legacy of poverty bequeathed by apartheid.

The solution to this state of affairs is the reintroduction of substantive uncertainty into the political system. This will allow the vote to be enhanced as leverage and thereby re-establish the accountability equation between political elites and citizens in South Africa. It won't resolve the problem. But it would complicate President Mbeki's life. Given that he can no longer take his position and ANC rule for granted, he will inevitably be compelled to take the interests and wishes of voters as seriously as he does more privileged stakeholders in society. Every time he is thus confronted with competing interests between the business community and the broader citizenry, he will be forced to make concessions both ways. As Margaret Legum cheekily put it in an intervention from the floor at a recent public meeting of the Institute for Democratic

Alternatives in South Africa (IDASA), "The president must be forced to look over his left shoulder as much as he does over his right".[10]

This conception of South Africa's strategic imperatives goes against the grain of the dominant thinking among progressives. Indeed, the reigning left-wing orthodoxy is that it is important for progressive forces to coalesce against counter-revolutionaries because South Africa is at a very delicate stage in its democratic transition (Cachalia 2004; Southall and Wood 1999). The strategic aim is thus to establish predictability and prioritise political order. It is this rationale that serves as the philosophical foundation for, and justification of, the continued alliance of the ANC, COSATU and SACP, corporatist institutions like NEDLAC, and the cooperative relations of much of civil society with government. There is perhaps no more eloquent an articulation of this strategic perspective than by the deputy General-Secretary of the South African Communist Party (SACP), Jeremy Cronin, in two separate interviews: the first being the now notorious one with Irish academic Helena Sheehan for which he was wrapped over the knuckles by the ANC leadership, and the second with Adam Habib and Imraan Valodia very soon after the ANC received its overwhelming electoral mandate in the 2004 elections. In the former interview, Cronin explicitly states, "what people don't realise is that breaking the alliance means splitting all three organisations. You are talking of 2 million COSATU members, more than 80 percent of which are ANC members" (Cronin 2002; Southall 2003:65). For this reason it is imperative to remain within the alliance, not only to ensure that the ANC is not handed over to the neo-liberals, but also because it is increasingly becoming possible to win political victories as the shine of the Washington consensus policies begin to erode. This optimism carries through to the more recent interview, where once again Cronin highlights the political possibilities that arise as a result of the contemporary crisis of the global economy. He concludes: "The strategic priority of the day in South Africa is to have a significant political majority capable of spearheading fundamental transformation" (Interview with Jeremy Cronin, 20 April 2004), which he maintains has the greatest likelihood of being realised through the ANC.

But has not the track record of this strategic engagement not been very positive? Is the predictability facilitated by the strategic choices of COSATU, the SACP and other progressives not the cause of the reinforcement of existing power relations, which fostered the shift to the

10 This public meeting took place in Cape Town on 10 March 2004.

right in macroeconomic policy in the first place? Is it then sensible for progressive activists and movements to continue to advocate for a strategic perspective that leads to systemic outcomes that undermine their own political and socio-economic programme? Is not substantive uncertainty, which enhances citizens' leverage over state elites more sensible if one's goal is a more human-centred development program? Of course there could be much debate on the precise institutional mechanisms that could facilitate substantive uncertainty. Some may maintain that it need only involve electoral reform and the emergence of social movements (Southall and Mattes 2004; Ballard, Habib and Valodia 2004), while others would suggest that it would require the former coupled with the break-up of the tripartite alliance and the abandonment of corporatist institutions (Habib and Taylor 2001; Habib and Desai 1997). All of this could facilitate uncertainty, and this is necessary for loosening up the existing configuration of power in South African society. What is important to note in this debate, however, is that it is immaterial for advocates of uncertainty to agree with a particular social movement or political party. What is important for them is the systemic effect of the viable presence of these movements and parties, which creates uncertainty, and thereby facilitates the accountability of state elites to the citizenry.

To return to the question: when will a sustainable shift in the state's economic programme occur? The answer: when there is substantive uncertainty reintroduced into the political system. That is the strategic task confronting South African society. Unfortunately this is not what progressive activists have wanted to hear, at least not in an election year. But so long as the realisation of substantive uncertainty is postponed, so long will the goals of development, poverty alleviation and egalitarianism elude South Africa's democratic transition.

References

Abedian, Iraj (2004) "Right Choice for the Driving Conditions", *Financial Mail*, 7 May 2004.

Alexander, N. (2002) *An Ordinary Country: Issues in the Transition from Apartheid to Democracy in South Africa*, Pietermaritzburg: University of Natal Press.

Ballard, R., Habib, A., and Valodia, I. (2004) "Social Movements in South Africa: Promoting Crisis or Stability?, Beal, J., Gelb, S., and Hassim, S. (eds.), *Fragile Stability: State and Society in Democratic South Africa*, Cape Town: HSRC Press.

Bond Patrick (2000) *Elite Transition: From Apartheid to Neoliberalism in South Africa*, London: Pluto Press.

Bratton, M. and van de Walle, N. (1997) *Democratic Experiments in Africa: Regime Transitions in Comparative Perspective*, Cambridge, Cambridge University Press.

Cachalia, F. (2004) "Globalisation Limits the ANC's Options for Easing Poverty", *Sunday Times*, 11 April 2004.

UNDP (2004).

Coalition Against Water Provision, Anti-Privatisation Forum and Public Citizen (2004) "Nothing for Mahala: The Forced Installation of Prepaid Meters in Stretford, Extension 4, Orange Farm, Johannesburg, South Africa", Centre for Civil Society, Research Report no. 16.

Cohen, Tim (2004) "Corporate South Africa must leave its Shell" *Business Day*, 4 February 2004.

COSATU (2004) "Why Workers Should Vote ANC", <http://www.cosatu.org.za/docs/2004>.

Cronin, Jeremy (2004) "If Public Debate is Dead, Who Pulled the Trigger?", *Sunday Times*, 28 March 2004.

Cronin, Jeremy (2002) "An Interview with Helena Sheehan", <http://www.comms.deu.ie/sheehanh/za/cronin02.htm>.

Daniel, J., Habib, A., and Southall, R.. (eds.) (2003) *The State of the Nation 2003-2004*, Cape Town: HSRC Press.

Department of Social Welfare (2002) "Report of the Committee of Inquiry into a Comprehensive System of Social Security in South Africa", Pretoria: Department of Social Development.

Erwin, Alec (1992) "Economic Reconstruction", *African Communist*, second quarter, pp. 13-23.

Habib, A. and Taylor, R. (2001) "Political Alliances and Parliamentary Opposition in South Africa", Roger Southall (ed.) *Opposition and Democracy in South Africa*, London: Frank Cass.

Habib, A. and Padyachee, V. (2000) "Economic Policy and Power Relations in South Africa's Transition to Democracy", *World Development* (28) 2, pp. 245-263.

Habib, A. and Desai A. (1997) "Labour Relations in Transition: The Rise of Corporatism in South Africa's Automobile Industry", *Journal of Modern African Studies*, (35) 3.

Huntington, S. (1991) *The Third Wave: Democratization in the Late Twentieth Century*, Norman, University of Oaklohoma Press.

Marx, Karl (1972) "The Eighteenth Brumaire of Louis Bonaparte", Robert Tucker (ed.), *The Marx-Engels Reader*, New York: W.W. Norton.

Mbeki, T. (2004a) "Address of the President of South Africa, Thabo Mbeki, to the First Joint Sitting of the Third Democratic Parliament", Cape Town, 21 May 2004.

Mbeki, T. (2004b) "State of the Nation Address of the President of South Africa, Thabo Mbeki: Houses of Parliament", Cape Town, 6 February 2004.

Mbeki, T. (2003) "Address of the President of South Africa, Thabo Mbeki, to the National Council of Provinces", 11 November 2003.

McDonald, David (2002) "The Bell Tolls for Thee: Cost Recovery, Cut-Offs and the Affordability of Municipal Services in South Africa", in McDonald, David and John Pape (eds.) *Cost Recovery and the Crisis of Service Delivery in South Africa*, London and Cape Town: Zed Press and HSRC Press.

Murray, M. (1994) *The Revolution Deferred: The Painful Birth of Post-Apartheid South Africa*, London: Verso.

O'Donnell, G. (1993) "On the State, Democratization, and some Conceptual Problems: A Latin American View with Some Glances at Some Post-Communist", *World Development*, (21) 8.

O'Donnell, G. and Schmitter, P. (1986) *Transitions from Authoritarian Rule: Tentative Conclusions about Uncertain Democracies*, Baltimore: Johns Hopkins University Press.

Padayachee, V. and Valodia, I. (2001) "Changing GEAR? The 2001 Budget and Economic Policy in South Africa", *Transformation*, no. 46, pp. 71-83.

Policy Coordination and Advisory Services (PCAS), "The Presidency, Towards a Ten Year Review: Synthesis Report on Implementation of Government Programmes", October 2003.

Schedler, A (2001) "Taking Uncertainty Seriously: The Blurred Boundaries of Democratic Transition and Consolidation", *Democratization*, (8) 4.

Southall, R (2003) "The State of Party Politics: Struggles within the Tripartite Alliance and the Decline of Opposition", in Daniel, J, Habib, A, and Southall, R. (eds.) *The State of the Nation 2003-2004*, Cape Town: HSRC Press, pp. 53-77.

Southall, R. and Wood, G. (1999) "COSATU, the ANC, and the Election: Wither the Alliance?", *Transformation*, no. 38, pp. 68-81.

Statistics South Africa (2003) "Statistical Release", P0210, Pretoria: Statistics South Africa.

Stiglitz, J (2003) *The Roaring Nineties,* W.W. Norton and Company: New York and London.

Sunday Times, 9 May 2004.

3. Labour and Politics in South Africa

Liv Tørres *

1. Politics and Labour – Hand in Hand?

While core labour standards,[1] such as the right to organise and bargain collectively, are generally regarded as international human rights, many view labour movements mobilising on the basis of these rights primarily as features of capitalist societies in western democracies. The economic consequences of labour rights have also been given far more attention than their political impact. At the same time, several labour movements in the south have spearheaded democratic transitions. The Congress of South African Trade Unions (COSATU) played a leading role in the anti-apartheid struggle in South Africa. Politics and labour, hand in hand, shaped the struggle and in turn laid the basis for the alliance between COSATU, the African National Congress (ANC) and the South African Communist Party (SACP). The alliance became an important part of the power configuration in the post-apartheid transition, highlighted by Habib elsewhere in this volume, and some would argue even more important than Parliament itself in forming the content and shape of public policy. At the same time, there are major tensions within the alliance centred around economic policies, HIV/AIDS and South Africa's approach towards Zimbabwe.

This chapter sets out to explore the role of labour in the South African reconstruction and development process with particular focus on the political dimension of trade unionism and the alliance as a site of

* Associate professor, Department of Political Science, University of Oslo.

1 The core labour standards refer to the ILO Conventions concerning the right to organise, to collective bargaining as well as the ban on child labour, forced labour and discrimination (ILO Conventions 29, 87, 98, 100, 105, 111, 138 and 182).

Peris Jones and Kristian Stokke (eds.), Democratising Development, *ISBN 90 04 14821 3, pp. 55-76.*

struggle and achievements. While most would see the strength and political outlook of labour movements primarily as determined by their economic base, political strength and strategies will also be shaped by the political setting and pacts developed when labour was formed. We trace the background to the alliance, explore the progress that has been achieved in the past decade and discuss its future challenges and prospects. The strength and success of the alliance will depend on its delivery, but also on the autonomy of its partners and their ability to mobilise. In the long term, however, the alliance may itself challenge the very same independence and ability to mobilise, which provides the basis for the strength of labour.

2. Comrades in Arms

Valenzuela (1992) argues that the characteristics of labour movements, their long-term political programmes and effects on national policies, as well as their internal organisational structures cannot be understood without factoring in their insertion into national political systems, the nature of the respective political regimes at the time and the characteristics of the political parties to which they established links.

The South African tripartite alliance emerged through decades of liberation struggle against the apartheid regime. The alliance between the ANC and SACP has the deepest roots, dating back to the Party's foundation in 1953.[2] While the SACP's sturdy trade union legacy made it a strong link between the ANC and the unions that were formed in the 50s, the activities and strategies of the SACP had become closely linked to the ANC in the following decades, including its subordination of trade union activities to ANC's nationalist aspirations (Eidelberg 2000). Simultaneously, the union federation South African Congress of Trade Unions (SACTU) was formed with a strong focus on political goals. When the ANC, SACP and SACTU were banned in the early 60s, they all became forced to operate in exile or underground inside the country. Their experiences did, however, provide an important learning curve for the new generation of trade unionists to surface inside

2 The links between the previous Communist Party of South Africa (CPSA) and the ANC were much looser. The relationship between ANC and SACP was strengthened after 1961 and the establishment of Umkhonto weSizwe, the ANCs military wing and the subsequent formation of a revolutionary council on which both organizations served.

South Africa. With SACTU's emphasis on political goals and relatively centralised structures, the new unions learnt that both their political struggle and organisational survival would depend on their strength on the shop floor.

A dominant part of the trade union movement that emerged in the 70s and 80s hence focussed on building strong shop floor structures and internal democracy. When the federation COSATU was formed in 1985, it merged strong political and "workerist" traditions, strategies focussed on labour issues and political campaigns and strong democratic structures with a core of charterist[3] tendencies at the centre (Tørres 2000). Although the COSATU launch represented a potential formidable advance for the ANC as an internal representative, it also posed a possible challenge by being formed on the basis of traditionally independent unions[4] and not predominantly by the pro-ANC unions.[5] During the 80s, however COSATU played a significant role in the internal struggle against apartheid, which in turn influenced its relationship to both the ANC and the SACP. Through the late 80s, links and contact were established between COSATU and the ANC/SACP in exile,[6] and while COSATU retained its independence, it also became regarded as the only legitimate trade union federation by the ANC.[7]

The alliance between COSATU, the ANC and the SACP developed within the context of the "negotiated revolution" where the national revolution would pave the way for a socialist revolution. Controversies remained, however, as to how the class struggle would be taken forward after democracy was achieved. Hopes were high amongst certain parts

3 The Freedom Charter (1955) formed the political base for the SACP, ANC and COSATU.

4 The Federation of South African Trade Unions (FOSATU).

5 In fact the pro-ANC United Democratic Front trade unions were soon absorbed by the ex-FOSATU unions.

6 A series of union seminars were organised by SACTU and COSATU in Lusaka and Harare in the 80s serving to bridge goals and tactics. In the early 90s, meetings between COSATU and ANC/SACP became more structured and oriented towards the "post-apartheid" South Africa. In 1990, COSATU-ANC workshops were for example held in Zimbabwe to plan policies for a post-apartheid government.

7 COSATU's stance as the ANC's labour ally was confirmed by the decision taken in 1990 to transfer to the federation the assets of the old exile union centre SACTU (Lodge 2002).

of the SACP and labour movement in the early 90s that SACP could be established as an independent party based on democratic socialism and leaning on the trade union movement. However, the SACP leadership determined to remain as a separate political party without autonomous political representation, *inside* the alliance with the ANC. The basis for the Tripartite Alliance, as it was to become known, was a commonly agreed programme for reconstruction and development. Thus the Alliance was sold both internally and externally as a "relationship" based on a shared programme, not a "marriage" lasting forever. But while COSATU's economic policy at the time, and to this day, has been one of growth through redistribution, the final version of the Reconstruction and Development Programme (RDP), was much watered down from the original COSATU version (Naidoo 2002).[8]

The moderated final version of the RDP programme should be seen to represent a "class compromise" on the background of the ANC representing a multi-class constituency. While many expected the ANC to retain a certain working class bias, there was also strong resistance among parts of the ANC leadership to anything that resembled a radical economic programme. While differences and tensions continued to bubble under the surface, the RDP, to some extent represented a general consensus of the liberation movement, proposing a state-led, market assisted transformation process, promising to accommodate capital, but not be subordinate to it (Naidoo 2002). The ANC adopted the RDP as its manifesto for the 1994 elections, while COSATU in turn embraced the ANC as its favourite election candidate and deployed key leaders into the ANC government, including into positions to oversee the implementation of the RDP. In the first year of democracy, hundreds of unionists went into government, including many of the best COSATU negotiators and operational managers (Naidoo 2002). In hindsight, COSATU paid a high price of organisational weakness in the short and medium term from this so-called "braindrain". At the same time, both COSATU and the ex-COSATU leaders were confronted with an increasing opposition to the RDP amongst ANC leaders.

In early 1996, the RDP Ministry was abruptly closed, on the basis that it had been "successfully integrated" into government. Shortly,

8 The RDPs first four drafts were the products of policy expertise associated with the trade union movement. Three further drafts were debated at meetings which built up a wider range of consensus between the ANC, the trade unions, the SACP, MDM affiliates and a range of NGOs (Lodge 2002).

thereafter, allegedly because of a currency "crisis", the Growth, Employment and Redistribution Strategy (GEAR)[9] was rapidly introduced as a "non-negotiable" programme. Although GEAR proponents claimed to be providing a macro-economic framework for the RDP, GEAR effectively reversed the RDP logic: rather than state-led, it was set to be led by the market and instead of the state accommodating capital, it was seen to be subordinating to it. While some would pinpoint a policy shift in the 2004 election year towards a more interventionist state-led economic strategy, the main components of GEAR policies are still in place.

3. Deliveries of the Alliance

For both labour, and the constituencies outside the alliance, the debates about the deliveries and impact of the alliance have gained momentum in the past few years. By the early 1990s, apartheid had skewed social protection heavily toward prosperous whites, leaving South Africa with a considerable development deficit and the new democratic government with major challenges for reconstruction. Expectations to social and economic improvements were high amongst the black population. Few expected all the social problems to have been solved a decade later, but most expected development trends to have turned in a more equitable direction. While several gains have been made, poverty, unemployment and labour market restructuring pose considerable challenges to internal relations in the alliance and the legitimacy it holds amongst its partners and the population.

Through GEAR, the government set restrictive targets for fiscal policy as well as aims for investments, trade and growth. It aimed to reduce the deficit relative to GDP from 5 to 3 percent before 1999, and stabilise tax revenues at 25 percent of the GDP. In practice, it had the effect of cutting government spending by 9 percent in real terms, while at the same time permitting a substantial increase in military spending together with moderate improvements in the social budget (Makgetla 2001). While the fiscal and tariff targets were realised in the following three years, South Africa also experienced a historically low rate

9 Growth, Employment and Redistribution: A Macroeconomic Strategy <www.finance.gov.za>. The summary of economic information leans heavily on Makgetla 2001 and 2004.

of investment,[10] rising capital outflows, massive job losses and sluggish growth.

The government demonstrated commitments to improve social protection for the historically deprived black communities, with a consequent focus on education, health, welfare, housing and infrastructure. In several areas, such as water, electricity and to some extent housing, delivery has been substantial. Yet, while economic growth has picked up in the past few years, South Africa is still facing a crisis of unemployment, poverty, and malnutrition combined with high food prices. Unemployment climbed from 16 per cent in 1995 to just below 30 per cent in late 2001. By the end of 2003, everyone, including government statistics, agreed that "strict" unemployment is at least 30 percent.[11] The Mesebetsi labour force survey (Tørres *et al.* 2002)[12] indicated unemployment to be even higher. In 2000, total unemployment reached nearly 32 percent under the strict definition and 45 percent of those not actively seeking jobs were included. The largest job losses have been in mining, manufacturing, the public service and agriculture. Even in the sectors where economic growth has picked up from the end of 2000, formal sector job losses have persisted.[13] While the RDP programme promised one million jobs in the subsequent five years from 1994, and GEAR 270.000 jobs per year, there have instead been massive job losses.[14]

10 Investment languished persistently at less than 20% of the GDP and fell to 14,9% in 2000, the lowest level since 1993 (SARB 2001). Between 1994 and 2001, foreign direct investment totalled R45 billion, while FDI out of SA came to R54 billion (Makgetla 2001).

11 In March 2004, unemployment was at 29% using the "narrow" definition that does not count as unemployed people who want paid work, but are too discouraged to actively seek it. Using the "broad" definition, i.e. also counting the latter group, the unemployment figure rises to 41 percent of the labour force.

12 The Mesebetsi Labour Force Survey was a sample survey of 10.000 households conducted by Fafo and the SA Department of Labour 2000 (see Tørres *et al.* 2000).

13 Women, people in non-urban areas and Africans have unemployment rates much higher than the average. Young African men in the 15 to 30 age group have an unemployment rate of more than 60 percent. The most vulnerable of all are however African women in the 15-30 age group living in rural areas.

14 Half of those who are currently looking for work have never worked before, reflecting the large numbers of young entrants into the labour market

Not only has unemployment increased dramatically, a large proportion of the jobs created is in the so-called informal sector with low wages, and neither benefits nor labour protection. According to the Mesebetsi survey, about 2,2 million, or 20 percent of the working population, work in the informal sector (excluding agriculture and domestic services).[15] This survey, as well as the official estimates, indicates that there has been considerable growth in informal sector employment over the past years. Statistics now indicate that only about 60 percent of employment is found in the formal sector.

A. *Income and Wealth*

After Brazil, South Africa demonstrates the largest inequality between rich and poor in the whole world. Some 60 percent of the employed were according to the Census 1996 reported to receive incomes of R1 500 or less a month. By 2000, the overall individual income mean is R2 419 per month, whilst the median is R1,309 per month, suggesting that income differentiation remains significant (Tørres *et al.* 2002). Africans earn on average R1,638 per month whereas Whites earn R6,131 monthly. White labourers earn on average R3,511 whereas African *managers* earn R4,550.

To the extent the economy has created jobs at all, they have been low-level, insecure and very poorly paid. As the following table indicates, the official statistics report an unmistakeable decline in real incomes over the past decade (see Makgetla 2004). The proportion of workers earning under R1000 a month in nominal terms has remained fairly stable at around 40 percent of the total. In 2004, 39 percent of the population earned under R1,000 a month, but the purchasing power of

every year. In shortage of job creation and efficient government "unemployment offices", most also struggle to get government assistance in looking for work. 40 percent of the unemployed in rural areas and 28 percent in urban areas say that this is one of their two greatest obstacles to finding work. About 60 percent of the unemployed go from door to door enquiring for jobs directly at various companies.

15 The informal sector includes employees, employers, self-employed people or family business workers who work for private sector enterprises with 20 or less employees and in enterprises that are not registered or incorporated and do not keep a set of accounts separate from the household budget.

R1000 had fallen by well over a half compared to ten years earlier (The People's Budget 2005).

Table 1. Workers' income, 1995 and 2002

	Household Survey, October 1995	Labour Force Survey, September 2002
Value of R1000 in constant 2000 rand	R1,406	R950
% of all workers earning:		
R0	0%	4%
R1-R999 a month	35%	35%
over R1,000 a month	64%	61%
Total	100%	100%
% of workers earning under R1,000	36%	39%

Source: Makgetla 2004

The apparent long-term fall in wages essentially results from the shift from formal to informal work. Hawking and subsistence agriculture together accounted for almost half of all employment growth reported between 1997 and 2002. And most of the reported new jobs earn well under R1000 a month. The same trend is emerging from the steady decline in labour's share of total national income, falling from 57 percent in 1990 to 51 percent by 2002 (Makgetla 2004). In 1995, the richest 20 percent of households had 63 percent of household income, whereas the poorest 20 percent had only 3 percent (CSS 1995, IES 1995). The total overall Gini (0,63) in 2000 was higher than the one for 1993-1994 at 0,59 (World Development Report 2000). About 10 percent of households receive some 50 percent of overall household income, while approximately 50 percent of households receive only about 10 percent of total household income in 2000.

Some argue that workers, the so-called "labour aristocracy" need to moderate wage demands in order to create jobs for more people. Another prevailing related myth is that it is the gains of the formal sector workers, which have created the pressures on the unemployed poor. Yet a further argument often presented is that the poor majority to a large extent survives on government grants and old age pensions in particular. In reality, however, half of the poorest households (with R286 per month), relies upon remittances from household members for their survival (Tørres *et al.* 2002). Wage moderation amongst workers, who are most often the ones paying remittances, may hence in fact aggravate poverty amongst the poorest. With two-thirds of the population inside the labour force and only about one third of the labour force in employment, each working man or woman has about 4,3 people to support. In conclusion, between 1995 and 2000, the share of the poorest 60 percent of households in the national income fell from 17 to 15 percent, with the biggest decline amongst the poorest households; the average African household income fell by 19 percent, to R26,000 a year and average white household incomes simultaneously rose by 16 percent, to R158,000 a year (Makgetla 2004).

B. Conditions of Employment and Institutional Change

In the past decade, new acts have improved and extended employment conditions and labour rights to virtually all workers, irrespective of race or sector; established dispute-settlement mechanisms based on conciliation and arbitration; supported sector-wide collective bargaining; and set up an ambitious skills-development strategy based on a one percent training levy paid by employers and Sector Education and Training Authorities (SETA's) responsible for distributing the funds to business.

Compared to the previous apartheid era and in comparison with many other middle income countries, formal sector workers in South Africa have extended access to benefits at work and relatively well-regulated working conditions. Yet, several challenges remain. Working hours in South Africa have traditionally been relatively long by international standards, and certainly compared to industrialised countries. The *Basic Conditions of Employment Act* (1997) reduced the standard working week to 45 hours. One quarter of working people report hours over 45, and 12 percent of respondents worked more than 55 hours.[16] In terms of working conditions and benefits, 44 percent of workers have access to annual leave, 45 percent to sick leave and 26 percent report access to maternity leave. Workers in the public sector, unionised workers and permanent employees have most often access to such benefits. Most workers also report to still not have contracts covering their employment relations. Written work contracts are not common in the private sector. Three out of four employees in the public sector report having a

16 Where no other reference is given, data is extracted from the Mesebetsi Labour Force Survey (Tørres *et al.* 2002).

written work contract, while only 39 percent of private sector employees report that this is the case.

The *Labour Relations Act* (LRA) 1996 is another crucial piece of legislation which was put in place on the basis of union demands for collective bargaining and after heavy rounds of negotiations with the social partners. Key innovations relate to the scope of union organisation, the structure of negotiations and dispute settlement. In firms with over 100 workers, trade unions can also establish workplace forums to promote consultation on issues such as work organisation, corporate downsizing and changes in production processes. Furthermore, for the first time, public servants, farm and domestic workers received the right to organise, and an agency fee was introduced into collective bargaining.

Union density, as a proportion of all the employed outside domestic work and agriculture, increased from 18 percent in 1985 to 40 percent in 2001. In the same period, membership doubled, from 1,4 million to 2,7 million, even though formal employment declined. In terms of the federations, COSATU remains the largest.[17] At its height in 2001, about 1,8 million workers were members of COSATU. Job losses brought membership figures down to 1,3 million by 2003. Simultaneously, approximately one third of formal sector workers report being covered by collective agreements (Tørres *et al.* 2002).

The Government has also instituted an *affirmative action programme.* And finally, the National Economic, Development and Labour Council (NEDLAC) was established in 1995 as a forum for discussions and negotiations between the social partners about labour laws, social issues and reconstruction. All in all, the government hence delivered substantial advances in certain socio-economic areas, completely uprooted and replaced old institutions and policies and simultaneously established a relatively progressive industrial relations system and system of social dialogue. At the same time, major challenges remain with rocketing unemployment and informal sector employment, with subsequent poverty and inequality. While changes have occurred in terms of black empowerment and gender improvements in the top layers of

17 Both the Federation of Unions of South Africa (FEDUSA) and the National Congress of Trade Unions (NACTU) reported about 500 000 members in 2002, but FEDUSA has grown relatively while NACTU has declined. A number of independent unions, account for about a million members. Both COSATU and NACTU represent mostly black, lower-level workers, while FEDUSA represents largely professionals and semi-professionals.

the private and public sector, the bottom of the labour market remains overwhelmingly black and poor.

4. Tensions Emerging in the Alliance

In spite of progress and deliveries on several issues, increased tensions have emerged in the tripartite alliance over the past decade. Inside the alliance, views will differ as to the benefits of the alliance and whether it should be maintained.

On the one hand, COSATU has managed to get many strategic advantages from its inside influence over policies, especially in the social area and particularly in the early years. The provision of basic services, including shelter, health care, water, electricity, education and so forth, is generally regarded as a major gain for the working class. Labour market reforms form other examples of gains made by labour in the past decade. The Labour Relations Act described above is generally depicted by the COSATU leadership as the first salvo fired by the democratic government in its efforts to replace the apartheid labour regime.[18] The possibility for more active intervention in the market has also clearly emerged in areas where the Alliance has taken a unified position, such as with the Mining Development Act and the Financial Sector Summit (COSATU 2002).

Others, less optimistic about the alliance, argue that several of the achievements, including on labour legislation and the Constitution, were made on the basis of mass mobilisation by labour. Furthermore, on key labour issues such as privatisation, rationalisation of public sector and tariff reductions, victories have been far apart. The COSATU call for a Basic Income Grant and massive job creation programmes have also been largely ignored. Likewise, COSATUs criticism of a market-led housing strategy and their strategies for trade and industrial policy, issues of monetary policies have also been voiced. The launch of GEAR as a "non-negotiable" is another example in point. Thus, in the final analysis, the degree of strategic advantage that has been gained from the alliance appears more modest. Indeed, the union movement may have achieved more advances (including statutorily binding agreements) at NEDLAC than it has through the Tripartite Alliance. In fact, COSATU recognises that rather than inside the Alliance, strategic engagements

18 As reflected in the address by COSATU General Secretary, Zwelinzima Vavi, at the SACP special Congress, 8th April 2005, Durban.

have normally taken place elsewhere.[19] Some would even argue that the alliance has been counterproductive for COSATU by eroding its membership base through the increased unemployment caused by the government's economic policies.

Real ideological and political differences have riveted the alliance on several occasions. Conflicts emerged for example at the SACP 1998 Congress when President Mandela and Deputy President Thabo Mbeki challenged the "left" to toe the line or leave the alliance (Southall 2003). COSATU expected the Ekurhuleni Declaration in March 2002 to provide a basis for settling policy disagreements in the Alliance, in the context of preparations for the Growth and Development Summit. The expected processes did not take place, however, and some ANC leaders were seen to mount fierce attacks on COSATU and the SACP in the run-up to and following the general strike later the same year. Likewise, tensions emerged at the 2002 ANC National Congress where discussions were rife about the possibility that the ANC might face an open contest for leadership for the first time. Such tensions and debates are not likely to end. At the same time, the alliance parties constituted a massive united front during the elections campaigns 2004. The ANC also realigned their policies more to the alliance partners with added focus on the role of the state and the government has in consequence made unemployment and the fight on poverty as priority number one.[20] However, several COSATU leaders pinpoint the contradictory and complex picture emerging and that it is premature to say that strategic policy shifts have taken place.

Those who argue for the end of the Tripartite Alliance maintain that the alliance is no longer a partnership of equal partners, but that the SACP and COSATU have become, and are being treated as, subordinate. Views also differ in the alliance on the role of COSTAU and of the alliance itself with the ANC sometimes seen by COSATU to regard the labour federation as a labour aristocracy or expected to vanguard the interests of the state, rather than that of the poor and the working-class. Critics highlight the several COSATU demands that have not

19 As expressed for example in Labour, Socio-Economic Transformation and the State – Reflections on South Africa's ten years of democracy. Address by Zwelinzima Vavi, COSATU General Secretary to the COSATU Conference Celebrating Ten Years of Democracy and Freedom, 5th March 2005.

20 As expressed amongst others in President Thabo Mbeki's State of the Nation Address, 21 May 2004.

been met, such as those made for the socialisation of the mining and financial sectors; a halt to the privatisation of public assets and the consolidation and expansion of public enterprises to drive state-led infrastructural development and job creation etc. And finally, there has been criticism of centralisation, lack of tolerance for divergent views, bureaucratisation at the expense of internal democracy[21] and of an apparent continued preference for the political habits of exiles rather than those of democracy. The criticisers suggest that an opposition party to the left of the ANC would force the government's economic policy to align better with the Constitutional and democratic imperatives (Naidoo 2002). The argument would be that a break-away of the COSATU and the SACP would make it possible to construct an opposition party of the left, whose socialist programme would enable it to attract a mass-based, popular following.

On another level, however, unions represent the left in the ANC's multi-class make-up, and are thus seen to play an important role in counter-veiling the influence of more conservative components within the ANC (see Naidoo 2002). Furthermore, as important as a left opposition may be, several argue that it is doubtful that a class-based agenda at this stage will outweigh race and ethnicity in the electoral stakes. Without good preparation, such a left opposition would be obliterated with little benefit to an actual left agenda. It is hard to predict the alternate political route of ANC policies had COSATU and the SACP not been in the Alliance. Some see today's ANC practices as being inherited from the exile period when priority was given to securing positions in a bureaucratic and military apparatus that would provide standing in the future and factionalism and patronage prevailed according to Southall (2003). Yet, others expect that this inheritance will become moderated with time and with the encounters with the democratic processes of the trade union movement and other social movements inside the country. The ANC may, according to these views, be subject to regressive tendencies, but not beyond possible redemption (Southall 2003). There are also those underlining that in a true alliance, there have to be compromises made between the interests of workers and those (i.e.

21 After deputy general secretary Jeremy Cronin of the SACP was quoted in an Irish newspaper for example arguing that "I think there are tendencies now of what some of us refer to as zanufication of the ANC" comparing the ANC to ZANU in Zimbabwe, he was censured by the ANC NEC and required to apologise, which he did.

the ANC) representing the state, including also the interests of capital, consumers, environmental groups etc. A final consideration is the attitudes of COSATU workers and shop stewards, who in many cases are also ANC's active members and party officials at the local level. Hence, while the COSATU leadership may experience tensions with the ANC, factory floor workers and shop stewards in general give relatively strong support to the alliance and to the ANC (Tørres 1996, 2004; Buhlungu 2004).

Labour is experiencing the difficult balancing act between cooperation and independence. On the one hand, it is seen as part and parcel of the Tripartite Alliance and hence also co-responsible for ANC policies. On the other hand, it is attempting to retain a strong image of independence. COSATU has on several occasions debated the balancing act between power and engagement, and between independence/opposition and co-operation. Using power through mobilisation is, however, often seen to annoy the ANC, irrespective of the cause or source (COSATU 2002). On the eve of COSATU's anti-privatisation strike in 2001 for example, President Mbeki launched a major attack on what he called the "ultra left" in COSATU.[22] Public "mudslinging" occurred again when COSATU went on another general strike against privatisation in 2002. Yet if COSATU does not use power, politicians and bureaucrats routinely say they do not have time to engage. COSATU has on several occasions pointed out that Alliance leadership has poor capacity to drive joint processes and that no collaborative policy development has taken place on the economy. The only preparations for the Growth and Development Summit in 2002 were for example undertaken at NEDLAC. Few Alliance Secretariat meetings are convened and hardly any real interaction takes place amongst the Alliance leadership otherwise, although this was identified as the key requirement in the bilateral discussions amongst others in the run-up to the Ekurhuleni Summit in 2002.

Those in favour of COSATU staying in the Tripartite Alliance argue that the ANC belongs to the broader liberation movement, and thus to give it up, and go into the "political wilderness" would be class suicide (Naidoo 2002). Moreover, they would argue that COSATU is independ-

22 The ANC Executive Committee argued in a confidential briefing document that an "ultra-left tendency" had emerged attempting to transform COSATU into a political formation independent of the ANC (ANC 2001).

ent, financially self-sufficient and worker-controlled, and therefore able to resist the dismal fate of trade union movements elsewhere in Africa in the post-liberation phase (Webster 2005). The Tripartite Alliance furthermore, does not prevent its members from building alliances with other social formations and movements. The internal tensions are also seen by some to be a natural consequence of the various organisations having different, but complementary backgrounds, views, interests and consistencies and as such a good basis for a relationship. And finally, it is sometimes argued that the ANC faces tight limits on its' actions because of domestic and, even more, international capital demands that government restrain spending, avoid inflation, open the economy to international competition and financial flows, and generally secure property rights (COSATU 2002). If government ignores these demands, it is argued, the result will be massive capital flight, which will wreck the economy.

Many, including people in the union movement see the influence of the alliance on government policy as low, or even practically zero. Yet, COSATUs best "card" may in fact be that the ANC itself may need the alliance more than COSATU does. While regarding COSATU often as a problem to be contained rather than as an asset, it is an important support base for elections. Furthermore, the idea of COSATU possibly launching a new party or supporting an independent SACP at elections is a scary thought to many ANC cadres. And there is little doubt that as tensions have grown between COSATU and the ANC over the past years, COSATU and the SACP have become closer.[23] At the same time, the ANC's views of the SACP have changed. Throughout the exile days, the SACP and its activists were highly regarded and the SACP provided key direction to the ANC. Just associating with the SACP, and even more being a member, brought respect and honour in the democratic movement,[24] but after the collapse of the Soviet Union, the SACP's role

23 The relationship between the SACP and COSATU has however also been fairly strenuous in periods. Continued differences remain in their respective attitudes to capital, to the role COSATU should play in the broader transformation of South Africa and when it comes to its relationship to the ANC.

24 The SACP was the first to be banned, in 1950. By the time the ANC was outlawed in 1960, it had already accumulated ten years of experience in underground work. It had developed connections outside the country, which it put at the service of the ANC. SACP cadre were amongst the most respected ANC leaders and M.K. operatives such as Joe Slovo, Moses Mabhida, Moses Kotane, and Chris Hani.

became increasingly contested and its policies more focussed and controversial.

As an alternative, or supplementing, channel of influence for COSATU, the bilateral Millennium Labour Council[25] emerged on the background of labour-government tensions and while formally being an institution under NEDLAC. It emerged in practice as an institution bringing senior business and labour leaders together to find common ground on matters of mutual interest without the government.[26] The ANC attracted widespread criticism also in COSATU for its 2002 endorsement of Robert Mugabe's Zanu, which stood accused of having rigged the elections in Zimbabwe. On HIV/AIDS issues, COSATU found alliance partners, through the Treatment Action Campaign, in order to put pressure on the government. The labour movement has developed several issue-based coalitions with other social movements, which can contest the role and policies of the state. In recent years, unions have for example developed joint campaigns with social movement through the Basic Income Grant coalition, the People's Budget coalition, and the Treatment Action Campaign as mentioned above, all taking forward issues of redistribution, and addressing priorities of the poor and the working class.

5. Labour and Politics Hand in Hand: Basis for Democracy and Delivery?

There are strong indications that the South African labour movement gained their political resources and capacity for mobilisation through collective bargaining, organising and strong shop floor structures (Tørres 2000, 2004). On that basis, labour took a principal role in the internal struggle for democracy and as such became a leading alliance partner also for the African National Congress (ANC). Economic de-

25 The Millennium Labour Council (MLC) was launched in July 2000. It is an "informal" bilateral body and comprises 12 leaders each from business and labour. The MLC aims to improve the social dialogue and to reach concrete agreements to tackle socio-economic problems facing South Africa.

26 The agreement reached on the LRA constitutes one example of successful negotiations in the MLC. Soon after the MLC's inception, government tabled proposed labour law amendments. The MLC engaged extensively on the matter, resulting in an agreement on a set of proposals, which constituted the basis for negotiation at NEDLAC.

velopments did politicise the working class in South Africa. But it also seems plausible that it was particularly through the joint existence of bargaining systems and strong internal organisation that labour gained the empowerment that made them collectively realise the need to act and the capacity to go through with it. The question remains however as to whether the same rights, resources and capacity for mobilisation remain pillars for democratic consolidation after the first phase of transitions have been passed and to what extent, and how, political involvement and alliances affect the strength and resources of the labour movement in the longer term.

For the time being, the alliance remains in place, and there is every indication that it will do so for at least the forthcoming ANC congress in 2007. Yet there can be no doubt equally that its foundations have been severely shaken by bitter infighting (Southall 2004). There is also little doubt that there will be severe fighting about whom, or rather *whose* candidate should take over as party leader, and presumably as president thereafter, after Thabo Mbeki. Yet, while several challenges have emerged for the alliance, few doubt that the ANC needs the alliance. An oppositional party on the left, launched by the SACP and supported by COSATU, would constitute severe competition to the ANC. Furthermore, a new development strategy, geared to structural change, is unlikely to be successful unless it is based upon broad consultation with business and labour. South Africa demonstrates a long history of codetermination and social dialogue from the early 90s through the National Economic Forum, the subsequent establishment and functioning of NEDLAC as well as negotiations by the social partners through numerous other forums.

In the longer period, infighting about political directions, combined with growing unemployment and poverty, increases the likelihood that an opposition party of the left will be established with strong backing from the SACP and COSATU. The question of political alliances has also been a controversial issue internally in COSATU with a strong minority actively working against it. From the very beginning the clothing and textile workers union (SACTWU) was against it because they wanted an independent labour movement. The Metal Workers Union (NUMSA) was also against the alliance, but primarily because it wanted stronger links with the SACP on the basis of a socialist platform. In addition to these groups, opposition has grown in parallel with growing frustration with what is perceived as lack of delivery from the ANC.

Valenzuela (1992) distinguishes between the various kinds of unions, and union-state relations, (found under democratic regimes) such as: the social democratic, the contestatory and the pressure group. Likewise, literature on state-labour relations distinguishes between pluralist, political, social movement unionism[27] and corporatist perspectives. The South African trade union movement in the 80s and early 90s would generally be characterised as social movement unionism while the relations and alliance developing after the first elections in 1994 could resemble the category of social democratic corporatism otherwise found in Scandinavia. Social democratic state-labour relations would see the relations between the state and labour not as a question of co-option, but rather of labour strategically using the political loopholes available to advance its own interests. Hence societal corporatism refers to a co-existence between the state and social partners, where the state consults with and delegates responsibilities to the unions in exchange for responsible behaviour. Societal corporatism developed gradually in several West European countries in the post-war period and generally goes together with some sort of centralised bargaining and/or social dialogue between the social partners.

Valenzuela argues that labour's independence from politics, and political parties, is crucial in processes of democratic transitions in order to avoid undermining labour. Others, including South African (and Scandinavian) trade unionists, would argue that labour movements can gain effective control of the state apparatus and use it to benefit workers and the democratic transition more generally. In the broader picture however, it all seems to depend on the ability of labour to balance carefully between alliance and independence, and between co-operation and protest.

As with other social organisations, labour movements are creatures of their past circumstances. As such, South African labour is in the short term bound to some extent by the close relations with the ANC developed through the struggle. A large majority of COSATU workers support the alliance. 75 percent of COSATU workers believed

27 Pluralists see unions primarily as economic and regard autonomy from the state as essential. Corporatist analyses arose on the other hand as a challenge to the pluralists' account of political processes and argue that unions are not autonomous but have tied their interests to the state. Theories on social movement unionism arose in turn as a reflection of the political role that labour took upon itself in countries such as Brazil, Poland and South Africa in struggles for democracy in close alliances with social movements and NGOs.

the Alliance should fight the elections in 1994 (Ginsburg and Webster 1995; Tørres 1995). Interestingly, even *unorganised* workers believed that union involvement in politics was a good thing and gave support to the Alliance in the early 90s (Tørres 1995). Yet, while 77 percent of COSATU workers believed that the ANC had worker interests at heart, there has been declining support for the alliance amongst workers since 1994. By late 1998, "only" 64 percent thought the alliance should contest the next elections together (Naidoo 1999). Webster (2005) finds, however, that amongst COSATU members, the support for the alliance has remained strong up to 2004. Workers' trust in the alliance will to some extent depend on delivery. Expectations of the government ran high after the elections in 1994. However, workers also indicate that they are aware of the constraints on the government. Simultaneously, workers repeatedly indicate that if their expectations are not met, they will readily engage in mass actions (Tørres 2003). COSATU workers are also more active in politics and civil society than non-unionised workers and are more politically aware, conscious, and sophisticated (Tørres 1995, 2003). COSATU workers repeatedly express that the alliance should be based on broad and in-depth consultation. A large majority of COSATU workers argue that the ANC should consult properly with its supporters on all issues (Naidoo 1999; Tørres 2003). Since the early 90s, workers have in fact been divided on whether workers can rely upon political parties to represent their interests (Ginsburg and Webster 1995), with large groups believing that unions are their best *political* representatives (Tørres 2003).

The future of the alliance will on this basis rely on concrete delivery, but more fundamentally and broadly on whether the alliance is seen to protect the interests of workers and the poor within the alliance, through both actual delivery and processes of consultation. By early 2005, the alliance has delivered mixed results for labour and the tensions have been growing between the alliance partners. Arguments reflected by Ballard and Habib elsewhere in this volume, about the alliance being seen as a barrier to development and/or to the substantive political uncertainty needed in South Africa as argued by Habib, may in fact be exaggerated when seeing the limited impact the alliance has had on concrete union demands. Irrespective of the impact in concrete policy areas, the alliance may of course be argued to have had an impact on the likelihood of a new party emerging and hence degree of substantive uncertainty as argued by Habib. It does seem likely, however, that such arguments hold more relevance for the SACP than for COSATU.

If the SACP should decide to stand for elections independently, or other parties were to emerge with backing from such constituencies, it would introduce a fair level of substantive uncertainty. Webster (2005) argues that the strength of governing parties will determine the likelihood of trade unions breaking the alliance with them. He concludes on that basis, that with the dominance of the ANC in South African politics and the support that the alliance holds amongst COSATU members, COSATU will be unlikely to withdraw. It may however be more correct to assume that withdrawal or not from the alliance holds little relevance as long as there are no other parties for COSATU to support. Hence, it may not necessarily be the strength of the governing party, but lack of alternatives, which has most impact on trade union strategies in this respect. For COSATU, the real strength of their bargaining power lies in their ability to mobilise and demonstrate collective action, whether inside or outside an alliance. With the existence of a new party, competition for COSATUs support would become more real and COSATUs bargaining cards more effective.

The election campaign 2004 did demonstrate an increasing overlap between the interests of COSATU and the priorities of the ANC. In the longer term, the balance between the needs of the state and the needs and interests of workers and trade unionists, will give the union movements major challenges. Whether the ANC in the alliance promotes the interests of workers *vis-à-vis* capital, will continue to depend on labour's strength and ability to mobilise.

Labour's participation in political alliances will to some extent imply that it needs to accept constraint and compromise, but the success of labour will ultimately depend upon the degree to which they have loyalty amongst their own *members*. Political alliances carry dangers of co-option if labour is short of resources in order to take effective part in them. Labour's gains *inside* the alliance will hence depend on its strength *outside*. In order for labour to influence or control public policy, they need the means and use of sanctions like strikes and stay-aways. For this, they need the internal support of the workers. Centralisation of decision-making in the unions may have left a "gap" on the shop floor, which needs to be urgently addressed and filled. In addition to meeting the political challenges towards the ANC and SACP, labour is hence currently concerned with building strategies and campaigns to address shop floor and "back to basics" issues. Socio-economic rights, and more specifically labour rights, served as a basis for the democratic struggle against apartheid in South Africa. In the years to come, labour's ability to mobilise on the basis of the same rights will determine its political influence, but also the consolidation of democracy. With weak political opposition in Parliament and lack of an effective multiparty system, the role of civil society and labour in particular, will remain crucial for democratic debate, transparency and delivery.

References

ANC (1997): Declaration and Resolutions of the Mafikeng Congress. <www.anc.gov.za>.

ANC (2001): *Briefing Notes on the Alliance.* Discussion Document, October 2001.

Buhlungu (2003): "The State of Trade Unionism in post-apartheid South Africa." in Daniel, J., et al. (eds.) The *State of the Nation. South Africa 2003 – 2004.* Cape Town: HSRC.

COSATU (2002): *Political Report to the COSATU CEC,* December 2002.

DPE (2000): *An Accelerated Agenda Towards the Restructuring of State Owned Enterprise: Policy Framework.* <www.dpe.gov.za>.

DTI (2001): *Driving Competitiveness: An Integrated Industrial Strategy For Sustainable Employment And Growth.* <www.dti.gov.za>.

Eidelberg, P.E. (2000): "The Tripartite Alliance on the Eve of the Millennium: COSATU, the ANC and the SACP," In Adler, G. and E. Webster (eds.) *Trade Unions and Democratization in South Africa, 1985 – 1997.* London: Macmillan Press.

Lodge, T. (2002): *Politics in South Africa. From Mandela to Mbeki.* Cape Town: David Philip.

National Treasury. (2001): *Budget Review 2001.* <www.finance.gov.za>.

Makgetla, N. (2001): *A framework for employment creation and development. Paper.*

Makgetla, N. (2004): *Unpacking the Employment data,* Paper COSATU.

Naidoo, R. (2002): The union movement and South Africa's transition, 1994 – 2003. Harold Wolpe Memorial Trust/Centre for Policy Studies Seminar, 23 June.

OECD (2002): *African Economic Outlook.* African Development Bank.

Reserve Bank (2001): *Quarterly Economic Bulletin.* September 2001. <www.resbank.co.za>.

Southall, R. (2003): "The state of party Politics: Struggles within the Tripartite Alliance and the decline of opposition" in Daniel, J. et al. (eds.) The *State of the Nation. South Africa 2003 – 2004*. Cape Town: HSRC.

Standing, G., J. Sender and J. Weeks (1996): *Restructuring the labour market: the South African challenge.* An ILO Country Review Geneva: International Labour Organisation.

Statistics South Africa (2001a): *South Africa in Transition.* <www.statssa.gov.za>.

Statistics South Africa (2001b): *Labour Force Survey 2000.* <www.statssa.gov.za>.

Statistics South Africa (2001c): *Survey of Total Employment and Earnings.* Data series from <www.statssa.gov.za>.

The People's Budget (2005): <http://www.cosatu.org.za/docs/2005/people%27s.pdf>.

Tørres, L. (2000): *Amandla – Ngawethu? The political role of labour in South Africa.*: PhD Thesis; Department of Political Science, University of Oslo.

Tørres, L. *et al.* (2002): *Mesebetsi Labour Force Survey: Topline Report.* Oslo: Fafo.

Tørres, L. (2004): *COSATU Workers Speak.* Paper NALEDI/COSATU.

Tørres, L. (2005): *Labour and social capital,* University of Oslo, Mimeo.

UNDP. (2001): *Human Development Report.* <www.undp.org>.

Valenzuela, J.S. (1992): "Labour movements and Political Systems: Some Variations", in Regini, M. (ed.) The Future of Labour Movements. London: Sage. pp. 53-101.

Webster, E. (2005): *Trade Unions, Social Movements and Left Parties: Governing in a Globalising World.* Paper presented to the COSATU Ten Years of Democracy Conference. March 2005.

4. Social Movements in Post-Apartheid South Africa: An Introduction*

Richard Ballard **

1. Introduction

Some of the most influential analysis of post-liberation mobilisation and opposition in Africa is pessimistic. Fanon observes that former liberation "militants disappear into the crowd and take the empty title of citizen" (Fanon 1967:137). Mamdani warns of the postcolonial "marriage between technicism and nationalism" resulting in the demobilisation of social movements (Mamdani 1996:21). For Mbembe, political opposition in a postcolonial context is different to opposition in a colonial context as a result of the local origins of the postcolonial elite. Whereas colonial relations are characterised by either resistance or cooperation against an external oppressor, postcolonial relations are convivial as a result of the familiarity between the population and now local elite (Mbembe 2001:104). Mbembe describes the outcome as a mutual "zombification" in which the dominant and dominated are left impotent.

> ... at any given moment in the postcolonial historical trajectory, the authoritarian mode can no longer be interpreted strictly in terms of surveillance, or the politics of coercion. The practices of ordinary citizens cannot always be read in terms of 'opposition to the state,' 'deconstructing power,' and 'disengagement.' In the postcolony, an 'intimate tyranny' links the rul-

* This chapter draws from a larger project on social movements located at the Centre for Civil Society and School of Development Studies at the University of KwaZulu-Natal. While this chapter is somewhat general, comprehensive case studies of particular movements can be accessed via the CCS web site <http://www.ukzn.ac.za/ccs/>.

** School of Development Studies and Centre for Civil Society, University of KwaZulu-Natal, <ballardr@ukzn.ac.za>.

Peris Jones and Kristian Stokke (eds.), Democratising Development, *ISBN 90 04 14821 3, pp. 77-100.*

> ers with the ruled – just as obscenity is only another aspect of munificence, and vulgarity a normal condition of state power. (Mbembe 2001:128)

Whereas the need for adversarial struggle for state capture against the illegitimate apartheid state was clear, such unity of purpose does not emerge in the context of a democratically elected government. Today's social movements are no longer affiliated to a political party working towards the capture of the state, as was the case prior to the democratic transition (Buhlungu 2004; Bond 2004). Oppositional movements of the democratic era are more fragmented on what it is that they oppose and what their political project is. Opponents of the state have to overcome the familiarity that characterises the postcolonial situation. For Desai, "It's like marching against your mother: stoning them, forsaking them, and decrying them" (in Wren Spaulding 2003).

Perhaps Mbembe's analysis manifests most clearly within the ruling alliance of the African National Congress (ANC), the Congress of South African Trade Unions (COSATU) and the South African Communist Party (SACP), along with the de facto membership of the South African National Civic Organisation (SANCO) (Zuern 2004). The pillars of the liberation movement were trade unions, centring the realm of production and the workplace, and civics which addressed issues related to consumption in the townships and villages. In post-apartheid South Africa, unions remain active, addressing policy on formal labour practice, government employment practice of civil servants, as well as the labour practice of businesses. However, their attempts to oppose the state's chosen economic path from within the ruling alliance has limited the extent to which it can block this path. The civic movement has been even more effectively neutralised, with SANCO being described recently as a "moribund ally", an "empty shell" with little capacity for opposition (Forrest 2003).

Yet despite certain aspects of Mbembe's glum predictions holding true, South Africans have not been reduced to passive recipients of the post-apartheid order. A large swathe of activism in South Africa is orientated against government policy on consumption issues. Community movements oppose the state's failure to provide affordable services (Bond 2004; Buhlungu 2004; Desai 2003; Dwyer 2004; Egan and Wafer 2004; Pape and McDonald 2002). Privatisation and cost recovery are seen as key components of this problem. They also oppose evictions and attempt to secure land tenure (Greenberg 2004; Oldfield and Stokke 2004). The state has been opposed on its HIV/AIDS policies and, in particular, its reluctance to provide antiretroviral treatment (Friedman and Mottiar 2004).

It is not necessarily the case that social movements oppose the state itself, and there is growing interest in the way struggles can confront corporations (Cock 2004), multilateral organisations (Rustomjee 2004), institutions (Cock 2004; Smith 2004), or even other parts of civil society (Kirsten, 2004). Corporations and the government are targeted on issues of pollution. Communities living alongside dirty industry have brought tremendous pressure on these industries and won significant gains in reduction of pollution. Movements also seek to counter various forms of social prejudice, which also manifests in government policy. Struggles against discrimination by sexual minorities, women, foreigners, and others, are often targeted both at state policies but have as a broader objective the disruption of social norms (Amisi and Ballard 2004; Dirsuweit 2004; Hassim 2004). Finally, there are movements that oppose multilateral organisations and foreign corporations in relation to unplayable or odious debt, or in terms of claiming compensation from businesses that operated in South Africa during apartheid. These include Jubilee, Jubilee South Africa and Jubilee South (Rustomjee 2004).

The intention of this chapter is to contextualise the emergence of a new set of social movements in South Africa, to examine some of their strategies and programmes, and to map out some of the lines of debate in relation to their politics. In particular, the discussion reflects on the predicaments that result from opposing a democratically elected government. Activists, for example, face the constant choice between participating in the processes of government and opposing government. A related choice is between holding to the view that good can be extracted from the government, despite what is seen as its misguided path, and the view that the government is more or less irredeemable and, by extension, to be replaced. For many activists, struggles in contemporary South Africa may be the building blocks of a new opposition the to state. Capitalism and the market remain a core concern, and the ANC's shift towards a pro-growth strategy based on market liberalisation and a restrained national budget is understood to be the primary cause of worsening poverty in South Africa. Such activists therefore define their project as a counter-hegemonic or anti-systemic one. To put it crudely, counter-hegemonic activists feel that the revolutionary economic change that was anticipated with democracy has yet to materialise, and this remains the major project. Some explicitly describe themselves as true custodians of the liberation tradition; a title, of course, also claimed by the ruling ANC party (Buhlungu 2004; McKinley and Naidoo 2004:19).

Yet the choice between participation and opposition with a view to rupture is, to some extent, academic. Struggles in post-apartheid South Africa respond, in the first instance, to particular manifestations of exclusion, poverty and marginality. They are very often local and immediate; they are pragmatic and quite logical responses to everyday hardships (Barchiesi 2004; Desai 2003; Egan and Wafer 2004). Activists operate to achieve direct relief for marginalised groupings on particular issues. Such activists do not focus primarily on opposing the state's economic path, although they may do so by default, but rather on more specific struggles. This is not to say that they necessarily agree with the current national programme but rather that they choose to focus their attention on particular gains in relation to particular issues. In such situations, engagement with the state may indeed be on the cards. The country has, after all, installed a democratically elected government and given it an overwhelming mandate to pursue its programmes for overcoming the injustices of apartheid. Regardless of the effectiveness of these programmes, rhetorical interest in resolving poverty in South Africa allows considerable room for activists to manoeuvre. They recognise that the current situation allows many opportunities to nudge, coerce or force the state and other institutions to address various aspects of marginality. In particular, movements make extensive and flexible use of the discourse of rights to add legitimacy to their activities (Greenstein 2003). Even the more militant movements who engage in technically illegal activities such as reconnections and land occupations use the language of rights to invest their activities with a sense that they are endorsed by a higher code of 'good'.

2. Changing Ideological and Political Landscape

In order to understand social movements since the transition, it is important to remind ourselves of ideological shifts in the political landscape. South Africa's liberation struggle was arguably one of the quintessential social movements of the 20th century. Culminating in the United Democratic Front in the 1980s, this movement brought together political parties, unions, civic organisations, religious organisations, NGOs, and international supporters in a focused attack on apartheid. The relationship between local struggles and the broader anti-apartheid movement was complex. Activist concerns:

> ... extended beyond the issue of state power. Specific local conditions and grievances, and issues of sheer survival in many localities throughout the country, fed into a strategy of overall political mobilisation ... The anti-apartheid struggle had a coherent centre as well as disparate, uncoordinated, locally focused and untidy margins, expressed in the proliferation of multiple terrains of struggle spread geographically and thematically all over the country. It was natural to attempt to unify these multiple strands into a force that could meet apartheid head-on, confront power with power, and present an overall challenge to the regime, forcing it to yield ground and embark on negotiations.(Greenstein 2003:11-12)

The end of apartheid per se was only one part of the objectives of this collective force. Many saw apartheid as a specific manifestation of capitalism (Johnstone 1982; Wolpe 1972), and the anti-apartheid movement was thus considered to be a class struggle as much as it was a confrontation of racism. Significant changes in the economy, as well as the advent of democracy, were seen by many to be necessary for the achievement of social justice. The movement was explicitly counter-hegemonic, and often framed its intent in terms of Marxist programmes of expansionist state spending on the poor, and an avoidance of free market doctrine that was gaining dominance under Reaganism and Thatcherism.

In the wake of the negotiated transition between 1990 and 1994, the dominant political party of this liberation movement became the uncontested ruling party whose share of parliamentary seats increased in the three successive democratic elections. While the new constitution conferred unprecedented rights on citizens, the condition of those excluded from the formal economy has remained extremely marginal. Intentions to operate expanding national budget as articulated in the Reconstruction and Development Programme – effectively the ANC government's election manifesto of the 1994 elections – were replaced with the Growth Employment and Redistribution programme in 1996. The result was shrinking national budgets in the second half of the 1990s, a trend only reversed at the start of the next decade. State rhetoric switched to the importance of growth enabled by economic liberalisation and improving the conditions for competitiveness. Little growth was achieved and it is widely recognised that poverty, inequality and unemployment have grown (Everatt 2003). Some amelioration comes in the form of welfare payouts such as child support grants and pensions, upon which many families depend as their sole source of income. The government also attempts to target the poor through the Poverty Relief Fund and the Community Based Public Works Programme. Employment Equity and Black Economic Empowerment are touted as attempts to redress past imbalances although most doubt that they effectively target poor people.

Considerable successes in infrastructural delivery and more limited success with land transfers have been offset by massive job losses and the resulting inability for many to pay for services (Desai 2003, Pape and McDonald 2002). The government's cost recovery approach to service delivery and its policies of privatisation have resulted in cost structures that are unaffordable to the poor (Bond 2004). Desai (2002) has argued that there is no longer a 'culture of non-payment' as there was in the 1980s intended to undermine the minority government, but rather an 'economics of non payment' whereby individuals simply cannot afford services as a result of their marginalisation from the formal sector. Yet the government responds as if this was a problem of discipline, cutting off services and evicting delinquent residents.

The reluctance to oppose has been evident in South Africa both within and outside the ruling alliance (Cronin 2002, Desai 2003, Saul 2001, 2002). After the transition, frameworks of opposition were in disarray (Marais 2001: 162). Many had hoped that the need for adversarial opposition was over, but the state's fiscal discipline embodied in GEAR from 1996 signalled for many a shift to more centrist policies. Opposition to the state's economic path was not to be found amongst political parties. Tellingly, the official opposition is now the white dominated and pro-free market Democratic Alliance which scored 12.37% of the electorate's support in the 2004 general election (also see Saul 2001). There is little evidence that the electorate is rallying around alternative economic paths amongst the other parties that polled more than 1% – namely the Inkatha Freedom Party, United Democratic Movement, Independent Democrats, New National Party (now absorbed into the ANC), and the African Christian Democratic Party.

As well as overwhelming support from the electorate and little significant parliamentary opposition, the ANC government has been given considerable space to explore this development model by its former liberation partners and supporters (Saul 2001). The critical voice of Unions, the Communist Party, and Civics was quietened through their alliance with the ruling party, notwithstanding important stands they have made (Cronin 2002, Desai 2003, Mantashe 2003). Many civil society organisations switched to a cooperative service delivery role (Boulle

1997, Marais 1997). Some movements such as the women's movement, civics and unions struggled to maintain any vigour as a result of the fact that many former activists had moved to government (Hassim 2004, Lumsden and Loftus 2003:19).

3. Post-Apartheid Hardships and the Rise of a New Generation of Social Movements

With the opposition parties representing economic principles that are broadly in line with the government's approach, more critical voices turned to civil society and social movements in particular (Bond 2004; Desai 2002, 2003; Pape and McDonald 2002; Saul 2001, 2002). As a result of the way the new democratic state drew many former activists into its project, there is little institutional continuity between liberation social movements and the current generation of social movements – although it should be recognised that many of the activists and leaders themselves were involved in the liberation struggle (Bond 2004). In effect, social movements had to be re-constituted and re-invented. The new generation of social movements appeared in earnest once the ANC's second term in office began. The Treatment Action Campaign (formed in 1998), Concerned Citizens Forum (1999), Anti-Eviction Campaign, Anti Privatisation Forum, Soweto Electricity Crisis Committee (2000), the Landless Peoples Movement, Coalition of South Africans for the Basic Income Grant (2001) and the Education Rights Project (2002), have been amongst the more enduring and visible struggles to have re-constituted a vibrant oppositional civil society. Countless unnamed small scale and ephemeral struggles have also emerged across the country.

Burawoy states that "[i]n the postcommunist era progressive struggles have moved away from distributional politics to focus on identity politics or what Nancy Fraser calls a politics of recognition"(Burawoy 2003:242). While the politics of recognition enters South Africa's social movements in fascinating and poorly understood ways (e.g. see Tarrow 1998:17, hooks 1990), the somewhat northern analysis that distribution is decreasingly relevant does not hold true at all. The emergence of a new set of struggles since the late 1990s must be located squarely within the high and growing level of poverty and inequality that characterises our society.

Yet while distributional issues are paramount in South Africa, it does not follow that the result is a union-led "class struggle" of the kind that many believed characterised the anti-apartheid movement. In this movement, worker struggles were seen to be the vanguard of the broader movement to capture the state and establish a socially just post-apartheid society. Since the transition, COSATU remains an important advocate of the interests of workers but its alliance with the ruling party has rendered it somewhat incapable of more forcefully expressing its stated opposition to the government's chosen economic path. COSATU has been pursuing a kind of minimum objective of simply defending against the further erosion of employment (Desai 2003). It also explored other remedies such as a universal basic income grant, advocated and mobilized through the Coalition of South Africans for the Basic Income Grant. This welfarist remedy is one to which to government appears singularly unreceptive.

Although of limited impact thus far, innovative new unions have emerged in response to the growth of the informal sector (Devenish and Skinner 2004). The recently closed Self Employed Women's Union in KwaZulu-Natal achieved significant success in forcing the recognition of more survivalist livelihoods in the informal economy. As a result of pressure from this group, the city of eThekwini no longer clears informal traders from the streets – a success yet to be achieved in Johannesburg whose managers appear convinced that vendors work against the achievement of a "world class city" and should therefore be cleared from the streets.

Some believe that without the commitment of unions, a new generation of social movements will be hamstrung. Russel and Swilling insist that "[t]he key to the revival of social movements on a significant scale will be whether the trade union federations allow their huge, nationally structured institutional resources and leadership cadre to support these nascent processes" (Russel and Swilling 2002:93). And for Saul, 'finding a way to more effectively to link trade unions and social movements (in a "structured moment" a political party?) for progressive purposes is just one off the many challenges, barbed and unpredictable, that must be on the agenda of the ANC leadership's critics' (Saul 2002). However, the 'muted' role of unions globally, as Harvey puts it, is forcing many to re-think their centrality (Harvey 2003b: 35, also see Desai in Wren Spaulding 2003). Their relationship to the politics of the poor has become indirect given that poverty is characterised by exclusion from the formal sector.

Buroway (2003) draws on Polanyi to suggest that counterhegemonic potential lies not only in the realm of production, as classically understood, but in the domain of consumption and the market:

> Everyone suffers from the market inasmuch as unrestrained it leads to the destruction of the environment, global warming, toxic wastes, the colonization of free time, and so forth. ... Whereas alienated and degraded labour may excite a limited alternative, it does not have the universalism of the market that touches everyone in multiple ways. It is the market, therefore, that offers possible grounds for counterhegemony. We see this everywhere but especially in the amalgam of movements against the many guises of globalization. (Buroway 2003:231)

Harvey argues that unions were in the ascendancy during an era of expanding reproduction (2003a:172). Once this became difficult to sustain, from the 1970s, capital sought to bolster its earnings through a return to "accumulation by dispossession". This involved privatisation of utilities, further attempts to end communal land ownership and other forms of crude appropriation. Harvey argues that the kinds of struggle that were appropriate in engaging with expanding reproduction and with accumulation by dispossession were different. These are diverse and inchoate precisely because of the variety of contexts and forms of dispossession taking place. Rather than being "postmodern" as they have sometimes been classified, Harvey argues that they are defensive responses to various attempts by capital to generate profit through dispossession (2003a:174).

In South Africa, as we have seen, issue-based movements emerge over issues such as evictions, landlessness, electricity and water cut-offs, lack of access to medicine, lack of access to education, pollution of living environments, privatisation, cost recovery and so on. The Anti-Eviction Campaign, the Anti-Privatisation Forum, the Concerned Citizens Forum, the Soweto Electricity Crisis committee and others oppose cost recovery for services. Through illegal reconnections, court injunctions and protest they attempt to expose the contradiction whereby councils demand payment from residents who do not have sufficient incomes. Further movements such as the Education Rights Project and the Treatment Action Campaign address other aspects of state delivery around schooling and health. These all relate to the inability of people to pay for what that they need and the failure of government to supply it at affordable prices. While these appear to be narrow single issue struggles, they reflect the systemic nature of poverty underpinned by high levels of unemployment (see Desai in Wren Spaulding 2003). As one delegate stated at the 2004 Social Movements Indaba meeting, "we are all movements of the unemployed".

While it is possible to attribute the hardships created by cost recovery and job losses on the state's economic model, some hardships have been created by other features of post-apartheid society. Although the Treatment Action Campaign has identified the behaviour of pharmaceutical corporations as highly problematic, a major focus was – in fact – on the government's denial that AIDS may be a disease at all and that antiretrovirals are an appropriate response (Friedman and Mottiar 2004). Various movements seek to counter other causes of marginality that are not explained by historical materialist analyses and their contemporary cousins of anti-neoliberalism, anti-globalisation. Instead, class is seen to interact in complex ways with racism, homophobia, xenophobia, patriarchy and other dimensions of exclusion that produce the marginality that people experience. In some cases, such as that of economic migrants and refugees, an identity may place one in the most marginal of positions in society, not only materially but also because of the xenophobic social and cultural exclusions that result from not being readily accepted into host groups. It is therefore vital to track grassroots protests against xenophobia and exclusion (Amisi and Ballard 2004). A variety of groups deal with the longstanding marginalisation felt by women who often bear the brunt of deprivation, such as the white ribbon campaign which opposes violence against women (Hassim 2004). Identity-related concerns are also taken up by gay organisations who have successfully overseen the passage of new legislation and who seek to counter social prejudice (Dirsuweit 2004).

Questions of citizenship, gender, and sexuality often exacerbate material disadvantage, and are not the indulgent concerns of a "classless" petit-bourgeoisie. Indeed, there is a notable absence in South Africa of new social movements of the kinds described in the industrialised world as – perhaps – middle class individuals concerned with social and economic justice who orient their energies to poor sectors of society. As we shall see below, one effect of this is the way in which the political projects of such movements is constructed by their leaderships.

4. Tactics

De Certeau distinguishes between the strategies of the powerful and the tactics of "the other":

> A tactic is a calculated action determined by the absence of a proper locus ... The space of a tactic is the space of the other. Thus it must play on and with a terrain imposed on it and organized by the law of a foreign power ... and seize on the wing the possibilities that offer themselves at any given moment. It must vigilantly make use of the cracks that particular conjunctions open in the surveillance of proprietary powers. It poaches them. It creates surprises in them. It can be where it is least expected. It is a guileful ruse. (De Certeau 1984:37)

Power is, therefore, not the exclusive property of elites, and the poor and marginalized are capable of influencing elites to take directions they might otherwise not have taken. In South Africa, extensive use has been made of tactics not sanctioned by authorities in order to hinder and oppose the state (Miraftab and Wills, forthcoming). These might include reconnections of electricity and water, occupations of land and houses, and protests deemed to be illegal.

Furthermore, it is not always necessary to operate outside of the legal framework in order to achieve results. Neither is it necessarily the case that an adversarial stance is required to deflect the state from its intentions. Grassroots organisations such as the Homeless Peoples Alliance prefer a 'politics of patience' with a high degree of "bureaucratic intimacy" in order to achieve the delivery of housing (Khan and Pieterse 2004). The Treatment Action Campaign has ranged between adversarial and cooperative at various points in its campaigns (Friedman and Mottiar 2004). Movements thus seek to reconstitute instruments of deprivation as instruments of change (Tarrow 1998:30). Notwithstanding alarmingly repressive behaviour at times, there has been an undeniable opening up of the state since the end of the apartheid regime. Increasingly, instruments and spaces have become available for the state to engage with civil society, and indeed, for civil society actors to challenge the state. The National Economic Development and Labour Council (NEDLAC), the media, the courts, the constitution, formalized attempts to have public input into policies, local governments' Integrated Development Plans, and even rhetorical support for mass demonstrations provide a significant repertoire of "in-system" mechanisms for influencing policy and challenging the government.

The new political, economic and social order is underwritten by a constitution that enshrines first and second generation rights, clauses that have been used by a number of social movements to either defend themselves or advance their campaigns. Badiou (2001) rails against the global focus on human rights arguing that it merely attempts to prevent universally defined evil. Unlike Marxism, he argues, human rights cannot imagine and work towards the good. The uncritical celebration of rights is indeed problematic in that they tend to result in the assumption that because one has a right to education, adequate housing and services that it must somehow be so. Even the reinforcement of a right in the constitutional court may not translate into material improvements in the lives of the poor, as the much celebrated Grootboom case shows.

Yet it is important to note the creative ways in which social movements in South Africa, even militant ones, have adopted and made use of the notion of rights. The Gay movement claims as a core success the fact that 35 pieces of legislation that affected sexual minorities have been changed in the last 10 years (Dirsuweit 2004). The Western Cape anti-eviction campaign is using constitutional clauses to prevent evictions and frustrate the state (Oldfield and Stokke 2004). Legislation is not only an end in itself. Kirsten reports that the development of gun control legislation was crucial to creating broader debate in society and therefore shifting norms around gun ownership (2004:23).

The claim to rights helps legitimate even illegal activities such as reconnections and occupations of property (Greenstein 2003:29). The use of the language of rights can amount to an attempt to call on a broader framework to legitimate and gain credibility for otherwise risky activities. Indeed such deployment, at times, bears little relation to actual legally inscribed rights (Greenstein 2003:24). The discourse of rights has advantages over other expressions of marginality such as 'needs' which appear somewhat subjective. Rights are supposedly objectively defined, codified in the constitution – regarded by almost all as sacrosanct – and are endorsed by elites. Rights can be the kind of tactic defined by de Certeau above: an opportunity afforded by official processes to demand that the state put its money where its mouth is. Through the legal system, the marginalised are able to challenge the state and thereby shift relations of power, particularly when combined with popular mobilisation (Greenstein 2003:21). Cock describes such strategies as potentially counter hegemonic (Cock 2004). Movements are, thus, not restricted to illegal activity in order to diametrically oppose the government but use parts of the state against itself.

5. State Responses

The state's intolerance of some protest and the illegality and confrontationalism of protest have been mutually constitutive of one other. The state has chosen, for example, not to approve some applications for protest. In March 2004 an application for the Anti Privatisation Forum to march on the opening of the constitutional court was declined and a decision to proceed resulted in 52 arrests – some of whom were simply members of the public who happened to be wearing red T shirts. On election day in April 2004, 62 members of the Landless Peoples Movement were arrested for conducting a protest. There is growing concern of the stigmatization of the 'ultra-left' and the desire to repress protests (Cronin 2002; Desai 2002, 2003; Greenstein 2003:30-1; Saul 2001, 2002; Vally 2003). The state maintains that whereby illegal tactics were justified under apartheid, such approaches should be considered insurrectionist against a legitimate democratic state (Sachs 2003:26).

It is clear that social movements have provided a substantial challenge to the government. Its repressive response betrays the extent to which movements have hit a nerve. This resentment is multi-faceted. The ANC dislikes the way in which social movements have been able to upstage it by, for example, organising a significantly larger march at the 2002 World Summit on Sustainable Development. Much is also made of the ANC's historical intolerance for dissent. Movements are regarded as impertinent, not showing sufficient respect for the government which believes, somewhat paternalistically, it has a mandate from the majority of the population to proceed the way it feels best. Movements also remind the ANC of its tendency towards centralism, which is in tension with participatory democracy (Greenstein 2003:9). In addition, Bond argues that movements, having targeted neoliberalism, are a threat to vested interests (Bond 2004:27).

Given the overwhelming electoral support the ANC continues to receive, its somewhat hysterical response to dissenting voices may initially seem to be an over-reaction. Yet they can be read as a shrewd attempt to monopolise the definition of legitimate expressions of citizenship. Miraftab and Wills (forthcoming) suggest that the effect of identifying and demonising the "ultra left" is to create a distinction between two kinds of civil society. On one hand is what the politically powerful consider to be legitimate civil society which engage in ways that the state sanctions. On the other are inauthentic kinds of civil society which operate outside of state-sanctioned spaces of participation. The state thus seeks to construct certain expressions of citizenship as more legitimate than others and thereby pull the rug out from under its most vociferous opponents who attempt to operate in spaces that it cannot control directly.

6. Political Project of Social Movements

At first glance, many movements appear to be concerned with particular issues such as cut-offs, evictions and privatisation (McKinley and Naidoo 2004:11). However, single issue causes become vehicles for achieving broader ideological objectives (Flacks 2004, quoted in Egan and Wafer 2004). Many radical activists and academics define their progressiveness in terms of the promotion of a socialist alternative and, in this sense, construct their counter-hegomic project as an anti-capitalist one. Ngwane argues unambiguously that "[s]ocial movements ... have to fight the state, destroy it and replace it with a workers' state" (Ngwane 2003:32). Particular campaigns around electricity or other narrow issues thus are taken to be a means to an end. The scale of focus is broadened from a particular issue to the state's economic path. The role of movement leaderships and intellectuals is crucial in imbuing a generalised impulse to mobilise and take action with a 'sense of strategic and political purpose' (Barchiesi 2004:5, also see Mngxitama 2004). Such intellectuals identify their ideology through markers such as: anti neo-liberalism, anti-capitalism, anti-GEAR, anti-globalisation, anti-marketism. A number of such voices gather in the Social Movements Indaba, which was convened in response to the World Summit for Sustainable Development in Johannesburg in 2002, and continues to meet periodically. These are movements such as the Anti Privatisation Forum, Anti Eviction Campaign, the Landless Peoples Movement, Concerned Citizens Forum, Jubilee South Africa, Environmental Justice Networking Forum, Rural Development Services Network, and others (Cock 2003: 20). One delegate at the Social Movements Indaba meeting of 2004 referred to their collective as the 'socialist movements'. There is a sense within the Social Movements Indaba that they constitute the 'real' social movements of the country in contrast to more collaborationist and reformist organisations. Ngwane differentiates between 'good' and 'bad' social movements (Ngwane 2003:32). Bond distinguishes between organisations

> that emerge in the implementation of formal social policies (such as welfare agencies or implementation-oriented NGOs) or the reproduction of daily life (mutual aid groupings) – and *movements*. The latter are both protest-oriented and utopian, in the sense of attempting to construct the community of a future society in the decay of the old. (Bond 2004:9-10)

Drawing on Tironi, Bond distinguishes between the desire for participation and the breaking of the social system or its rupture (Bond 2004: 10). Social movements, then, tend to be imagined as the 'hinge' around which society can be diverted in a new direction (Hetherington 1998:10). This is particularly the case in South Africa where the legacy of the liberation movement has put many in the habit of viewing social movements as agents for cataclysmic social change. Collaboration with the state is seen as pointless as it represents bourgeois interests (Buhlungu 2004, Sachs 2003). The test of an authentic movement, from this perspective, is whether it holds a vision for a socialist alternative or at least opposes the state's neo-liberal growth path. From this perspective, successes in relation to particular issues such as the provision of HIV treatment is not unambiguously good unless it is attached to this broader project. Indeed it can be harmful. Leaders of the TAC are derided for their simultaneous criticism of the government's failure to deliver HIV treatment, and proclaiming to be a loyal card-carrying member of the ANC (Friedman and Mottiar 2004). The decision to work with the government on the delivery of antiretrovirals – now that it has decided to supply them – is seen not as a success, but rather to have compromised their ability to oppose the state vociferously in the future.

The responsibility for a utopian future is thrust upon local level struggles by the poor. In the process, effects are confused and conflated with intentions. While it might be possible to say that community struggles are – by default – anti-neo-liberal, it does not follow that they set out with this ideology in mind. Mark Heywood of the TAC suggested at a conference in Durban in October 2004 that revolutionary social movements as defined by the left were a figment of their imagination. While his sentiments created a stir, they did bring to the fore, as Ferial Haffajee (2004) has noted, the necessity to distinguish between ideal types and reality on the ground. As Harvey recognised, there is no necessary link between what he calls "insurgent movements against accumulation by dispossession" and a socialist political programme. Many such movements would, in fact, resent being "co-opted by socialist developmentalism" (Harvey 2003:166). Strategic rhetoric, then, should become an object of analysis in and of itself. The spectre of empire, globalisation, neoliberalism, the Washington consensus, and the ANC government's compliance with these, are attempts to solidify and personify as a recognisable adversary an otherwise dauntingly amorphous world system. They are discursive tools as much as they are objective descriptors of the way the world works. They are intended to have the same symbolic effect as the evils of apartheid and capitalism had in the past, to be vanquished by the morally righteous. To fire up the troops it is necessary to know who the bad guys are, and to clearly draw the battle lines. They provide a black and white, good and bad reading which attempts to squeeze out ambiguity and exert an order on the world (see Bauman 1991 on ambivalence).

Many struggles do not seek rupture or even necessarily a socialist alternative. While some activists involved may be mindful of, and even sympathetic to, these objectives, their primary focus is a local or issue specific struggle. Drawing on Castells' notion of "militant metropolitan dwellers", Desai points to movements that 'concentrate on fighting in their own locality and are often animated by the immediacy of their situation' (Desai 2003). They do this "without any grand ideology" (Desai 2003). Desai speaks of movements where the poor defend the little that they have (Desai in Wren Spaulding 2003). They do not address anti-IMF or World Bank struggles, or anti-state politics directly not because they disagree with them necessarily, but because they are operating at a local and immediate scale.

Is it necessarily the case, then, that progressive politics is impossible in the absence of a long term objective to "overthrow the capitalist system" (Ngwane 2004 cited in Bond 2004:29)? Some question whether the objective of the seizure of state power should be the benchmark of radical action, the qualifying property of the truly progressive. For Mngxitama (2004), "[r]evolutionary theory as we know it has become suspect, together with the old answers it prescribed"(Mngxitama 2004). Greenstein (2003) deploys some of the writings of post-Marxists such as Laclau and Mouffe to reflect anew on movements that do not position themselves as revolutionary. Is it possible to achieve counter-hegemonic goals outside of the traditional trajectory specified by socialism? Such movements can claim to be progressive in as much as they challenge existing power relations, although such challenges are not cast as a political revolutionary project. They therefore seek to challenge state power without merely "replacing one set of relations of domination with another" (Greenstein 2003:16). Or rather, they do not imagine that the only way to oppose state power is to seek to overthrow the state. Cock argues that new forms of mobilisation best described with Williams' phrase "militant particularisms" (Cock 2004). To quote Barchiesi, politics of the multitude is "non-teleological" and seeks to "open up previously unchartered terrains of political possibility and lines of advance" (Barchiesi 2004:6-7).

For post-Marxists, then, it does not follow that the absence of a socialist programme renders one unprogressive. While local struggles often focus on particular sites or situations, they are not confined to them and can expose and contribute to broader struggles (Low and Lawrence-Zúñiga 2003:18). Small scale, locally embedded actions can contest broader relations of dominance and subordination. It is therefore limiting to say with some disappointment, as Guha does of Indian rebellions, that they failed to overcome their parochialism and transform into a national liberation movement (2000:6). As South Africans well know, liberation movements are indeed an opportunity for dramatic progress. Yet state capture often disappoints many who were hoping for a better deal and they cannot therefore be seen as the be all and end all of radical activity. As Laclau and Mouffe have argued, the political nature of struggles is not confined to parties and the state, but is rather any 'type of action whose objective is the transformation of a social relation which constructs a subject in a relationship of subordination' (Laclau and Mouffe 1985:153). The existence of a range of struggles, even if not coordinated in a national liberation movement, can result in a "chain of equivalence" that confronts and transforms relations with dominant powers.

Such movements avoid black and white analysis which flattens the complexities that confront activists. They possess higher tolerance for ambiguity, uncertainty, the absence of road maps. This requires novel reflection on complex ethical choices rather than resorting to the well known scripts (Bauman 1993). Committed socialists such as Harvey believe that the innovation of embedded politics is an inadequate replacement for macro-politics.

> The danger ... is of seeing all such struggles against dispossession as by definition 'progressive' or, even worse, of placing them under some homogenizing banner like that of Hardt and Negri's 'multitude' that will

> magically rise up to inherit the earth. This, I think, is where the real political difficulty lies. (Harvey 2003a:168-9)

The problem in South Africa, though, is that any attempt to trump up a moral equivalence between the apartheid state and the post apartheid state on the grounds of the latter's continued adherence to capitalism is simply not going to ride with the majority of the population, as the continued loyalty to the ANC in the face of growing economic exclusion attests. A programme of state capture would be a non-starter when the present state is led by a recent liberation movement which continues to embody so strongly national aspirations. Or rather, aspirations have been channelled through a nationalist project which resonates with the population despite enduring poverty.

7. Conclusion

Mbembe's characterisation of postcolonial opposition is indeed evident in the elite's expectation of acquiescence, in the very existence of an alliance with unions and the communist party, and in activists own anxieties in opposing former comrades. However, Mbembe's fatalistic expectation of mutual zombification is contradicted by the reality of various movements across South Africa who have transformed the political landscape in post-apartheid South Africa (Barchiesi 2004:4). The obvious tangible effect of social movements on the political landscape of the country is that they represent the interest of the poor and marginalised and apply pressure on the government to pay greater attention to the welfare of these groups. This is an avenue for marginalised people and those interested in the plight of the marginalised to impact on material distribution, on social exclusion, and on claiming a certain degree of influence and power over state itself. In a context where the formal political system has failed to produce a significant political party to the left of the ANC to more directly champion the cause of the poor, social movements restore a degree of political balance in favour of the poor.

Most movements have had a direct or indirect influence on policy. Some, such as Self Employed Women's Union, Treatment Action Campaign, Homeless Peoples Alliance, have explicitly set out to influence state policy through engagement and negotiation. Others have influenced state policy through, in effect, making certain courses the state wanted to pursue more difficult for them. Social movements are setting boundaries and limits to state activity (or inactivity) that might not otherwise be there. Resistance comes to redefine what the government sees as the path of least resistance, so to speak. Pro-poor policies suddenly seem attractive in comparison to being tied up in expensive and time consuming court proceedings or being faced with hostile protestors.

It might be argued that the impact of social movements is manifesting in the government's rhetorical shifts away from the austerity of the 1990s. Many remain sceptical that this will translate in to a meaningful change in the lives of South Africa's jobless. It may well be argued, furthermore, that such shifts are the twin of the strategy of repression. For Harvey, drawing on Gramsci, "[t]he power of the hegemon ... is fashioned out of and expressed through an ever-shifting balance between coercion and consensus" (Harvey 2003a:37-38). Realising that it has opened the door for others to gain support through more explicitly worded anti-poverty manifestos, the ANC government shifted to recapture this ground in the build up to the 2004 election.

Within movements, there are debates around participation and reformism versus opposition and rupture. These positions speak to a somewhat hypothetical ideal rather than to the reality of the current effect of social movements. It is arguable that, at times, activists and critics alike place excessive focus on the extreme end point of some radical action, which is revolutionary political change. Mobilisation by the poor has unsettled the elite's presumption that it can proceed how it feels best. In and of itself, this is both radical and counter-hegemonic.

References

Amisi, Baruti and Richard Ballard (2004): "Refugee organisation and struggle in South Africa", Research report for the Globalisation Marginalisation and New Social Movements Project. Durban: University of KwaZulu-Natal.

Badiou, Alain (2001): *Ethics*. London: Verso.

Barchiesi, Branco (2004): "Classes, Multitudes and the Politics of Community: Movements in Post-apartheid South Africa" presented at *How Class Works* Conference State University of New York at Stony Brook, 10-12 June 2004 and at the annual Congress of the South African Sociological Association, Bloemfontien, University of the Free State 27-30 June 2004.

Bauman, Zygmunt (1991): *Modernity and Ambivalence*. Cambridge, UK: Polity press.

Bauman, Zygmunt and Benedetto Vecchi (2004): *Identity*. Cambridge, UK: Polity press.

Bond, Patrick (2004): "South Africa's Resurgent Urban Social Movements: The Case of Johannesburg, 1984, 1994, 2004" Centre for Civil Society Research Report No. 22, Durban: University of KwaZulu-Natal.

Boulle, J. (1997): "Putting the voluntary sector back on the map." *Development Update* 1(1).

Buhlungu, Sakhela (2004): "The Anti-Privatisation Forum: A Profile of a Post-Apartheid Social Movement" Research report for the Globalisation Marginalisation and New Social Movements Project. Durban: University of KwaZulu Natal.

Burawoy, Michael (2003): "For a Sociological Marxism: The Complementary Convergence of Antonio Gransci and Karl Polanyi" in *Politics and Society*. Vol. 31, no. 2, pp. 193-261.

Cock, Jacklyn (2003): "Local Social Movements: Some questions from the 'back alleys' of South Africa" *South African Labour Bulletin*. Vol 27, no. 3, pp. 19-21.

Cock, Jacklyn (2004): "Connecting the Red, Brown and Green: The Environmental Justice Movement in South Africa" Research report for the Globalisation Marginalisation and New Social Movements Project. Durban: University of KwaZulu Natal.

Cronin, Jeremy (2002): "Post-Apartheid South Africa: A Reply to John S. Saul" *Monthly Review*. 54(7) <http://www.monthlyreview.org/1202cronin.htm>.

de Certeau, M. (1984): *The Practice of Everyday Life*. Berkeley, University of California Press.

Desai, Ashwin (2002): *We are the Poors*. New York: Monthly Review Press.

Desai, Ashwin (2003): "Neoliberalism and Resistance in South Africa" *Monthly Review*. 54(8) <http://www.monthlyreview.org/0103desai.htm>.

Devenish, Annie and Caroline Skinner (2004): "The Self Employed Womens Union" Research report for the Globalisation Marginalisation and New Social Movements Project. Durban: University of KwaZulu Natal.

Dirsuweit, Teresa (2004): "The problem of identities: The lesbian, gay, bisexual, trangender and intersex social movement in South Africa" Research report for the Globalisation Marginalisation and New Social Movements Project. Durban: University of KwaZulu Natal.

Dwyer, Peter (2004): "The Contentious Politics of the Concerned Citizens Forum (CCF)" Research report for the Globalisation Marginalisation and New Social Movements Project. Durban: University of KwaZulu Natal.

Egan, Anthony and Alex Wafer (2004): "The Soweto Electricity Crisis Committee" Research report for the Globalisation Marginalisation and New Social Movements Project. Durban: University of KwaZulu Natal.

Everatt, David (2003): "The Politics of Poverty" *The Real State of the Nation: South Africa After 1990 – Development Update Special Edition*. vol. 4, no. 3, pp. 75-99.

Fanon, Frantz (1967): *The Wretched of the Earth*. Harmondsworth England: Penguin Books.

Forrest, D. (2003): "Social Movements: 'Ultra-left' or 'Global Citizens'?" *Mail and Guardian*. 31 February, pp. 9-11.

Friedman, Steven and Shauna Mottiar (2004): "A Rewarding Engagement?: The Treatment Action Campaign and the Politics of HIV/AIDS" Research report for the Globalisation Marginalisation and New Social Movements Project. Durban: University of KwaZulu Natal.

Greenberg, Stephen (2004): "The Landless People's Movement and the Failure of Post-apartheid Land Reform" Research report for the Globalisation Marginalisation and New Social Movements Project. Durban: University of KwaZulu Natal.

Greenstein, Ran (2003): "Civil Society, Social Movements and Power in South Africa" unpublished RAU Sociology seminar paper <http://general.rau.ac.za/sociology/Greenstein.pdf>.

Guha Ranajit (2000): "On Some Aspects of the Historiography of Colonial India" in Chaturvedi, Vinayak (ed.) *Mapping Subaltern Studies and the Postcolonial*. London and New York: Verso, pp. 1-7.

Haffajee, F. (2004): "Fact, Fiction and the New Left" *Mail & Guardian*, 11-17 June 2004.

Harvey, David (2003a): *The New Imperialism*. Oxford: Oxford University Press.

Harvey, David (2003b): "The 'New Imperialism' and the Left". *Debate: Voices from the South African Left*. 9, pp. 31-35.

Hassim, Shireen (2004): "Voices, Hierarchies and Spaces: Reconfiguring the Women's Movement in Democratic South Africa" Research report for the Globalisation Marginalisation and New Social Movements Project. Durban: University of KwaZulu Natal.

Hetherington, K. (1998): *Expressions of Identity: Space, Performance, Politics*. London: Sage.

Hooks, bell (1990): *Yearning: Race, Gender and Cultural Politics*. Boston MA: South End Press.

Johnstone, Frederick A. (1982): "'Most Painful to Our Hearts': South Africa Through the Eyes of the New School" *Canadian Journal of African Studies*. vol. 16, no. 1, pp 5-26.

Khan, Firoz and Edgar Pieterse (2004): "The Homeless People's Alliance: Purposive Creation and Ambiguated Realities" Research report for the Globalisation Marginalisation and New Social Movements Project. Durban: University of KwaZulu Natal.

Kirsten, Adéle (2004): "The Role of Social Movements in Gun Control: An International Comparison between South Africa, Brazil and Australia" *Centre for Civil Society Research Report No. 21.*

Laclau, Ernesto and Chantal Mouffe (1985): *Hegemony and Socialist Strategy: towards a radical democratic politics*. London and New York: Verso.

Low, S.M. and Lawrence-Zúñiga (2003): "Locating Culture" in S.M. Low and Lawrence-Zúñiga (eds.) *The Anthropology of Space and Place: Locating Culture*. Malden, MA: Blackwell.

Lumsden, F. and A. Loftus. (2003): "Inanda's Struggle for Water Through Pipes and Tunnels: Exploring State-civil Society Relations in a Post apartheid Informal Settlement." CCS Research Report.

Mamdani, Mahmood (1996): *Citizen and Subject: Contemporary Africa and the Legacy of Late Colonialism*. Princeton NJ: Princeton University Press.

Mantashe, Gwede (2003): "Trade Unions and Social Movements in South Africa" *South African Labour Bulletin*. Vol. 27, no. 6, pp 33-34.

Marais, Hein (1997): "The RDP: is there life after GEAR?" *Development Update*. 1(1).

Marais, Hein (2001): *South Africa: Limits to Change: The Political Economy of Transition*. London: Zed Books.

Mbembe, Achille (2001): *On the Postcolony*. Berkeley and LA: University of California Press.

McKinley, Dale and Prishani Naidoo (2004): "New Social Movements in South Africa: A Story in Creation" *Development Update*. Vol. 5, no. 2 pp. 9-22.

Miraftab, Faranak and Shana Wills (forthcoming): "Insurgency and Spaces of Active Citizenship: The Story of Western Cape Anti-Eviction Campaign in South Africa" *Journal of Planning Education and Research*.

Mngxitama, Andile (2004): "Let black voices speak for the voiceless", *Mail and Guardian* 22 Jun 2004. <http://archive.mg.co.za/>.

Ngwane, Trevor (2003): "The Anti-Privatisation Forum (APF)" *South African Labour Bulletin*. Vol 27, no. 3, pp. 31-32.

Oldfield, Sophie and Kristian Stokke (2004): "Building unity in diversity: Social movement activism in the Western Cape Anti-Eviction Campaign" Research report for the Globalisation Marginalisation and New Social Movements Project. Durban: University of KwaZulu Natal.

Pape, John and David McDonald (2002): "Introduction" in McDonald, David and John Pape (eds.) *Cost Recovery and the Crisis of Service Delivery in South Africa*. Cape Town: Human Sciences Research Council Publishers. pp. 1-14.

Russel, B and M. Swilling (2002): *The Size and Scope of the Non-profit Sector in South Africa*. Durban and Johannesburg: Centre for Civil Society, University of Natal, and the Graduate School of Public and Development Management, University of the Witwatersrand.

Rustomjee, Cyrus (2004): "From Economic Debt to Moral Debt: The Campaigns of Jubilee South Africa" Research report for the Globalisation Marginalisation and New Social Movements Project. Durban: University of KwaZulu Natal.

Sachs, Michael (2003): "'We Don't Want the Fucking Vote' Social movements and demagogues in a South Africa's young democracy" *South African Labour Bulletin*. 37(6), pp 23-27.

Saul, John (2001): "Cry for the Beloved Country: The Post-Apartheid Denouement" *Montly Review*. 52(8) pp. 1-51.

Saul, John (2002): "Starting from Scratch?: A Reply to Jeremy S. Cronin" *Monthly Review*. 54(7) <http://www.monthlyreview.org/1202saul.htm>.

Smith, Myriam (2004): "Questioning Heteronormativity: Lesbian and Gay Challenges to Education Practice in British Columbia, Canada" *Social Movement Studies*. Vol. 3, no. 2.

Tarrow, Sidney 1998 (1993): *Power in Movement: Social Movements and Contentious Politics*. UK: Cambridge University Press.

Vally, S. (2003): "The Iron Fist and the Velvet Glove," *Mail and Guardian*. 20 December p. 24.

Wolpe, Harold (1972): "Capitalism and Cheap Labour Power – From Segregation to Apartheid" *Economy and Society*. vol. 1, no. 4, pp. 425-456.

Wren Spaulding, Holly (2003): "The New Tools of Liberation in South Africa. An interview with Ashwin Desai" *Z Magazine* Vol. 16, no 3 <http://zmagsite.zmag.org/Mar2003/wren0303.html>.

Zuern, Elke (2004): "Continuity in Contradiction? The Prospects for a National Civic Movement in a Democratic State: SANCO and the ANC in Post-Apartheid South Africa" Research report for the Globalisation Marginalisation and New Social Movements Project. Durban: University of Kwa-Zulu Natal.

5. Poverty, Inequality and the Social Wage: Balancing the Books in Post-Apartheid South Africa?

*Julian May and Nina Hunter**

1. Introduction

The months leading up to the ten year celebrations of South Africa's democracy witnessed intense debate over trends in the incidence and severity of poverty in the post-apartheid era. Reaching agreement over what has happened to income distribution and well-being has been complicated by errors found in recent official statistics. This has been compounded by the multitude of methodologies that have been applied to the analysis of poverty, some of which with popular appeal but of doubtful rigour. In addition, the Office of the President of South Africa has questioned the findings of both the official statistics agency and other studies, and suggestions that poverty and inequality have increased have been rebuffed. This response has gone so far as to suggest that an unspecified ideological agenda has been followed by research showing that the post-apartheid poverty strategy has achieved less than might have been hoped for (*Sunday Times*, 2004).

Poverty reduction was again placed at the heart of government policy by the State of the Nation address that immediately preceded the 10 year celebration. In this speech, President Thabo Mbeki identified the development of a social safety net as the third leg of South Africa's poverty strategy (Mbeki 2004). Later in the speech, we learn that this encompasses not only social welfare but also the delivery of services and infrastructure and that this leg provides the link between interventions hoping to boost the activities in the "First" (the modern and integrated) and "Second" (underdeveloped and isolated) economies thereby absorbing those dependent upon social welfare and ensuring sustainable

* Associate Professor and Research Fellow, School of Development Studies, University of KwaZulu-Natal, South Africa.

Peris Jones and Kristian Stokke (eds.), Democratising Development, *ISBN 90 04 14821 3, pp. 101-129.*

poverty reduction. Social policy, the mix of interventions concerned with welfare, protection, rights and access to essential services that have somehow seemed inimical to respectable economic practice, is thus brought to the fore of South Africa's poverty reduction strategy. Social policy has also become entangled in the measurement of poverty itself through attempts to include such expenditure as a part of the calculation of the "social wage" in South Africa.

In this chapter we examine social policy expenditure in terms of its likely impact on the severity and incidence of poverty in the first decade of democracy, where this evidence is available. Although it is tempting to speculate as to the changes in poverty that might have taken place in South Africa during the post-apartheid era, the data that are currently available do not permit such analysis to be made with confidence. Instead we will start by reviewing what we think is known and then make mention of poverty analysis that points towards what might be anticipated once the official statistics have been corrected. After clarifying the terminology used, we will then review the major elements of the "social wage" to which the South Africa government has been allocating resources. Finally, we will critically examine what may be learnt from adopting a social wage accounting methodology when reviewing the first 10 years of social policy in post-apartheid South Africa.

2. South Africa's Poverty Profile: "Singular, not to say Grotesque"[1]

At PPP$11 240 per annum in 2001, South Africa's per capita GDP corrected for purchasing power parity (PPP) places it as one of the 50 wealthiest nations, while the strikingly poor social indicators of the country result in South Africa being ranked 111th of 175 countries in terms of its Human Development Index (HDI) in 2001, down on its ranking of 93rd in 1992 (UNDP, 2002).[2] Despite being among the 35 largest economies in the world, the country now has life expectancies among the 30 worst while projections of mortality suggest that these will deteriorate further as deaths from the AIDS epidemic increase (UNDP 2003; UNDP 2004; Dorrington *et al.* 2001:25).

1 As exclaimed by Sherlock Holmes in "The Adventure of the Six Napoleons".

2 The HDI calculated by the South African Human Development Report (UNDP 2003:150) would place South Africa at 115th place for 2003.

At the time of the transition in 1993, South Africa was described by the World Bank as among the world's most unequal economies, with a Gini co-efficient measuring 0.58. More recent analysis using the 1996 Population Census data put the Gini co-efficient for income as high as 0.68, worse than that of Brazil and of 33 other developing countries (Marais 1998:106). Woolard and Leibbrandt (2001:22) show that in 1995, six percent of South Africa's population captured over 40 percent of income. This experience of income inequality carries over to the social indicators as well, with the HDI reported by the UNDP revealing significant spatial and racial differences within South Africa. In 1991, while white South Africans had an HDI similar to that of Canada or Israel, the HDI score for Africans was lower than that of Egypt and Swaziland, and a provincial comparison shows that the score for the Limpopo Province was lower than that of neighbouring Zimbabwe (May *et al.* 2000:23). Although there were some improvements in the HDI among some groups by 2000, South Africa is one of a handful of countries that has experienced a decline in the HDI since 1995, while the racial aspect of the South African situation remains unchanged with the gap having widened between the index of the poorest province which is mostly African and richest province which has the highest proportion of whites in South Africa (UNDP, 2003).

Despite conceptual and measurement problems, most analysts would still agree with Lipton (1997:1003) as to the usefulness of income or consumption based poverty when evaluating progress made by policy interventions. At the start of South Africa's transition in 1993 almost half of the population, some 19 million people, were categorised as poor using a national consumption-based poverty line with over 60 percent of Africans being poor compared to just one percent of the white population (Klasen 1997). The World Development Report of 2000 uses the same data to show that 11.5 percent of the South African population lived on less than PPP$1 per day, while 35.8 percent of the population lived on less than PPP$2 per day (World Bank 2000:64). At that time, poverty rates in South Africa could thus be compared to countries such as Bolivia (11.3 percent), Colombia (11.0 percent) or Cote d'Ivoire (12.3 percent) in terms of the PPP$1 per day measure of poverty.

More recent South African measures of poverty based on a minimum acceptable standard of living suggest that poverty is more severe than the rather arbitrary international rules of thumb would imply. Woolard and Leibbrandt (2001) use a range of thresholds to provide a rigorous analysis of poverty in South Africa in the period until 1995.[3] Using data from the 1995 Income and Expenditure Survey (IES), they conclude that some 40 to 50 percent of South Africans could still be categorised as poor in 1995, while 25 percent could be categorised as ultra-poor. They also found that the poverty rate was far higher in rural than in urban areas (65 percent of individuals compared to 22 percent) and 27 percent of rural dwellers were below half the poverty line, and thus were likely to also be chronically poor in the sense of being unable to escape poverty over time. In line with other studies, the Eastern Cape emerged as the poorest province in South Africa, containing 27 percent of those likely to be chronically poor while KwaZulu-Natal and Limpopo Province accounted for 19 and 17 percent of the chronically poor respectively (Woolard and Leibbrandt 2001:59-60). Also in 1995, the poverty gap, a measure of the depth of poverty calculated to show the amount that is needed annually to wipe out poverty through a perfectly targeted transfer to the poor, was about R15 billion, or about four percent of GDP. In the case of the two poorest provinces, Eastern Cape and Limpopo Province, the poverty gap amounted to 11 percent and 21 percent of the provincial Gross Geographic Product (GGP), respectively (May *et al.* 2000:20) which provides some sense of the challenge faced by these regions.

Changes in the incidence and depth of poverty since 1995 are less clear due to both problems with the data and the apparent reluctance of the government to adopt an official poverty line. Instead a multitude of approaches have been used by different agencies for different purposes, some of which may have important implications for both policy development and implementation. As an example, a household minimum income of R800 has been used for means testing for one of the social grants, a figure that has remained without adjustment since the mid 1990's. The use of different thresholds and different methods produces a different ordering of the provinces in terms of the incidence of poverty from that used by government and donors for geographic targeting. Thus while the more conventional money-metric approach based on per capita income and the Human Development Index show that the three poorest provinces are Limpopo, Eastern Cape and KwaZulu-

3 For most of their analysis Woolard and Leibbrandt (2001:56) settle on the Household Subsistence Level and $1 a day "International" line (R3509.00 and R2200 per annum per adult equivalence in 1995 Rand). The latter may be thought of as the ultra-poverty line.

Natal (Woolard and Leibbrandt 2001), other methodologies lead to the politically strategic province of KwaZulu-Natal losing its status as the third poorest province alternatively to the Free State or Northern Cape depending on the technique being used.

Notwithstanding this confusion, most analysis points to an increase in the numbers of people who are poor. Using large sample surveys collected by Statistics South Africa between 1994 and 1998, Budlender (2000:93) suggests that both poverty and inequality may have increased, a finding supported by an official publication using the results of the 2000 Income and Expenditure Survey (IES) (Statistics South Africa 2002). The IES shows that average annual per capita income in 1995 was reported to be R12 135 adjusted to 2000 prices, higher than the per capita income of R11 755 per annum reported in 2000. However many analysts have raised serious concerns with the quality of the data collected by the IES 2000, pointing to methodological and weighting problems and evidence of sloppy fieldwork and data processing (Meth and Dias 2004:61; van der Berg and Louw 2003:2). In a brave attempt to make use of this data, Meth and Dias (2004) employ a mix of procedures to adjust for these problems and conclude that the case for an increase in the numbers of people in poverty seems convincing. They find that the numbers of people in the lower of two expenditure groups identified as encompassing the potentially poor increased by about 2.9 million people between 1995 and 2000 while the numbers in the higher band increased by 1.4 million people (Meth and Dias 2004:63). Thus they estimate that there were 22 million people in poverty in 2002, an increase of at least 2.4 million from 1999 when applying the same methodology. Attempting to take account of transfers to the poor from government in the form of water, electricity, health care, housing, sanitation, education and transport, they amend this estimate to an increase of two million people (Meth and Dias 2004:81).[4] Finally van der Berg and Louw (2003:18) adopt an absolute poverty threshold in order to categorise the population into poor and non-poor, and show that the numbers in poverty reached 17 million people in 2000, an increase of 1.2 million people from 1995.

A recent Statistics South Africa report (Statistics South Africa 2002) analyses data from the 2000 Income and Expenditure Survey, and

4 Referred to as a social wage as an attempt to take into account government reaction to the Stats SA data.

shows the continued high levels of income inequality in South Africa. Examination of the data shows that the top decile in the distribution accounts for 49 percent of total expenditure compared to just eight per cent accounted for by the bottom four deciles, suggesting little change in income inequality since 1993. Van der Berg and Burger (2002:10-11) try to take account of shifts in social spending in terms of their impact on the distribution of income adjusted for non-cash transfers. Noting that per capita incomes of the African elite have almost caught up with those of the white population, they calculate a Gini coefficient for South Africa of 0.66, similar to most other studies. Turning their attention to the impact of social spending, they show that social spending on the African population has increase from 51 percent in the immediate transition period to 80 percent in 1997. When income is calculated adjusted for South Africa's relative progressive taxes and for the strongly progressive non-cash transfers that are made, they conclude that the Gini coefficient can be re-estimated to 0.44. In particular, they conclude that fairly good targeting of Old Age Pensions and Disability Grants have resulted in rural areas receiving an unusually fair share of social spending compared to the situation in many developing countries. However, they do not attempt to measure the impact that this social spending might have had on the well-being of the poor, noting that the quality of the service delivered substantially determines this. As an example, while inequalities in terms of inputs to education might have narrowed, the outcomes in terms of education attainment have not (van der Berg and Burger 2002:18).

Seeking reasons for persistent poverty, Bhorat and Poswell (2002:51) examine the impact of trade and technology on employment dynamics in South Africa since 1995. They conclude that economic growth in the post-apartheid period has resulted in weak employment growth among highly skilled workers, while unskilled workers and those in poor households have carried the adjustment costs of greater openness. Indeed, since internationally most empirical analysis supports the view that growth is important for the reduction of poverty, the sluggish growth in the South African economy observed throughout the 1990's, together with persistent and growing unemployment gives little hope that substantial poverty reduction would even have been possible. This expectation is further reinforced by other findings which point to the poor performance achieved by highly unequal economies such as South Africa in terms of translating growth into poverty reduction (Hanmer and Naschold 2001). May *et al.* (2004) reflect on this evidence and arguing that progress along the current growth path will not be sufficient to reduce poverty, call for stronger action to address these market failures through further transfers and redistribution. They suggest that such policies form part of the microeconomic strategy being sought by government in various budget and State of the Nation addresses (Manuel 2001, 2002; Mbeki 2001).

This examination of the data available in South Africa suggests that it is reasonable to conclude that poverty and inequality has persisted through-out the first 10 years of South Africa's democracy. While an important reason for these disappointing trends is the legacy of the apartheid, global economic trends, the way in which South Africa had re-integrated with the global economy, and national macro-economic policy have also contributed. As a way of thinking through what alternatives might be adopted, it is pertinent to recall that Titmuss (1968:155-159) in his collection of essays on the welfare state argues that social policy represents actions undertaken by government for a variety of political reasons to provide for a range of needs that the market does not or cannot satisfy for certain segments of the population. These take account of needs arising from the unequal allocation of the costs and benefits of economic growth, including those that are the future consequences of such growth. He includes children, the elderly, the disabled and the poor more broadly as the intended beneficiaries of such spending, describing such expenditure as compensation for "... bearing part of the social costs of other people's progress" (Titmuss 1968:159).

There is a perhaps surprising level of consensus in South Africa that an important component of the post-apartheid response to the "singular if not grotesque" poverty profile should be through a reallocation of government budgets towards such social spending and on those identified as target groups by Titmuss. Most of these are groups who have carried not only the social costs of apartheid era policies, but also the costs of struggle and of post-apartheid economic restructuring. The rewards of growth previously reaped by the white minority, have more recently being garnered by South Africa's new elites. Placed in that context, it is not surprising that disagreement emerges over the method, extent, duration and purpose of such spending as well as the balance of these interventions and other more conventional economic policies since these are decisions that determine the scale of costs and benefits allocated to the non-poor and poor respectively. These political choices of compensation and redistribution are often obscured by the confusing way in which policy options are described, and we will first try to clarify the terminologies being used before reviewing trends in social spending since 1994.

3. Social Security, Social Protection and the Social Wage

The terms social security, social safety nets, social protection and the social wage have tended to be used indiscriminately when applied to social policy in South Africa. However, there is an element of hierarchy in the strict usage of the terms that should be kept in mind. As a point of departure, the United Nations define social security as:

> ... the protection which society provides for its members through a series of public measures against the economic and social distress that otherwise would be caused by the stoppage or substantial reduction of earnings resulting from sickness, maternity, employment injury, invalidity and death; the provision of medical care; and the provision of subsidies for families with children. (Midgley 1996:3)

This suggests an overlap with the notion of social safety nets used (recently) in the context of developing countries. In this regard, the World Bank (2000) defines safety nets as: *... formal and informal measures that protect people from the worst effects of low income and poverty"*, while Lipton (1997:1004) lists the provision of safety nets as one aspect of an emerging consensus on poverty, noting the concern that such nets need to be targeted and should not crowd out private savings, work or charity. Safety nets are seen to go beyond short-term interventions expected to assist in times of transitory crisis and extend to assisting low-income households in times of income fluctuations (Cook *et al.* 2003:17; Devereux 2003:1).

Social protection has also been used interchangeably with safety nets although social protection suggests a broader array of policies including interventions in labour markets, actions taken to reduce exposure to risk, and improving the capacity of people to protect themselves from hazards and unforeseen negative events. Social protection also evokes a dimension of social norms and citizenship rights. The British Department for International Development regard social protection as referring to: "*... public actions taken in response to levels of vulnerability, risk and deprivation which are deemed to be socially unacceptable within a given polity or society*" (Norton *et al.* 2001:7). Although the World Bank's definition of social protection also incorporates risk management, this definition seems to focus more on individual responsibility and less on preventing such circumstances in the first place (Holzmann and Jorgensen 2000:3).

Thus social protection may be obtained through inclusion as a member in an insurance scheme by virtue of payment or of some other contribution and is sometimes referred to as social insurance, and the contribution made and benefits received are clearly specified and may be compulsory. Alternatively, protection may be obtained as a broader right of citizenship which entitles access to a range of usually government-financed cash or in-kind benefits. This is often made available for the protection of the most vulnerable persons in society and implies some form of rationing; such as through means testing, although universal protection is preferred in some countries. This is referred to as social assistance, the term adopted in South Africa, and defined by Norton *et al.* (2001:10) as:

> ... public actions which are designed to transfer resources to groups deemed eligible due to deprivation. Deprivation may be defined by low income, or in terms of other dimensions of poverty (eg. social or nutritional status).

Finally, Dreze and Sen (1991:16) distinguish between social security for protection and social security for promotion. Social security for protection is concerned with preventing a decline in living standards, especially in terms of basic needs and refers to more immediate interventions. Interventions of both insurance, conditional on membership and participation in a scheme, and assistance, conditional on citizenship and eligibility for support, could be included in this group. Social security for promotion is concerned with the enhancement of living conditions and addressing constant deprivation or what has been referred to earlier as chronic poverty. While it is the direct concern of social security for protection to address moments of vulnerability, promotion interventions operate over a longer time frame and seek to build assets, enhance living standards and expand capabilities. Promotion interventions may thus adopt policies of redistribution and may support what is now being termed pro-poor growth.

To add to the confusion, the notion of a social wage is evoked by some to capture the value of all of these forms of social spending that accrue to poorer segments of the population. The social wage has commonly been taken to refer to public social spending on health, education and housing (Harding 1982:13; Sefton 2002:1). However, agreement on what constitutes the social wage, how this is to be measured and how the social wage relates to the concepts already described has not been reached. As an example, Rankin (1997) argues that the social wage is the income accruing to the public interest, and thus is that slice of a country's national income that is paid over in return for the use of social inputs. Shaikh and Tonak (1994:164) see the social wage as the value of all government services received, less taxes that are paid, while Bowles and Gintis (1982) talk of "citizen wage expenditures". Meade (1972) and others go so far as to equate a social wage with a universal basic income. Certainly we can take it that this is not what is meant by the South African government. Instead, the South African view seems to include the social spending on health, education and housing already mentioned but also includes public works, electricity and water connections and even land reform as part of the social wage (ANC Today 2003).

For the purposes of this chapter, we will confine the analysis to interventions that provide social security for protection regarding these as constituting a minimum basket that makes up the social wage. Although important, social spending on other forms of micro-economic reforms such as asset redistribution and market regulation that could be thought of as social security interventions of promotion is difficult to analyse as the data required for their measurement and, more importantly, for their distribution are not yet available. We will therefore examine selected public expenditure in a number of areas or domains. These domains are social grants, non-employment benefits, family allowances, disaster relief and social assistance for service delivery including housing and also water supply and sanitation. One of the public works programmes (Community Based Public Works Programme) is also reviewed. We will return to the composition of the social wage in the final section.

4. Social Spending in South Africa: 1994-2002

The post-apartheid South Africa Constitution guarantees a number of rights to its citizens that require government interventions. These include the right to have access to health care services, including reproductive health care; sufficient food and water; and social security, including, if they are unable to support themselves and their dependants, appropriate social assistance. Access to adequate housing and basic education are also catered for and the Constitution requires that the state takes "... *reasonable legislative and other measures, within its available resources, to achieve the progressive realisation of each of these rights*" (Section 27).

Although implementation is at best patchy in terms of coverage and quality, the government has attempted to provide for these rights through an array of state-funded and state-run programmes, some of which predate the transition period. Programmes include:

- Long-term and medium term cash transfers, including the state Old Age Pension, Disability Grant, Grant-in-Aid, Child Support Grant and Foster Care Grant;
- Short-term cash or in-kind cash and in-kind transfers for crisis situations, including Social Relief Fund, Disaster Relief Fund, Refugee Relief Fund, the Special Programme for Food Security and in-kind transfers during food crisis through the National Food Emergency Fund;
- Employment generating programmes, including the Poverty Alleviation Projects, Community Based Public Works Programme, the Flagship Programme for Unemployed Women and their Children, Working for Water Programme and Working for the Coast Programme;
- Education, including Early Childhood Development and free primary and secondary education;
- Health protection programmes, including Primary Health Care, the Integrated Nutrition Programme, Primary School Nutrition Programme, Prevention of Blindness/Vision 2020, Free Health Care Services and Protein Energy Malnutrition Scheme;
- Assistance with accessing services, including Consolidated Municipal Infrastructure Programme, Community Water Supply and Sanitation, Electricity Basic Support Services Tariff Strategy, Integrated Sustainable Rural Development Strategy, Rural Infrastructure Strategy and Free Basic Services Coordination and the National Housing Subsidy Scheme;
- Assistance for people with special needs, including Home-based/ Community Care Programme for Children and Families Affected and Infected by HIV/AIDS and Assistive Devices for the Disabled.

The 2003 Intergovernmental Fiscal Review (National Treasury 2003b) argues that increased budgets for these programmes in 2003/04 reaffirm the commitment of provinces to deliver more and better quality services. Reflecting this, recent South African budgets have been heralded by some as being both pro-poor and pro-growth and as putting in practice the commitments contained in the Constitution. Thus in per capita terms, it is true that real social service expenditure is set to increase by five percent in 2003/04 and at an annual average real rate of four percent between 2002/03 and 2005/06. The 2003 Budget Review points to education, health, welfare and other social services as taking up 58.3 percent of non-interest allocations in 2003/04, having risen from 52.9 percent a decade ago (National Treasury, 2003a:16). Total expenditure on social services at the national and provincial level as a percentage of general government expenditure rose by 6.4 percent between 1990 and 2001, to constitute almost half of general government expenditure in 2001 (National Treasury 2000a:145). Of particular significance is the fivefold increase in the budget for HIV/AIDS and TB prevention and treatment. In 2003/04 a new provincial transfer was introduced to meet the costs of the phased-in extension of the Child Support Grant to children up to their 14th birthday (National Treasury 2003a). This is intended to assist with meeting increasing demand for grants. The number of grant beneficiaries has risen from 2.9 million in September 1998 to 5.6 million in 2003.[5]

The Department of Finance undertook an incidence analysis in 1999 to measure government's effectiveness in redistributing income and to evaluate the appropriateness of spending patterns. This study focused on approximately 60 percent of expenditure, namely education, health, the social grants, water provision and housing, between 1993 and 1997. The study concluded that the first years after the transition saw a substantial shift of social spending from the affluent to the more disadvantaged in society. Social spending is also said to be relatively well targeted to poor people as a result of, amongst others, changes in the composition of social spending, housing programmes and infrastructure, including water provision. In addition, shifts between programmes have occurred, such as the increasing emphasis on primary health care, and more appropriate targeting, such as the shift in educator resources to the poor (National Treasury 2000a). These actions are estimated to have increased the share of expenditure on the poorest quintile of households from 27.4 to 30.7 percent, while the share of the richest quintile declined from 12.7 to 8.7 percent (National Treasury 2000a:145). They have resulted in a modest increase in the budget defi-

5 Voucher Generation Report, August 1998; August 2003, Department of Social Development.

cit to GDP ratio compared to the forecast in November 2002, and the expansionary fiscal policy is thus said not to have come at the expense of fiscal discipline, a preoccupation of the post-apartheid government.[6]

Provincial expenditure on social services provides a better idea of what is taking place with regard to spending since most social service spending occurs at this level. Although the 2003 provincial budgets show strong real growth in spending of 7.5 percent in 2003/04, as Table 1 shows, when expressed as a percentage of general government expenditure, the proportion of social service spending has shown little change since 1995.

Table 1: Social Service Expenditure as a % of General Government Expenditure

Financial Year	Education	Health	Social Security & Welfare	Other	Total
1994/5	22.0	10.2	9.3	3.5	45.0
1995/6	21.9	10.2	9.6	5.1	46.8
1996/7	22.5	13.2	8.6	1.9	46.2
1997/8	22.0	11.3	11.6	3.7	48.6
1998/9	21.6	11.8	12.1	3.7	49.2
1999/00	21.3	11.4	12.1	3.7	48.5
2000/01	21.1	11.5	11.8	3.8	48.2
2001/02	20.3	11.6	12.0	3.8	47.7

Source: Hunter et al. *(2003:71) derived from National Treasury, 1994, 1995, 1997, 2000a, 2001a, 2002, 2003a*

Spending on education has remained relatively constant at between 20 and 22 percent of general provincial government spending, while spending on health has also remained constant after an initial spurt in expenditure in the 1996/97 financial year. Of particular relevance for poorer households, the Department of Health administers a Primary Health Care (PHC) programme, which provides free health care for certain vulnerable groups, including pregnant women and children under six. Currently 20 percent of the total health budget is spent on basic health care, of which PHC is the central component (CICSSS, 2002). The Financial and Fiscal Commission (FFC) notes that this increase in

6 The budget deficit to GDP projections have increased from -2.2 to -2.4 percent in 2003/04 and -2.1 to -2.4 percent in 2004/05.

the budget for "basic health services", was largely achieved through a budgetary shift away from hospitals. However, a key problem identified is the slow movement of personnel to primary health care facilities. Other problems noted include the fact that budgets do not reflect actual spending, and are not co-ordinated with plans or national policy priorities (de Bruyn *et al.* 1998).

Welfare spending has grown inconsistently but markedly over the period. From 1996 until 1998 this amount grew by about 10 percent, and fell slightly thereafter. In sum, expenditure on social services makes up just under half of general provincial government expenditure, and this percentage has increased over time, although it declined slightly in 2001/02. Social service spending has made up just over 85 percent of provincial expenditure from 1999 to 2001. Currently, although increasing in real terms, the shares of education and health in total provincial spending are expected to decline steadily, while the share of social development is expected to increase by 4.2 percent over the period 2002/03 to 2005/06 (National Treasury 2003b:16).

The system of social grants has been one of the most important aspects of the poverty reduction strategy of both the apartheid and post-apartheid governments. Overseen by the national Department of Social Development (DSD), and administered by DSD at the provincial level, applications for these grants are taken and payments made at district welfare offices. It can be seen in Table 2 that social security grants account for the vast bulk of social development expenditure at the provincial level and although remaining at approximately the same proportion of social development expenditure, have steadily increased in value in current prices.

Table 2: Provincial Social Expenditure on Social Security Grants

Financial Year	Transfer payments (Rm)	Of which social security grants (Rm)	% on social security grants
1997/98	16383	15521	88.4
1998/99	17015	16167	87.7
1999/00	17700	16120	83.2
2000/01	18970	18039	86.3
2001/02	21554	20510	86.0

Source: Hunter et al., *(2003:74) derived from National Treasury 2001b, 2003b*

The impact that these grants have made on the poor has been well documented and the income benefit of these transfers can be easily examined using data collected for any standard survey of income and consumption such as the Income and Expenditure Surveys of 1995 and 2000. Among others, Haddad and Zeller (1997) point to the fact that the Old Age Pension in South Africa has become a safety net for non-target groups, in particular for children in the pension receiving households. Calculations by the Committee of Inquiry into a Comprehensive Social Security System[7] indicate that in the absence of social assistance transfers 58 percent of South African households would fall below the subsistence level of R401 per adult equivalent. The Taylor Committee further notes that existing social security programmes reduce the average poverty gap by 23 percent (CICSSS 2002:59). The grants are means tested and are targeted: the Old Age Pension is available for the elderly (females 60 and over, and males 65 and over); disabled adults and children may receive grants for their disability; relatively small Child Support Grants are targeted at poor children (but received by their primary caregiver); Foster Care Grants may be received by those legally fostering the child of other parents.[8] Some analysts (Chernick and Reschovsky 2000:28) calculate that nearly 88 percent of the eligible are in fact receiving the Old Age Pension, pointing to near universal coverage. However, the uptake of some of the grants is hampered by complicated administrative processes that may prevent many of the eligible from

7 Hereafter referred to as the Taylor Committee.

8 Other grants – the War Veteran's Pension and the Grant-in-Aid – are also available for very few beneficiaries.

accessing them. In order to access the grants identity documents and birth certificates in the case of children are amongst the documents required by district welfare offices. Many of those living in rural areas do not have these documents, which are obtainable from another government department that is experiencing efficiency and capacity problems, namely the Department of Home Affairs.

The Community Based Public Works Programme (CBPWP) is another short-term programme and aims at poverty alleviation, skills training, delivery of needed assets and capacity building. Specific objectives include the generation of temporary employment on a large scale during the construction of community assets which should improve the living standards and quality of life of the poorest. In addition, the CBPWP aims to create permanent income-generating activities through the operation and maintenance of community productive assets, and to build capacity of local development organizations and local government structures to manage community development ventures. An evaluation completed on the programme highlights room for improvement on its implementation. Concerns include an inequitable geographic spread of projects; a lack of proper administrative co-ordination between ministries that have jurisdiction over public works; a lack of capacity for implementation; and lack of monitoring and evaluation of the programme. The Department of Public Works has taken into account the findings of the evaluation, and have realigned the CBPWP. The changes include targeting at the district level rather than at provincial level; the use of District Councils and NGOs as programme implementing agents; placing emphasis on assets capable of providing continued benefits such as directly productive, labour saving and road access infrastructure; project appraisal and approval and monitoring (CICSSS 2001).

Turning to other areas of government expenditure that might be included as a social wage, van der Berg (1999) notes that improved access of the poor to social services such as improved sanitation, access to health services, nutrition and housing, may improve other aspects of their life while not necessarily improving their cash income. As already noted, a number of such programmes are run at the provincial level and allocating these forms of social spending to the incomes of the poor has been one of the strategies adopted by the government when attempting to calculate a social wage for South Africa.

Access to basic services forms the other major component of imputations intending to take account of the social wage. According to Hunter *et al.* (2003), the Consolidated Municipal Infrastructure Programme (CMIP) has the intention of enabling municipalities to provide at least basic levels of services to low income households. The aim of the programme is to support municipalities, particularly those in urban areas, through a grant fund to provide municipal infrastructure in order to improve quality of life and build sustainable communities. The CMIP also makes available capital grants to municipalities to provide services and facilities such as water, roads, storm water drainage, solid waste disposal, community lighting, clinics, cemeteries, and multi-purpose community and sports facilities to the needy (CICSSS 2001). The programme funds low-income households up to a certain ceiling amount per household. Funding is provided to municipalities on an application basis (National Treasury 2000b).

The bulk of the burden of inadequate water supply in South Africa is carried by the rural poor, particularly women, who due to a lack of access to running water have to walk long distances to fetch water. A policy for the provision of a free basic level of services was established, and in February 2001 it was announced that government would ensure that poor households are provided with a basic supply of water free of charge. The primary aim of the Community Water Supply and Sanitation (CWSS) scheme is to provide basic water and sanitation services to those that have not benefited from them in the past, particularly those in rural areas, and in so doing alleviate poverty.

Table 3 shows that the budget available to local government for the CMIP is on the decline. In 1997/1998 the transfers peaked at R1382 million. The operating budget for the CWSS has steadily increased while the capital budget for the same programme has declined (Hunter *et al.* 2003).

Table 3: National Transfers to Local Government for Conditional Grant Programmes (R million)

Financial Year	CMIP	CWSS (Operating)	CWSS (Capital)
1995/96	126	0	496
1996/97	540	497	321
1997/98	1382	493	1429
1998/99	703	599	520
1999/00	696	710	429

Source: Hunter et al. *(2003:127) derived from National Treasury (2000b:135)*

Finally, in terms of housing, Section 26 of the Constitution grants South African citizens the right to have access to adequate housing. In respecting this right, the Department of Housing has assisted vulnerable and previously disadvantaged groups with housing subsidies through the National Housing Subsidy Scheme (Human Rights Commission 2000). The housing subsidy programme comprises of a once off capital subsidy to households whose income is below R3 500 per month. Information on the number of houses completed or under construction and provincial expenditure on housing can be seen in Table 4. On average total provincial expenditure on housing comes to just more than a percent of general government expenditure. In 1997/98 there was a peak in expenditure likely due to the high number of houses built in this financial year. The number of subsidies approved has climbed year by year since 1998/99, but dropped markedly in 2001/02. The number of houses completed or under construction has also declined in recent years, indicating a slowing in delivery.

Table 4: Delivery of Housing

Financial year	Subsidies approved	Houses completed/under construction	Total provincial exp. as % of general gov. exp.	Total prov. exp. as % of GDP
1994/1995			1.0	0.3
1995/1996	743,439	192,032	0.7	0.2
1996/1997			1.2	0.3
1997/1998		323,303	1.7	0.5
1998/1999	225,980	227,947	1.6	0.4
1999/2000	233,531	263,763	1.3	0.3
2000/2001	246,988	204,507	1.3	0.4
2001/2002	226,101	124,291	1.2	0.3

Source: Hunter et al. *(2003:104) derived from National Treasury (2003b), Department of Housing, own calculations from Department of Housing, South African Reserve Bank (SARB), time series KBP6016J, and SARB, time series KBP4184F*

The National Treasury (2003b:167) notes the number of subsidies approved up to December 2002 as follows: 1 502 614 subsidies to all beneficiaries, 783 935 subsidies to male headed households, and 718 679 subsidies to female headed households. Approximately 88 per cent of approved subsidies were project-linked. Project-linked subsidies help beneficiaries acquire ownership of fixed residential properties for the first time through projects approved by provincial housing departments. Seven percent of subsidies were individual subsidies, and in this instance beneficiaries are helped to acquire ownership of fixed residential properties for the first time, and buy existing homes or homes in projects not approved by provincial housing departments.

This review of the South African government's social spending during the first 10 years of democracy supports the view that the first years after the political transition saw a large and significant shift of social spending away from the more affluent to the formerly disadvantaged members of the population. It also suggests that social spending has been redistributive and relatively well targeted to reach those most in need of it (van der Berg 2001). Furthermore, the post-apartheid government launched new programmes and expanded and revised existing programmes to deal with asset and capability poverty. The Taylor Committee notes that in many cases, these programmes have been innovative, responsive, well conceived and potentially well targeted. (CICSSS 2002).

5. The Social Wage: Opening Pandora's Box?

In its Ten Year Review (Government of South Africa 2003), the government dismisses the data presented earlier that shows persistent poverty and instead argues that the positive patterns of social expenditure have resulted in declining poverty and narrowing inequality. Reports such as the UNDP's Human Development Report for South Africa that have suggested otherwise have been sharply critiqued, while studies showing the persistence of poverty have been described as being excessively pessimistic. Adapting and stretching a more cautious analysis (namely, van der Berg and Burger 2002), the Office of the President has associated increases in social expenditure with improving the "social wage" prevailing in South Africa. However attempting to redefine income and poverty to show improvements in the incidence and severity of poverty may be of questionable value, and if undertaken more carefully may open up a Pandora's Box of commentary.

Rankin (1997:6) proposes a useful set of social wage accounting principles and views the social wage fund (the resources available to be distributed through such expenditure) as comprising three components: revenue from income tax (personal and corporate), revenue from indirect taxes (e.g. VAT) and the value added by state owned enterprises and other public investments in capital markets. Giving up on government revenue through tax cuts represents a transfer of the social wage to the beneficiaries of such relief. Thus, in South Africa, the total value of income tax cuts proposed by Budget 2003 was R15 billion in 2003/04, of which R13.4 billion takes the form of personal income tax reductions. Most of these benefits accrue to people earning low wages in the formal sector, but will not reach those who are categorised as poor. In fact, the South African Council of Churches notes that "... even those taxpayers who benefit least – those earning between R27,000 and R35,000 a year – will see R720 more next year, or R100 more than the additional support given to pensioners." (SACC 2003).

Moreover, the assumption that the entire value of social expenditure can be allocated to poor beneficiaries as additional income is also questionable. The Taylor Committee describes South Africa's social security system as neither adequate nor comprehensive and note that at the time at which the report was written – 2002 – there was no income support programme for children between the ages of nine and 18,[9] adults between 18 and 59 and no general assistance for households where no one is employed. In addition, the Taylor Committee finds that much of what is referred to as social security derives from the European concept which has as its fundamental assumption that social security will develop around formal sector employment. Instead, the Taylor Committee has noted that the development paths of African economies and third world countries more generally may require a new look at social protection systems that are more appropriate to the needs of these countries (CICSSS 2002). The social grants do not provide comprehensive coverage for all those in need. Unless they are able to access the Disability Grant, adults are by and large excluded from this framework of assistance. It is only possible for the UIF to be received by the unemployed for a maximum of six months and then only by those who were registered with the Fund, for the most part the formally employed. Some of the poorest households are those containing adults and children in which no-one receives a grant. The situation becomes even less promising when the values of the Grants are corrected for inflation as Meth (2004) has done.

9 Eligibility for the Child Support Grant was extended from children aged under seven years to those under nine years on 1 April 2003. From 1 April 2004 those aged under 11 were eligible for the Grant, and from 1 April 2005 the primary caregivers of children under the age of 14 will be eligible to apply.

Table 5: Value of Old Age Pension and Child Support Grant (R/month)

	Old age pension		Child support grant	
Year	Nominal Value	Value in 2002 prices	Nominal Value	Value in 2002 prices
July '95	410	708	-	-
July '96	430	693	-	-
July '97	470	694	-	-
July '98	490	671	100	137
July '99	520	668	100	129
July '00	540	649	100	120
July '01	570	647	110	125
October '02	640	640	140	140
April '03	700	652	160	149

Source: Derived from Meth (2004:12)

As Table 5 shows, while the real value of the Child Support Grant has been rising since 2000, the Old Age Pension has declined between 1995 and 2002, and only in 2003 begins to increase once more.

Problems can be identified in other aspects of the delivery of social security spending. For example, public education expenditure has been argued to not be pro-poor, since the share going to the poor and the ultra-poor is substantially smaller than their share of the population (de Bruyn *et al.* 1998). Moreover, although in South Africa education should be free, in practice schools require school fees and other costs (such as uniforms, school books and stationery, transport to school) are making it increasingly more difficult for the poorest to access basic education (Buthelezi 2004). In the case of non-cash transfers in the form of services, expenditure is declining in real terms while administrative and institutional barriers to access persist. More importantly, due to privatisation and the impact of cost recovery policies, services may well be the "Weakest Link" in South Africa's poverty reduction strategy. Hunter *et al.* (2003) note that the CWSS has suffered from a lack of institutional capacity and integration has resulted in a fragmented approach with responsibilities for sanitation spread across different government departments, with no one department taking complete responsibility. A lack of forward planning that should take future trends in population density into account has been noted (CICSSS 2001). The CMIP has also been described as containing "elements which work against the poor" which include application procedures and financial criteria that may create barriers and the fact that the programme is targeted to areas that already have some sort of infrastructure (Budlender 1999). As a result, for the most part it is rural areas, the "poorer" municipalities and marginalised communities that are disadvantaged (Hunter *et al.* 2003).

In addition, the provision of water and electricity is facing a mounting crisis in terms of the impact of the cost recovery policies that have been adopted. McDonald (2002:168) reports that 22 percent of households in a nationally representative survey stated that they were in arrears for water, while 13 percent were in arrears for electricity. Half of those in arrears reported that they would be unable to pay these off. Using these data, McDonald goes on to estimate that 3.25 million people have experienced a suspension in water services due to non-payment and an equal number have had electricity services suspended. Citing statistics from the Department of Provincial and Local government, he shows that there were 256 000 electricity disconnections and 133 000 water disconnections in the last three months of 2001. In each instance poor households were those most affected (McDonald 2002:170). In this respect at least, the credibility accorded by the South African government to the market as the instrument of regulation appears to have been misplaced, resulting in disconnections, indebtedness and further hardship. For some, these policies are regarded as the result of a neo-liberal agenda being pursued by the post-apartheid government and have been robustly attacked as being fundamentally poor unfriendly while benefiting big business (Bond 2000; Desai 2004; McDonald 2002).

Why then in the face of poor data, weak analytical capacity, generally favourable trends in cash transfers but unfavourable trends in the delivery of services, does the South African government feel the need to open a new line of argument around a social wage? As Rankin (1997) shows, the information demands for social wage accounting are formidable, and official statistics and analytical capacity in South Africa, while perhaps better than many other developing countries, are not adequate for an economy and society of its size and complexity. And as we have shown, even the comparatively simple measurement of poverty had not been properly undertaken by the official statistics agency within the first decade of South Africa's transition. Furthermore, the proper calculation of how the social wage fund has been allocated in terms of to whom transfers have been made, may well result in the politically embarrassing conclusion that post-apartheid policies have not been as redistributive as a simple incidence analysis would portray. Certainly the rural poor, once identified as a priority target group, are unlikely to have benefited from measures that promoted fiscal austerity or user charges while perhaps more appropriate target groups in the current epoch, such as the long-term unemployed, the homeless and the ill, may have been adversely affected by policies such as high interest rates, privatisation or inconsistent responses to HIV/AIDS. Instead, there is a risk that more confusion will result, and more attention devoted to activities of political thrust and parry instead of basic research, the generation of reliable statistics and informed decision making that benefits the poor.

6. Conclusion

Despite the plethora of household surveys, and increasing capacity in government and in the research community to use such data, even the simplest forms of poverty measurement have remained out of reach in South Africa or when attempted, have been dogged by controversy. With sufficient care, the data that are available can be used to reveal persistent poverty in the post-apartheid period and widening inequality although the inclusion of selective aspects of social wage accounting does improve this situation. In some situations uncertainty over trends in poverty and inequality may be of benefit to an insecure government. In South Africa, however, there seems no need for this to continue in the third term of reaffirmed government. An appropriate and official yardstick by which poverty changes can be determined and compared is essential together with the introduction of instruments for the collection of official statistics. Along with other indicators of well-being, this yardstick can then be consistently used for policy development and to assess progress.

Recognising the deep and persistent impact of apartheid on South Africa's social and economic institutions would permit a more realistic assessment of which policy interventions are appropriate and in what sequence. This includes dealing with "awkward" issues such as changing family structure, the role of subsistence and informal economy production, migration and the efficiency of markets when allocating resources to the poor. It is not surprising that solving the many distortions put in place by the colonial and apartheid governments has proven to be a difficult task, and it is one that will require more than one decade of democratic governance to achieve. It is perhaps not surprising that the new democratic South African government adopted many of the strategies that it deemed necessary to achieve macro-economic stability. Alternatives may have been difficult to defend in an era in which the state was being rolled back across the world while balancing the books in post-apartheid South Africa may have required more than a commitment to the socio-economic rights of the poor. Rather the policies of stabilisation, openness to trade and the protection of property rights would have attracted influential support among national and international stakeholders.

The recognition by government that micro-economic reforms are now required is an important recent development in terms of providing better compensation to those who bear the "... social cost of other people's progress". But more is required. Micro-economic reforms are not simply the introduction of a suite of supply-side instruments that are hoped to boost formal sector production, but should also include social policies of the kind described in this paper that assist those who have borne "apartheid's assault on the poor". Improving the coverage, depth and efficacy of these policies are among the matching demand-side instruments that might improve the efficiency with which South Africa is able to translate the recent hopeful macro-economic trends into a sustained reduction in poverty. Larger grants, dispensing with means testing and a universal or basic income grant are all options that might be considered.

As for the social wage, given the problems faced with data and the analytical challenges that we face in understanding poverty in South Africa, we question whether more concepts and more complex measurement procedures will be helpful. Such concepts may serve some purpose by rendering redistributive processes more legitimate in the eyes of elites, by being cast as Third Way reforms of the Blair/Schroeder ilk, while simultaneously appeasing segments of the ruling party's support base especially in the labour movement. However, there is an equal chance that they obfuscate real trends in poverty and inequality, and detract attention away from the real challenge of restructuring the economic base of South Africa. As an example, partly including the social wage into poverty analysis largely does away with the apparently puzzling finding of increased poverty in the face of increased social spending. By so doing, the real decline in income experienced by those who have lost employment is obscured, as is the impact on income earning capacity due to HIV/AIDS. It is to be hoped then that the cluttering of poverty analysis was a side effect of the 2004 election year and that the "social wage" no more than riposte to critical analyses recently made of South Africa's progress since 1994.[10] Even if this is so, the South African

10 A fencing term to refer to an offensive action made immediately after a parry of the opponent's attack.

government should be mindful that critical analytical comment assists better policy formulation while misleading or incomplete information will hinder poverty reduction still further.

References

ANC Today, (2003), Government has improved the lives of the poor, *ANC Today*, Vol 3, No 43, 31 October-6 November, 2003.

Bhorat, H., and Poswell, L. (2002): *Employment and Household Poverty: The Effects of Trade, Investment and Technology*, Overseas Development Group; Institute of Development Studies: Discussion Paper 14.

Bond, P., (2000): *Elite Transition: From Apartheid to neoliberalism in South Africa*, Wits University Press.

Bowles, S., and Gintis, H., (1982): The crisis of liberal democratic capitalism: The case of the United States, *Politics and Society*, 11(1): 51-93.

Budlender, D., (1999): Women and the local government. In: D. Budlender (ed.) *The Fourth Women's Budget*. Cape Town, Idasa. p. 16-65.

Budlender, D., (2000), Earnings Inequality in South Africa, 1995-1998, in Statistics South Africa (2000), *Measuring Poverty*, Statistics South Africa, Pretoria.

Buthelezi, T., (2004): *An investigation of schooling costs as a contributor to dropping out of school in KZN: Policy implications for poverty alleviation*, Unpublished Masters of Development Studies dissertation, School of Development Studies, University of KwaZulu-Natal.

Chernick, H., and Reschovsky, A., (2000): *Designing an Intergovernmental Grant System for the New South Africa*. Paper prepared for presentation at the Annual Research Conference of the Association for Public Policy Analysis and Management, Seattle, Washington, 2-4 November.

Committee of Inquiry into a Comprehensive Social Security System (CICSSS), (2001): *Current Government Measures to Address Poverty and Meet Basic Needs*, Draft Input Document.

Committee of Inquiry into a Comprehensive Social Security System (CICSSS), (2002): *Transforming the Present – Protecting the Future* (Draft Consolidated Report), March, <http://www.welfare.gov.za>.

Cook, S., Kabeer, N. and Suwannarat, G., (2003): *Social Protection in Asia*, New Delhi, Har-Anand Publications.

De Bruyn, J., McIntyre, D., Mthethwa, N., Naidoo, K., Ntenga, L., Pillay, P., and Pintusewitz, C., (1998): *Public Expenditure on Basic Social Services in South Africa*. An FFC report for UNICEF and UNDP. Midrand: Financial and Fiscal Commission.

Desai, A., (2004): *Neoliberalism and resistance in South Africa*, Cubasiglo XXI, 15/01/2004, downloaded from <http://www.nodo50.org/cubasigloXXI/taller/desai1_150104.htm>.

Devereux, S., (2003): *Policy Options for Increasing the Contribution of Social Protection to Food Security*, Sussex, IDS.

Dorrington, R., Bourne, E., Bradshaw, D., Lauscher, R. and Timaeus, I., (2001): *The impact of HIV/AIDS on adult mortality in South Africa*, Technical Report, Burden of Disease Research Unity, Medical Research Council, Cape Town.

Dreze, J. and Sen, A., (1991): Public Action for Social Security: Foundations and Strategy, in E. Ahmad, J. Dreze, J. Hills and A. Sen (Eds.), *Social Security in Developing Countries*, (1-40), Oxford, Clarendon Press.

Financial and Fiscal Commission (FFC), (1997): *Local Government in a System of Inter-governmental Fiscal Relations in South Africa*. Discussion Document, Financial and Fiscal Commission, Midrand.

Government of South Africa, (2003): *Towards 10 Years of Freedom: Review*, downloaded from <http://www.10years.gov.za/review/documents.htm> on 12 April, 2004.

Haddad, L. and Zeller, M., (1999): Can social security programmes do more with less? General issues and the challenges for Southern Africa, *Development Southern Africa*, Vol 14, No. 2: 125-149.

Harding, A., (1982): An Introduction to the Social Wage, *Social Security Journal*, December.

Hanmer, L. and Naschold, F., (2000): Attaining the International Development Targets: Will growth be enough?, *Development Policy Review*, Vol 18: 11-36.

Holzmann, R. and Jorgensen, S., (2000): *Social Risk Management: A New Conceptual Framework for Social Protection and Beyond*, World Bank Discussion Paper No. 0006, Washington D. C., World Bank.

Human Rights Commission. (2000): *Fourth Annual Report (1998-1999)*. Johannesburg, South African Human Rights Commission.

Hunter, N., Hyman, I., Krige, D., and Olivier, M., with Dekker, A., Khandlhela, M., and May, J., (2003): *Draft South African Social Protection and Expenditure Review*, University of Natal, Durban and Rand Afrikaans University.

Klasen, S., (1997): Poverty and Inequality in South Africa: An Analysis of the 1993 SALDRU Survey. *Social Indicators Research*, Vol 41:51-94.

Lipton, M., (1997): Editorial: Poverty – Are the Holes in the Consensus. *World Development*, Vol 25, No. 7:1003-1006.

Manuel, T., (2001): *Budget Speech, 21 February 2001*, <www.treasury.gov.za>.

Manuel, T., (2002): *Budget Speech, 20 February 2002*, <www.treasury.gov.za>.

Marais, H., (1998): *South Africa: Limits to Change, the Political Economy of Transformation*, Zed Books, London.

May, J., Carter, M. and Padayachee, V., (2004): Is Poverty and Inequality Leading to Poor Growth?, *South African Labour Bulletin*, 28(2): 18-20.

May, J., Woolard, I. and Klaasen, S., (2000): The nature and measurement of poverty and inequality, (with Ingrid Woolard and Stephan Klasen) in May, J., (ed), *Poverty and Inequality in South Africa: Meeting the Challenge*, David Phillip and Zed Press, Cape Town and London, pp. 19-50.

Mbeki, T., (2001): *State of the Nation address at the opening of parliament, 9 February 2001*, <www.gov.za>.

Mbeki, T., (2004): *State of the Nation address by the President of South Africa*, Thabo Mbeki, to the joint sitting of the Houses of Parliament, Cape Town, 21 May 2004, <http://www.gov.za/speeches/sotn2004.htm>, downloaded at 14:10, 22 May, 2004.

McDonald, D.A., (2002): The Bells Tolls for Thee: Cost recovery, cutoffs and the affordability of municipal services in South Africa, in McDonald, D.A. and J. Pape, *Cost Recovery and the Crisis of Service Delivery in South Africa*, HRSC Press, Pretoria.

Meade, J.E., (1972): Poverty in the Welfare State, *Oxford Economic Papers*, 24(3), 289-326.

Meth, C., (2004): *What has happened to poverty in South Africa as unemployment has increased?* Version 4, unpublished report, School of Development Studies, University of KwaZulu-Natal.

Meth, C. and Dias, R., (2004): Increases in poverty in South Africa, 1999-2002, *Development Southern Africa*, 21(1), 59-86.

Midgley, J., (1996): Challenges Facing Social Security, in J. Midgley and M. B. Tracy (Eds.), *Challenges to Social Security*, (pp. 1-18), Westport, Connecticut, Auburn House.

National Treasury, (1994): *Budget Review 1994*, Pretoria, National Treasury.

National Treasury, (1995): *Budget Review 1995*, Pretoria, National Treasury.

National Treasury, (1997): *Budget Review 1997*, Pretoria, National Treasury.

National Treasury, (2000a): *Budget Review 2000*, Pretoria, National Treasury.

National Treasury, (2000b): *Intergovernmental Fiscal Review 2000*, Pretoria, National Treasury.

National Treasury, (2001a): *Budget Review 2001*, Pretoria, National Treasury.

National Treasury, (2001b): *Intergovernmental Fiscal Review 2001*, Pretoria, National Treasury.

National Treasury, (2002): *Budget Review 2002*, Pretoria, National Treasury.

National Treasury, (2003a): *Budget Review 2003*, Pretoria, National Treasury.

National Treasury, (2003b): *Intergovernmental Fiscal Review 2003*, Pretoria, National Treasury.

Norton, A., Conway, T. and Foster, M., (2001): *Social Protection Concepts and Approaches: Implications for Policy and Practice in International Development*, London, ODI.

Rankin, K., (1997): *The social wage as a definitive component of political parties' philosophies*, revised version of a paper to the Conference of New Zealand Political Studies Association, 8-10 July, 1996, downloaded from <http:/ www.geocities.com/Athens/Academcy/1223/krnknsocw_wp.html> on 13 May, 2004.

South African Council of Churches (SACC), (2003): *"We Can Do More to End Poverty"*, South African Council of Churches, downloaded from <http:// www.sacc-ct.org.za/budget02.html> on 22 May, 2004.

Sefton, T., (2002): *Recent changes in the Distribution of the Social Wage*, Centre for the Analysis of Social Exclusion Working Paper 62, London School of Economics, London.

Shaikh, A., and Tonak, A., (1994): *Measuring the Wealth of Nations: The Political Economy of National Accounts*, Cambridge University Press.

Statistics South Africa (SSA), (2002): *Income and Expenditure of Households 2000 – Statistical Release PO111*, Pretoria, Statistics South Africa.

Sunday Times, (2004): *Research Or Advocacy?* UN Reports Irks Government, posted 9th May, <http://allafrica.com/stories/200405100483.html>.

Titmuss., R.M., (1968): *Commitment to Welfare*, London: Allen and Unwin.

United Nations Development Programme (UNDP), (2002): *Human Development Report 2000* (New York: United Nations Development Programme, Oxford University Press).

United Nations Development Programme (UNDP), (2003): *South African Human Development Report, 2003*, Pretoria, United National Development Programme.

United Nations Development Programme (UNDP), (2004): *Human Development Indicators, 2003*, <http://hdr.undp.org/reports/global/2003/indicator/index.html>, downloaded 15:00, 22 May, 2004.

Van der Berg, S., (1999): *Social Policy to Address Poverty*, DPRU Working Paper 99/30, Development Policy Research Unit, University of Cape Town.

Van der Berg, S., (2001): Redistribution through the Budget: Public Expenditure Incidence in South Africa, 1993-1997, *Social Dynamics*, 27(1), 140-164.

Van der Berg, S. and Louw, M., (2003): *Changing patterns of South African income distribution: Towards time series estimates of distribution and poverty*, paper to the Conderence of the Economic Society of South Africa, Stellenbosch, 17-19 September, 2003.

Van der Berg, S. and Burger, R., (2002): *The stories behind the numbers: An investigation of efforts to deliver services to the South African poor*, report prepared for the World Bank, University of Stellenbosch, Stellenbosch.

Woolard, I, and Leibbrandt, M., (2001): Measuring Poverty in South Africa, (in) Bhorat, H., Leibbrandt, M., Maziya, M., van der Berg. S and I. Woolard, *Fighting poverty: Labour Markets and Inequality in South Africa*, University of Cape Town Press, Cape Town.

World Bank, (2000): *World Development Report 2000/2001, Attacking Poverty*, Oxford University Press, New York.

6. The Judicial Enforcement of Socio-Economic Rights: The *Grootboom* Case

Albie Sachs *

Mrs Grootboom[1] decided she had had enough. She and her two children and her sister with three children, lived in a shack in an area not far from Cape Town. The winter rains were approaching and she decided she could not bear another season in a water-logged area. Altogether, about 5000 people lived in similar circumstances in the settlement, without clean water, sewage and refuse removal services and with virtually no electricity. Many had applied to the municipality for subsidised low-cost housing and had been on waiting lists for as long as seven years, with no relief in sight. Faced with the prospect of remaining indefinitely in intolerable conditions, Mrs Grootboom and nearly a thousand adults and children moved to a nearby vacant hill-side. The land had, in fact, been set aside for low-cost housing. Negotiations with the owner and the local council followed, but without success. Eventually a court order was issued declaring them to be in unlawful occupation of the land and requiring them to be evicted. They were then forcibly removed, prematurely and inhumanely, at the expense of the municipality. Their makeshift homes were bulldozed and burnt and their possessions destroyed. Many of the residents were not even present to salvage what meagre belongings they could.

Desperate and homeless, they moved onto a local sports field. The bitter winter rains of the Cape were arriving and they had little more than plastic sheeting for protection. They approached an attorney who wrote to the council describing the intolerable conditions under which they were living and demanded that the council meet its constitutional obligations and provide them with temporary accommodation. Dissat-

* Justice of the Constitutional Court of South Africa.

1 The name Grootboom is the Afrikaans version of an African name meaning "Big Tree".

Peris Jones and Kristian Stokke (eds.), Democratising Development, *ISBN 90 04 14821 3, pp. 131-152.*

isfied with the municipality's response to the letter, the group launched an urgent application in the High Court. And so Mrs Grootboom gave her name to what many consider to be a case at the cutting-edge of world jurisprudence. The question her case raised was: could social and economic rights be regarded as fundamental rights enforceable directly[2] by the courts, and if so, how?

The South African Constitution[3] provides as follows:

Section 26

Housing

(1) Everyone has the right to have access to adequate housing.

(2) The state must take reasonable legislative and other measures within its available resources, to achieve the progressive realisation of this right.

(3) No one may be evicted from their home, or have their home demolished without an order of court made after considering all the relevant circumstances. No legislation may permit arbitrary evictions.

The High Court ordered the municipality to provide temporary shelter pending the outcome of the application, so that the Court would not be compelled to determine the difficult and important questions under pressure of approaching rains.

At the hearing the state acknowledged the dire circumstances in which the applicants found themselves. It contended, however, that these were the inherited consequences of past injustice, and not indications of a failure to meet current constitutional obligations. On the contrary, it argued, it was meeting these obligations by means of implementing a massive housing programme which enabled millions of poor people to move from leaking and makeshift shacks without secure tenure to weather-proof homes to which they had full title. Three quarters of a million families had already been able to move into completely subsidised homes, serviced with electricity and water, and millions more would benefit in future as the housing programme unrolled.

2 Nearly all modern states have legislation which the courts enforce, concerning housing, health, education and welfare. The issue was whether a right to housing flowed directly from the Constitution and as such had binding and overriding legal force in relation to legislation and policy on housing.

3 Act 108 of 1996.

The High Court accepted that the state in fact was meeting its obligation progressively to realise the right of access to adequate housing in terms of section 26(2) of the Constitution. The Court went on to hold, however, that the state had failed to meet further and special obligations which it owed to the children involved. The Bill of Rights provides:

> *Section 28*
> **Children**
> (1) Every child has the right—
> . . .
> (c) to basic nutrition, shelter, basic health care services and social services (emphasis added).

The Court pointed out that the right of the child to shelter was not qualified by reference to progressive realisation within available resources. The shelter envisaged by the section might be less than adequate housing, but at the very least the state had an obligation to provide the children with some protection from the elements. Furthermore, since the children could not be separated from their parents, the Court ordered that all the people concerned should be given at least elementary protection.

The state took the case on appeal to the Constitutional Court.[4] I might mention that we were helped at the hearing in a most considerable way by the participation of the Human Rights Commission[5] and the Community Law Centre of the University of the Western Cape. Counsel for the Legal Resources Centre[6] appeared on their behalf and succeed-

4 The Constitutional Court was established in 1994 after the country's first democratic election, in terms of the Interim Constitution of RSA Act 200 of 1993, and was confirmed as the highest court in the land in respect of all constitutional matters in the Final Constitution, n. 4 above. Its decision in respect of this issue was reported as *Government of the Republic of South Africa and others v Grootboom and Others* 2001 (1) SA 46 (CC); 2000(11) BCLR 1169 (CC).

5 The Human Rights Commission is a "Chapter Nine" body established in terms of section 184 of the Constitution, as a state institution supporting constitutional democracy. It has a monitoring and assessing function, which includes aiming sure that the values and rights of the Constitution are observed, respected, and promoted at all levels.

6 The Legal Resources Centre is a non-profit, non-governmental public interest law centre which provides legal assistance to vulnerable and mar-

ed in broadening the debate so as to require the Court to consider the rights of all South Africans to shelter, whether they had children or not, in terms of section 26 of the Constitution. The case showed the extent to which creative lawyers can help the poor to secure their basic rights.

How did the provision dealing with the right of access to adequate housing come to be in the Constitution? And the same question may be asked of similar provisions in the Bill of Rights dealing with access to health care, food, water and social security. How did they all come to be placed in the Constitution as fundamental rights which the state was obliged to realise progressively within its available resources? The existence of this cluster of social and economic rights in the Bill of Rights added to the task facing our Court. In determining the scope of the right of access to adequate housing we would not only be resolving the case of Mrs Grootboom and others, we would also start exploring the whole question of the status of socio-economic rights, and more particularly the extent of the state's duty in fulfilling them.

My own direct confrontation with the question started in the mid-1980s when I was a law professor in exile in Mozambique. A group of black law students at the University of Natal-Durban established a body called the Anti-Bill of Rights Committee. What?!? Not Anti-Apartheid, but Anti-Bill of Rights. I was jolted by the notion of idealistic persons belonging to the oppressed community, part of the struggle for a non-racial democracy, being opposed to the idea of a Bill of Rights. Yet I understood and sympathised with much of their motivation. They saw a Bill of Rights as a document established in advance by a privileged white minority to block any future moves towards social and economic transformation. The Bill of Rights would defend the unjust socio-economic situation created by apartheid, guarantee property rights in terms of which whites owned 87% of the land and 95% of productive capital, and impose extreme limits on the capacity of the democratic state to equalise access to wealth. Ultimately, the poor would remain poor, albeit formally liberated, and the rich would get richer, though technically not advantaged. As I heard one commentator put it, the Bill of Rights would in effect be a "Bill of Whites".

Yet a number of forward-looking white judges and academics had advanced the need for a Bill of Rights in the hope that it would facili-

ginalized communities in South Africa who are disadvantaged by reason of social, economic, and historical circumstances. For further information, see LRC mission statement at <www.lrc.org.za>.

tate the achievement of majority rule. Their reasoning had been that while ensuring the vote to everyone and outlawing discrimination, a Bill of Rights would re-assure whites that they had a constitutionally-protected future in the country. Such is the dialectic of legal development, however, that concepts that assuage the anxieties of the whites, inevitably arouse the concerns of the blacks.

I was determined to keep the dialectic from congealing in that unsatisfactory form. I wrote a paper espousing the need for an "Anti-Anti-Bill of Rights Committee". I started by pointing out that every revolution was impossible until it happened, then it became inevitable. It was in this unstable context that we had to consider a future Bill of Rights. The notion the law students had of a Bill of Rights was unduly narrow, presupposing that the function of a Bill of Rights was simply to limit the power of government. Yet there was no reason why the Bill of Rights should not also be an instrument for advancing the claims of the dispossessed. At this point I introduced into the discourse the theme of the three generations of rights.

The first generation encompassed the classic civil and political rights which emerged from the French and American Revolutions. These were the fundamental rights of citizens and free persons, which had to be spelt out unequivocally in any post-liberation document.

The second generation of rights dealt with entitlements concerning housing, health, education and welfare, and were introduced in Germany under Bismarck in the late 19th Century. These rights were taken up in the Russian Revolution and later came to be central to national policy in the so-called welfare states of the 20th Century. So they were developed in authoritarian, revolutionary and social democratic countries. After the Second World War these rights gained strong international favour and were integrated with civil and political rights into the Universal Declaration of Human Rights. They were subsequently entrenched in the International Convention on Economic, Social and Cultural Rights, which, though adopted separately from the International Convention on Civil and Political Rights, enjoyed equal legal status.

The concept of a third generation of rights, and, indeed, the whole notion of clustering rights in generational terms, was developed in the late 1970s by a Czech lawyer working at the United Nations. His concern was primarily with the right to a clean and healthy environment, a collective right which he could not fit easily into any known category of basic human rights. Hence he coined the idea of a third generation of rights which by its nature would belong to the whole community and to future generations, and not just to individuals. Other similar rights, sometimes referred to as solidarity rights, were the right to development and the right to peace. One analyst referred to the three generations of rights as "blue rights" (civil and political), "red rights" (socio-economic) and "green rights" (as above).[7]

When political prisoners were released in South Africa and exiles like myself able to return, serious negotiations about a new constitutional order began, and the debate on the enforcement of social and economic rights entered a new and pressing phase. Three distinct positions emerged. There were those who argued that such rights should be seen as aspirational only, and not be embodied in any way in the constitution. A second current favoured incorporating such rights in the constitution, but giving them the status of guiding principles only and not making them enforceable by the courts. The third position was that appropriate language should be found to make them justiciable as enforceable constitutional rights.

The only precedents we could find pointed towards the midway position, that is, to incorporating socio-economic rights in the constitution merely as non-justiciable directives of state policy. Thus when the Irish won independence from Britain they included socio-economic rights in their constitution but made it clear such rights would not be enforceable by the courts.[8] Similarly, when India won its independence after World War Two, its Constituent Assembly adopted a constitution which included socio-economic rights simply as directives of state policy, making it clear that they were not in themselves to be enforceable by the courts.[9] I mention in passing that the Indian Supreme Court went on to interpret these rights in a creative way, so using them to give tex-

7 Professor Kader Asmal, then at the University of the Western Cape and recently Minister of Education, used these descriptions during the debates preceding the drafting of the Constitution.

8 Article 45 of the Irish Constitution states that: "The principles of social policy set forth in this Article are intended for the general guidance of the Oireachtas. The application of those principles in the making of laws shall be the care of the Oireachtas exclusively, and shall not be cognisable by any Court under any of the provisions of this Constitution."

9 Part IV of the Indian Constitution contains these Directive Principles of State Policy. Article 37 states that: "The provisions contained in this Part shall not be enforced by any court, but the principles therein laid down are nevertheless fundamental in the governance of the country and it shall be the duty of the State to apply these principles in making laws."

ture and substance to the fundamental civil and political rights directly enforceable in the courts.[10] In the South African debate there was strong support for having separate chapters in the Constitution to deal with rights that were to be enforceable and those that were to be understood simply as directives of state policy.

It was at about this time, in the early 1990s, that I had the pleasure of being invited to spend a week in Paris as a guest of Robert Badinter, President of the Conseil Constitucionelle. Ronald Dworkin happened to be in Paris at the time. I was hoping to receive from him comments on the Draft Bill of Rights produced by the ANC Constitutional Committee, and in particular on the provisions for socio-economic rights. As a sweetener I was able to invite him to see the original copy of the Declaration of the Rights of Man in the Palais Royale. I recall Ronald Dworkin's cautious observations. As we descended the steps of the Palais he indicated his doubts as to whether it was appropriate to include extensive and detailed social and economic rights as fundamental rights in a constitution. He pointed out that equal protection was a powerful and principled instrument that could be used to strengthen the position of those whom racial policies had forced to live in disadvantage at the margins of society. I spent much time pondering over his words. The problem as I saw it was not simply to prevent the continuation of discrimination, but to ensure that everyone was entitled at least to the minimum decencies of life. There was a connection between the two, but not a complete overlap. As eventually drafted, the equality clause in our Constitution came to occupy a central role in the new Bill of Rights.[11] Yet it did not go beyond prohibiting negative discriminatory

---

10 Thus, in *Olga Tellis v. Bombay Municipal Corporation* (1985) 3 SCC 545, the Indian Supreme Court held that the right to life, which could not be taken away except by due process of law, included more than just the right to bodily being. Read together with the Directives of State Policy, the right to life included the right to a decent human existence. This meant that pavement dwellers could not be evicted from their rudimentary shelters without due process of law.

11 Section 9 of the Constitution provides:

Equality

(1) Everyone is equal before the law and has the right to equal protection and benefit of the law.

(2) Equality includes the full and equal enjoyment of all rights and freedoms. To promote the achievement of equality, legislative and

conduct and facilitating ameliorative action to redress patterns of disadvantage. It did not require positive action on the part of the state to enable people to live in conditions consistent with at least the minimum standards of human dignity.

During the final stages of the drafting of the Constitution the arguments on the enforcement of social and economic rights became particularly heated. The conservative position was that because judges were not accountable to the electorate, it was not appropriate for them to be embroiled in debates over social and economic policy. Relying on separation of powers arguments, supporters of this position argued that the judiciary should not be involved in decisions that had major implications for governmental spending. They pointed out that this was precisely what bodies were democratically elected to deal with. They feared that inevitably the courts would find their authority diminished through being sucked into taking positions on what were essentially political rather than legal matters.

If confirmation were necessary, my eight years on the Court underline for me the overall wisdom of starting off with such an approach. Normally it is not for us to decide on how resources should best be used. This is not simply because of the need not to get involved in questions affecting the budget. The enforcement of political and civil rights will, after all, often involve intrusion on the budget, such as when the court orders the holding of elections or the provision of legal aid. The deeper question is whether it is institutionally appropriate for judges to take positions on highly controversial questions of the kind that are hotly debated during elections. The answer must in general be no. Whether government policy is wise or stupid is something for public opinion and the electorate to

other measures designed to protect or advance persons, or categories of persons, disadvantaged by unfair discrimination may be taken.

(3) The state may not unfairly discriminate directly or indirectly against anyone on one or more grounds, including race, gender, sex, pregnancy, marital status, ethnic or social origin, colour, sexual orientation, age, disability, religion, conscience, belief, culture, language and birth.

(4) No person may unfairly discriminate directly or indirectly against anyone on one or more grounds in terms of subsection (3). National legislation must be enacted to prevent or prohibit unfair discrimination.

(5) Discrimination on one or more of the grounds listed in subsection (3) is unfair unless it is established that the discrimination is fair.

decide, not for the judges. In a constitutional democracy this must be the general rule. I stress, the general rule, not the invariable one.

My view is that there are in reality a restricted number of circumstances involving highly contentious matters where it is actually an advantage for judges not to be accountable to the electorate. When you see yourself as having a constitutional duty to defend deep core values which are part of emerging world jurisprudence and of evolving constitutional notions in your own country, you become sharply aware of the constitutional connection between the maintenance of judicial independence and the protection of human dignity.

The very notion of entrenching rights is to provide a basic framework of constitutional regard for every human being. It is not the duty of courts to side with one section of society against another, however powerful or weak they might be and however sympathetic to their claims individual judges might feel. But there is every reason why it should be incumbent on the courts to see to it that basic respect for the dignity of every person is maintained at all times. That is why we have fundamental rights. The Bill of Rights is there not simply to protect the vested interests of those that have, but to secure basic dignity for those that have not. The key question, then is not whether unelected judges should ever take positions on controversial political questions. It is to define in a principled way the limited and functionally manageable circumstances in which the judicial responsibility for being the ultimate protector of human dignity compels them to enter what might be politically contested terrain. It is precisely in situations where political leaders may have difficulty withstanding populist pressures, and where human dignity is most at risk, that it becomes an advantage that judges are not accountable. It is at these moments that the judicial function expresses itself in its purest form. The judges, able to rely on the independence guaranteed to them by the Constitution, ensure that justice is done to all without fear, favour or prejudice.[12]

---

12 Section 6 (1) of Schedule 2 of the Constitution contains the Oath or Solemn Affirmation of Judicial Officers as follows "... I, A. B., swear/solemnly affirm that, as a Judge of the Constitutional Court/Supreme Court of Appeal/High Court/E. F. Court, I will be faithful to the Republic of South Africa, will uphold and protect the Constitution and the human rights entrenched in it, and will administer justice to all persons alike without fear, favour or prejudice, in accordance with the Constitution and the law. (In the case of an oath: So help me God.)"

In my opinion, then, the greatest problem concerning judicial enforcement of social and economic rights is not one of institutional *legitimacy*. The Constitution itself requires the courts to ensure respect for such rights. The real difficulty is that of institutional *capacity*. It is in this connection that the more radical objection to our suitability to enforce socio-economic rights comes into play. The objection from radical quarters to judges enforcing social and economic rights suggests that we are likely to get it all wrong. They point to the social class from which we judges traditionally have been drawn, and the nature of our legal thinking which tends to look at questions in abstract and formulaic ways that end up favouring the status quo. But even where our background and modes of thought might predispose us differently, there can be little doubt that it is inappropriate for judges who in general know very little about the practicalities of housing, land and other social realities, to pronounce on these issues. That is what Parliament is there for. It has hearings and receives inputs from a variety of people with special expertise in particular areas. The very nature of the political process calls for compromise and a balancing out of interests, something to be applauded in an open and democratic society based on principles of give-and-take rather than of all-or-nothing.

Yet, though compromise on questions of practicality and use of resources is valuable, compromise on matters of deep principle is dangerous. Thus, the securing of maximum support, which is part and parcel of the political process, is intrinsically different from the principled balancing that in matters involving fundamental rights is central to the judicial function. We are institutionally completely unsuited to take decisions on houses, hospitals, schools and electricity. We just do not have the know-how and the capacity to handle those questions. But we do know about human dignity, we do know about oppression and we do know about things that reduce a human being to a status below that which a democratic society would regard as tolerable.

An implication of placing social and economic rights in a constitution is to say that decisions which, however well-intended, might have the consequence of producing intolerable hardship, cannot be left solely in the hands of overburdened administrators and legislators. Efficiency is one of the great principles of government. The utilitarian principle of producing the greatest good for the greatest number might well be the starting-off point for the use of public resources. But the qualitative element, based on respect for the dignity of each one of us, should never be left out. This is where the vision of the judiciary, tunnelled in the unshakable direction of securing respect for human dignity, comes into its own.

I suspect that behind the technical and political science arguments advanced against the judicial enforcement of socio-economic rights, lies a basic concern that somehow the involvement of the courts in this area will lead to a dilution of their respect for fundamental civil and political rights. Put another way, there is a fear that in pursuit of the right to bread, the right to freedom will be submerged. Anxiety on this score has historical foundations. Certain states have contended that in order to achieve national development and to improve the conditions of the impoverished masses they have had to suppress freedom of speech and do away with multi-party democracy and spurn an open society. Can it be, though, that people want freedom without bread, or bread without freedom? In South Africa the struggle for the vote and for freedom of movement and speech was always inseparable from the right to housing, health and education. Bureaucratic authoritarianism was intrinsic to apartheid. People simply did not count as human beings. The restoration of dignity for all South Africans accordingly requires the simultaneous creation of material conditions for a dignified life and development of increased respect for the personality and rights of each one of us.

Both freedom and bread are necessary for the all-round human being. Instead of undermining each other, they are interrelated and interdependent.[13]

It heaps indignity upon indignity to say that the poor are not interested in the franchise or the right to speak their mind or the right to be treated fairly, but only in a full stomach. The experience in South Africa was that in general terms the greatest sacrifices for freedom were made by those who were the poorest and most dispossessed. Yet the constitutional vision is deeply impoverished if it is limited to allowing a person dying of hunger simply to curse the government with his or her last breath. Where the struggle for survival is overwhelming, freedom to vote and the right to criticise the government become remote from the

13 As Amartya Sen has shown, in open and democratic societies you do not get famine, because shortages of food are dealt with in ways in which there is public accountability for distribution. In dictatorships, on the other hand, where you have the same quantity of food, you get famine and starvation because what grain is available is secretly hoarded and siphoned off to the rich. See Amartya Sen and Jean Dreze, *Hunger and Public Action* Oxford: Clarendon Press, 1989.

exigencies of daily existence. In a society in which people are not simply striving to survive but where they are educated, where they can read and study and learn about the world, they can make informed political decisions and exercise meaningful self-determination.

The inter-relatedness of the different generations of rights helps resolve some of the libertarian versus communitarian tensions on the question of the enforcement of social and economic rights. An extreme libertarian approach to Mrs Grootboom's situation would have secured to her the right to be left alone, with unrestricted freedom to denounce the government as the rain pelted down. Yet she did not want the state to leave her alone when the rains came. She wanted to be able to call upon the state to ensure that she and her children had a roof over their heads. On the other hand, if a radical communitarian approach had been adopted, the invasion by herself and a thousand others of privately owned land would, without more, have been justified. The fact was, however, that apart from the rights of the landowner, there were other individuals in the queue for formal housing due to be built on that land whose rights were also being affected. In my opinion, the approach that our Constitution required us to adopt was neither purely libertarian nor simply communitarian, but dignitarian. It is respect for human dignity that unites the right to be autonomous with the need to recognise that we are all social beings. Thus, the fundamental right of all human beings to have their basic human dignity respected becomes the link between freedom and bread.

Before I get to the manner in which the Court dealt with Mrs Grootboom's problem, I must mention the one previous case that had come to us concerning the enforcement of socio-economic rights. It was an extremely poignant matter, brought to us by someone close to death. It dealt with the right of access to healthcare and in particular to emergency medical treatment.[14]

Mr Soobramoney, who was suffering from chronic renal failure and other heart and sugar-related problems, approached our Court asking us to order the state hospital dialysis service to keep death away for as long as possible. He had previously received a session of life-saving dialysis treatment at a state hospital, but was told that he did not qualify for further treatment because limited resources meant that only thirty per cent of persons suffering from chronic renal failure could be treated.

14 *Soobramoney v. Minister of Health, Kwa Zulu-Natal* 1998(1) SA 765 (CC); 1997(12) BCLR 1696 (CC).

Priority was given to those who could benefit from renal transplants and since he was a badly placed candidate for such transplants, he had to stay at the back of the queue. Mr Soobramoney survived for some time on dialysis in the private medical sector, but when his family's funds ran out, he once more sought free treatment from a state hospital. On being turned away he went to court, claiming his constitutional rights were being denied. He relied on section 27 of the Constitution which provides:

> *Section 27*
> **Health care, food, water and social security**
> (1) Everyone has the right to have access to—
> (a) health care services, including reproductive health care;
> ...
> (2) The state must take reasonable legislative and other measures within its available resources, to achieve the progressive realisation of each of these rights.
> (3) No one may be refused emergency medical treatment.

This was a most painful case. Effectively, it was up to the eleven men and women on the Court to decide whether this man lived or died. There was no precedent to guide us, all we had was the text of the Constitution.

We decided firstly that his claim based on the right to emergency medical treatment had to be rejected. In our view, this right to emergency care could be claimed by or on behalf of someone who collapsed suddenly or and who was the victim of sudden trauma. It did not apply to chronic medical conditions, even if they reached life threatening proportions. If all chronic illnesses were to be regarded as emergency cases entitled to treatment at state expense, there would be no funds left in the health budget for other pressing health services such as mother and child care, health education or immunization, the prevention and treatment of diseases such as TB, cancer and malaria and the amelioration of HIV/AIDS. We did not accept that the Constitution should be read in a way which would produce such distorted allocation of resources.

As far as the right of access to health care was concerned, the Court found that the access granted by the state health services to Mr Soobramoney had not been shown to be unreasonable. The evidence from the hospital showed that their plan was eminently rational and non-discriminatory, and accordingly his claim on this ground failed as well.

In the course of argument, I said to counsel that I appreciated the dignity with which his client had approached the Court, and that if resources were co-existent with compassion, the case would have been easy to determine. And in my written judgment concurring with the main judgment I pointed out that the problem in all cases concerned with enforcing socio-economic rights is precisely that resources are always limited. In this context I stated that social and economic rights by their very nature involved rationing. Such rationing should not be considered a restriction of or limitation on the right of access to health care, but the very condition for its proper exercise. Socio-economic rights in this respect are different in their mode of enjoyment, if not in their essence, from civil and political rights. The right to free speech is not by its nature rationed. Everybody can speak their mind just as everybody above a certain age can vote. Difficult problems may arise in terms of their practical exercise, for example in relation to access to public broadcasting or having the financial means to establish independent media or running an election campaign. But the rights are fully-fledged from the start, and not subject to progressive realisation. If A expresses him or herself or votes in a certain way, this does not prevent B from expressing him or herself or from voting in the same or different ways. The progressive realisation of socio-economic rights within available resources, on the other hand, indicates that a system of apportionment is fundamental to their very being. I am not sure as to the full implications of this distinction, both in terms of conceptualising the nature of the right and in respect of determining appropriate remedies for a breach. Yet I am convinced that the exercise of a right that by its nature is shared, often competitively, with other holders of the right, must have different legal characteristics from the exercise of a classical individual civil right that is autonomous and complete in itself.

The right to treatment of a particular kind thus cannot be equated with the right to vote. This does not make the right of access to health care inferior in any qualitative sense to the right to vote, but different in its mode of protection. This difference is expressly recognised in the Constitution through the notion of requiring the state to take measures progressively to realise the right of access to health care. Thus, the state fulfils its duty in respect of providing such access as much by its measures to provide safe water, clean air and basic nutrition for the whole community, as it does by providing a place in a hospital and expensive curative treatment for an individual. What is important is that the reach of health programmes becomes progressively larger and that every individual has a right to be considered fairly and without discrimination for treatment within each programme.

Mrs Grootboom's case confronted us fully with what is meant by the statement that rights must be taken seriously. Constitutionally-demanded seriousness can be undermined in two opposite ways. Judges can either be overly eager to secure favourable headlines for being sympathetic to the poor, or else be unduly formalistic, passive and uncaring about the real lives of real people. I think we were all aware of the need to avoid judicial populism, that is, to resist any temptation to make orders that captured the popular imagination, but which could not be carried out effectively in practice. Yet our oath to do justice to all required us to give meaning and content to the socio-economic rights as set out in our Bill of Rights. The situation in which Mrs Grootboom and the others found themselves clamoured for some kind of response. The constitutionally protected right of access to adequate housing would have no meaning if a thousand people, as a result of state action, were left without a place to lay their heads and without even minimal shelter, only a spot on a sports field and a piece of plastic sheeting. The problem facing us was how to find a secure jurisprudential foundation for responding to their situation and how to provide a remedy consonant with our limited institutional capacity and capable of meaningful enforcement.

We were urged by the *amicus* to base our decision on the concept of a minimum core of rights as outlined by the United Nations Committee on Economic, Social and Cultural Rights.[15] We declined to do so. In

---

15 See *Government of RSA and Others v. Grootboom and Others* note 4 at para 29:

> "In particular they argued that in interpreting this section, we should adopt an approach similar to that taken by the committee in paragraph 10 of general comment 3 issued in 1990, in which the committee found that socio-economic rights contain a minimum core:
>
> 10. On the basis of the extensive experience gained by the Committee, as well as by the body that preceded it, over a period of more than a decade of examining States parties' reports the Committee is of the view that minimum core obligation to ensure the satisfaction of, at the very least, minimum essential levels of each of the rights is incumbent upon every State party. Thus, for example, a State party in which any significant number of individuals is deprived of essential foodstuffs, of essential primary health care, of basic shelter and housing, or of the most basic forms of education, is prima facie, failing to discharge its obligations under the Covenant. If the Covenant were to be read in such a way as not to establish such a minimum core ob-

the first place, our Constitution speaks directly on the subject and has language sufficiently expressive to provide a basic guide. In the second place we had no clear evidence before us as to how such a minimum core could be established, other than by reference to people dropping below the level that basic requirements of human dignity necessitated. In a unanimous judgment prepared by Justice Zak Yacoob, it was held that the key concept in the provisions on access to adequate housing was the obligation on the state to take "reasonable legislative and other measures" progressively to realise the right. We felt that the concept of reasonable measures was one capable of being adjudicated on by our Court. If the measures failed to meet the standard of reasonableness then the state would be in breach of its constitutional obligations. In deciding whether the measure met this standard the Court would acknowledge the special expertise of the government in this area and the fact that a wide range of policy choices would be consistent with reasonableness. Yet, however impressive the state housing programme was, it made no provision for persons such as Mrs Grootboom who found themselves in situations of such crisis and desperation that their dignity was being seriously assailed. In other words, however reasonable the programme was in its broad reach, it had one serious gap which prevented it from satisfying the constitutional requirement of being reasonable. There was no comprehensive plan, or indeed, any national plan at all, to deal with homeless people in situations of extreme desperation, such as victims of disaster, or persons in Mrs Grootboom's situation.

The fact that some relief had already been given to such persons (relief which was extended and consolidated pending our decision) left us free to deal with the level of unreasonableness, of which the situation of Mrs Grootboom was a symptom. We accordingly declared the housing programme of the state to be unreasonable and in conflict with the constitution to the extent that "it failed to make reasonable provision

ligation, it would be largely deprived of its raison d'être. By the same token, it must be noted that any assessment as to whether a State has discharged its minimum core obligation must also take account of resource constraints applying within the country concerned. Article 2(1) obligates each state party to take necessary steps 'to the maximum of its available resources'. In order for a State party to be able to attribute its failure to meet at least its minimum core obligations to a lack of available resources it must demonstrate that every effort has been made to use all resources that are at its disposition in an effort to satisfy, as a matter of priority, those minimum obligations."

within its available resources for people ... with no access to land, no roof over their heads, and who were living in intolerable conditions or crisis situations".[16]

Having made that declaration, that is, having established the nature of the state's obligations in this area, we then left it to the state to decide how best in practice it could remedy its failure. Thus, we left it open to the state to decide as to whether the programme should operate nationally, provincially or locally, and as to how a programme of emergency shelter should best be developed. We expressly left it up to the state to decide how best to deal with emergency situations, that is whether the programme would involve only providing dry land on which people could erect shelters, or whether it would provide both land and houses or whether it would be more efficacious for the state to provide sufficient financial assistance for the affected persons to make their own housing arrangements. There would be further policy choices open to the state, for example, whether to establish medium density housing or provide subsidies for the private sector construction industry. Similarly, it was left to the state to decide where it was to get the money for the emergency programme. It could take it from the formal housing programme, it could take it from defence, it could raise new taxes, it could take it from anywhere, except, I should add, from the judges' salaries!

It was in this way that we sought to balance out the need to protect the fundamental dignity of human beings on the one hand, with recognition of the fact that it was the role of the state, in respect of which its institutional capacity was superior to that of the Court, to determine the priorities, texture and detail of the manner in which it should fulfil its responsibilities.

In making what we regarded as a principled determination capable of being operational and effective, we were strongly influenced by the way in which the rights set out in our Bill of Rights are interrelated and interdependent. We made it plain that the right of access to housing could not be separated from the right to human dignity.[17] This meant that a purely quantitative response by the state to its obligations would not be enough, even if, by international standards, it made extraordinary provision for access to formal housing. The qualitative dimension could never be lost sight of. Our Constitution says that in interpreting

16 *Id.*, at para. 99.

17 Section 10 of the Constitution states that "[e]veryone has inherent dignity and the right to have their dignity respected and protected".

our Bill of Rights we must promote the values of human dignity, equality and freedom.[18] It was respect for these values, and especially the value of human dignity, that guided us in this case, as it orients us in all matters concerning the Bill of Rights.

The next major case concerning the enforcement of socio-economic rights was not long in coming, nor was it any less dramatic. It concerned the right of access to health care in the context of the HIV/AIDS pandemic which has hit our country severely.[19] In particular, it related to the right of pregnant women living with HIV to receive, in all state hospitals where it could be managed, the drug Nevirapine, which would substantially cut the transmission to the newborn baby of the virus. To reiterate, the Constitution provides as follows:

> Section 27
> **Health care, food, water and social security**
> (1) Everyone has the right to have access to –
> (a) health care services, including reproductive health care;
> ...
> (2) The state must take reasonable legislative and other measures within its available resources, to achieve the progressive realisation of each of these rights.
> (3) No one may be refused emergency medical treatment.

The case provoked intense emotion in our country. It was brought by the Treatment Action Campaign (TAC), described by its counsel as the most lively and effective civil society organisation in South Africa, and became known as the *TAC* case. It was a matter of public knowledge that the TAC had mobilised tens of thousands of people living with HIV not simply to see themselves as marginalised victims of a terrible disease, but as people actively determining their lives as best they could. Many of them had learnt in the struggle against apartheid how to com-

18 Section 39 of the Constitution provides that:
Interpretation of Bill of Rights
(1) When interpreting the Bill of Rights, a court, tribunal or forum –
(a) must promote the values that underlie an open and democratic society based on human dignity, equality and freedom;
...

19 *Minister of Health and Others v. Treatment Action Campaign and Others (1)* 2002(10) BCLR 1033 (CC).

bine street campaigning with the use of the media and development of litigation. Their constitutional complaint was that the government was unreasonable and in default of its constitutional obligations to the extent that it restricted the supply of Nevirapine to only two state hospitals on a two-year trial basis in each of the nine provinces. They pointed to the fact that the drug was being supplied to the state without cost for five years, and that its safety could not be in issue because it could freely be bought over the counter in the private sector. Furthermore doctors and nurses in medical facilities outside of the eighteen selected sites were in a position and eager to dispense it.

Counsel for the state argued forcefully that the questions raised belonged to government policy and were accordingly outside the domain of the judiciary. Simply put, it was not for judges to prescribe drugs. In essence, his argument based itself on the separation of powers doctrine. If accepted, its effect would have been significantly to curtail the scope of our decision in *Grootboom*.

Counsel arguing in support of the TAC position, on the other hand, contended that the decision in *Grootboom* did not go far enough. He challenged us to reconsider the reasoning of the Court in that case to the extent that it combined sections 26(1) and (2). In particular he argued that section 26(1) gave an independent right to each individual to have access to adequate housing, and not just a right to require government to put a reasonable programme in place. The Bill of Rights was based on the notion of individual rights. The duty on the state to take reasonable measures to secure these rights should be seen as additional to the individual rights, and not as fully subsuming the content of individual rights. In dealing with how these individual rights should be determined, he relied strongly on the minimum core notion as advanced by the United Nations Committee on Economic, Social and Cultural Rights. He stated that such a minimum core should be established on a case by case basis in terms of ensuring that at least the minimum decencies for a dignified life were provided to each individual. The effect of his argument was that the Constitution required more from the judiciary than an insistence that the state design and implement reasonable housing programmes. In his view, section 26(1) required the courts to come to the assistance of any individual whose life circumstances fell below the minimum core of entitlements consistent with the maintenance of human dignity.

I recall vividly an exchange between counsel and myself on this score. I put to him the following question: Does he mean that somebody living up in the mountains can come to court and say he wants water from a tap, even if the money spent on meeting his particular claim could be used to furnish water for 10,000 people living lower down on the plains? That was an emotional argument, he replied. No, I suggested, it was part of determining how the Constitution must be understood in terms of encouraging the best use of scarce resources to realise social and economic rights. I continued: could it be that the Constitution implied that those individuals with the sharpest elbows (and the best lawyers) would get a house, water and electricity? Should the Constitution be read as handing over to each judge in each court the right and duty to decide who should have priority access to social goods in short supply? Yes, he replied, if the individuals concerned were below the level of existence consistent with dignity. And so the dialogue continued.

In any event the judgment of the Court rejected the argument advanced by counsel. It did not reject the minimum core notion, the satisfaction of which the United Nations Committee on Social, Economic and Cultural Rights had declared to be obligatory for all states. It implied, however, that such minimum core obligation could be satisfied through broad governmental programmes aimed at meeting minimum needs and did not have to be met by acknowledging individual entitlements enforceable in the courts. Such entitlements would be completely unmanageable, and would end up discrediting the whole notion of social and economic rights, to the detriment of those most in need.

From a public point of view, however, the main interest was in how we would deal with the argument by counsel for the Minister of Health that, whatever our personal views, it was constitutionally inappropriate for us as judges to determine health policies. In response to this separation of powers argument, the judgment emphasised that it is the Constitution itself that gives the Constitutional Court the express task of enforcing constitutional rights. Accordingly, we would not be unduly interfering with government when we enforced rights spelt out in the Constitution, even if by so doing we intruded on questions of policy. Far from not respecting the separation of powers, we were in fact fulfilling our obligation in terms of that doctrine when we used our judicial authority to ensure that the Constitution was respected. In our view, the restriction to eighteen sites of the supply of a drug that was apparently safe, efficacious and inexpensive was not reasonable. Accordingly, we prepared a judgment ordering the Ministry of Health to make Nevirapine available in all public facilities where the doctors called for it and were in a position to control its proper use.

We had been asked also to require the Ministry to report back to the Court within a certain period of time as to what steps it had taken to fulfil its obligations. The judgment refused to do that. It pointed out that the government had responded correctly in the past in terms of complying with orders that came from the Court, and we had no reason to suspect it would not do so in the present case. I mention in passing that one cannot overemphasise the need that dialogue between the different branches of government be civil in tone and reasonable in substance. We view ourselves not as being in a contestationary relationship with government, but in a constitutional conversation with them. Just as we expect them to give respect to our role as an independent judiciary, so must we accord respect to them for doing what the Constitution requires them to do. I prefer not to use the term "deference" to describe our relationship. Rather it is a question of giving full acknowledgment to the functional and institutional roles given by the Constitution to the different branches of government.

As we were going into Court to deliver this judgment my colleague Sandile Ngcobo playfully offered me a handkerchief and asked: "Albie, are you going to cry today, will you need it?" He was referring to my reaction previously to a judgment of our Court which he had written, and about which, in my travels I had frequently spoken. It concerned somebody living with HIV who had applied for a job as a steward on the South African Airways, passed all the entrance exams, and been declared ineligible because of his HIV status.[20] South African Airways had said, amongst other things, that British Airways did not employ people in his situation because its customers might flee to a different airline. In his judgment, my colleague had firmly rejected the proposition that the commercial practices of other airlines could determine the constitutional rights of South Africans. The very fact that people were subject to prejudice was a reason for the court to intervene. He had therefore declared the applicant to be a victim of unfair discrimination and ordered South African Airways to employ him. The courtroom had been packed with people wearing T-shirts saying "HIV Positive". There had been complete silence as we handed down judgment. As we had gone out to the passage at the back I had heard cheering, and found myself crying. It had not just been because of emotion about the impact of AIDS on our country. The tears had come because of an overwhelming

20 *Hoffmann v. South African Airways* 2001 (1) SA 1 (CC); 2000 (11) BCLR 1211 (CC).

sense of pride at being a member of a court that protected fundamental values and secured dignity for all human beings. "No problem, Sandile. Today I'm prepared," was my response to his offer.

When we filed into court to deliver the judgment I saw that once more it was packed with people – young and old, men and women, black and white, the nation – wearing T-shirts marked "HIV Positive". There were also journalists from all over the world. The atmosphere was heavy as Arthur Chaskalson, the Chief Justice, in a magisterial voice read out a summary of our decision. The gist of our judgment was clear: since the drugs were available without cost and were deemed safe enough for use in the private sector and in the test sites, limiting their supply on the grounds that the government wanted to do further research on operational problems, was not reasonable. It had to be borne in mind that large numbers of children were unnecessarily going to be born with HIV in the meantime, and that doctors had said clearly that they wanted to prescribe the drugs but were prevented from doing so by directives from the Ministry. Once more after the judgment was given there was total silence. We filed out of the court and stood together for a moment in the passage behind. Then cheering erupted. And once more, I cried.

7. Social Rights Litigation as Transformation: South African Perspectives

Siri Gloppen

1. Introduction

This chapter analyses the role of litigation as a strategy to fulfil the social rights laid down in the South African Constitution. Critically examining litigation as a means to bring the constitutional provisions to life, it explores how aspects of the social, political and legal context condition the litigation process. Focus is on the social rights cases that the South African Constitutional Court has decided over the past decade. Comparative perspectives set the South Africa experience in relief, and inform the theoretical framework structuring the analysis.[1] The aim is to shed light on what has been achieved through social rights litigation; what has facilitated these achievements; and future prospects for social rights litigation in South Africa. Furthermore, it aims to extract some general insights regarding the potential and limits of litigation as a strategy for advancing social rights.

2. What Are Socio-Economic Rights?

An extensive discussion of the status of social rights is provided by Peris Jones and Kristian Stokke in the introduction to this volume. For the purpose of this chapter it thus suffices to note that the terms *socio-eco-*

1 Earlier drafts were presented to the workshop on "Human Rights, Democracy and Social Transformation: When do Rights Work?" (University of the Witwatersrand, November 2003) and the seminar on "Making Socio-Economic Rights Justiciable: the South African Experience" (Centre for Human Rights, Oslo, October 2003). I am grateful to the participants, and to colleagues in the CMI's "Courts in Transition" programme and research network, for valuable contributions.

Peris Jones and Kristian Stokke (eds.), Democratising Development, *ISBN 90 04 14821 3, pp. 153-180.*

nomic rights and *social rights* are used interchangeably to refer to rights which correspond to a particular set of international human rights norms, most centrally reflected in the UN Convention on Economic, Social and Cultural Rights (CESCR). The South African Constitution echoes these norms when it recognises rights to housing, health care, food, water, social security and education, with special protection of these rights for children (in Sections 25-31).[2] Hence, I see these provisions as constitutionalised human rights norms. As such they have a dual legal and normative validity. Their validity as positive law stems from their genesis – being the outcome of a legitimate procedure, in this case a democratic constitution-making process.[3] They can also claim validity as international human rights norms, legally binding on states that are party to the relevant treaties, in this case principally the CESCR (which South Africa has signed but not ratified). Furthermore, these rights form part of the value system that UN member states commit to upon joining the organisation, and should be regarded as international common law, binding on all states. Social rights litigation refers to litigation aiming at giving effect to these international human rights norms.

3. By Litigation Alone?

Is litigation worthwhile as a strategy to fulfil social rights? Traditionally, social rights have been regarded as a matter to be mobilised around and fought for on the political arena, through parties and interest groups, elections and demonstrations, and to be implemented by means of social policy. When included in the Constitution, they have been regarded as (utopian) directive principles for state policy, reflecting political aspirations, not justiciable rights to be administered by the courts.[4]

There are arguments to support this view. Leaving issues of socio-economic rights to judges is held to undermine the political process at its very core, running a stick into the wheel of democracy, obstructing

---

2 Constitution of the Republic of South Africa Act 108 of 1996. (Hereafter "the Constitution"). On the relationship between the South African constitutional rights and international human rights norms see Dugard (2000).

3 See H.L.A. Hart (1961) on legal validity and rules of recognition.

4 See discussion on conceptions of social rights in Jones and Stokke, this volume.

its proper functioning.[5] Questions regarding fairness in the distribution of scarce resources, and the adequacy of particular social policies, are at the heart of politics. To move these essentially political questions into the courtroom is considered unacceptable on normative grounds, as well as imprudent. Judges are not particularly well-equipped to deal with issues involving economic and social policies, where the room for rational disagreement is wide (Fuller 1978). Blurring the line between the legal domain and the domain of politics might also do a disservice to the rule of law and undermine the courts' authority, particularly in contexts where realisation of these rights for all is a utopian goal.

Sociologists of law argue that litigation is ill-suited as a strategy to advance social rights since the legal system tends to favour vested interests.[6] Judges almost invariably belong to the social elite, and are rarely responsive to the concerns of marginalised groups. And the law itself reflects the prevailing power-relations. Hence, courts are unlikely to work in favour of the disadvantaged whose social rights are most at risk. To spend energy and resources on litigation rather than political mobilisation is prone to be fruitless, even counterproductive, as it serves to unduly legitimise the law in the eyes of the poor and hamper prospects of social transformation (Hunt 1993).

These are strong arguments. Against this backdrop, it is reasonable to discard litigation as a suitable strategy in the fight for social rights. Yet, those who have followed South African legal politics over the past decade may hold a different view. On some crucial social rights issues, where the political system has failed dismally to respond to mobilisation through political channels, legal mobilisation has achieved significant results. This is most striking with regard to the constitutional challenges brought against the governments' HIV/AIDS policy.[7] And in

5 The metaphor is borrowed from Seip (1974). See also Gloppen (2000) and Roux (2004).

6 From the 1920s legal realists argued that, contrary to legal formalist beliefs judges do not primarily decide cases on the basis of legal rules or principles. What is decisive is how the facts of the case strike the judge and what on this basis seems just or adequate (Leiter 1996). Later studies have documented the importance of class, race and gender as determinants of legal practices (Baumgartner 1996).

7 Most importantly in the *Treatment Action Campaign (TAC)* case (CCT 2002). Constitutional Court judgments are accessible at <http://www.concourt.gov.za/>. Reviews of cases discussed here can be found on the

the *Grootboom* case (CCT 2000), when a poor community forcibly removed off public land turned to the courts for relief, the South African courts demonstrated their willingness to take seriously the social rights of poor and vulnerable groups.[8]

South African social rights jurisprudence does not stand out as a counter-majoritarian "stick". On the contrary, the courts seem to have removed obstructions to democracy's functioning, without usurping the political domain and can be regarded as performing their fundamental democratic duty of "unblocking the channels of democracy" (Ely 1980).

These landmark and well-publicised cases of successful legal mobilisation on social rights issues have focused considerable attention on social rights litigation. The South African experience has raised hopes, domestically and abroad regarding what litigation can achieve. It is thus appropriate to ask whether this optimism is justified. What are the potentials and limitations of social rights litigation? Can the achievements be replicated – at other times and places – or did they depend on a particular set of social, legal and political circumstances?

To address these questions I first "dissect" the litigation process and discuss factors interacting to determine whether social rights litigation succeeds or fails. The framework is subsequently used to analyse the South African experiences: To what extent are these factors present? What was their impact? A better understanding of factors that were decisive in the past may indicate likely future developments, and aid processes of judicial reform.

4. The Anatomy of Social Rights Litigation

To understand what enables social rights litigation, it is useful to break the process down into stages, as illustrated in figure 1.

Community Law Centre website <http://communitylawcentre.org.za/ser/casereviews.php>.

8 Albie Sachs gives a moving analysis of this case and the basis for the Court's reasoning, elsewhere in this volume.

Figure 1: The Anatomy of the Litigation Process

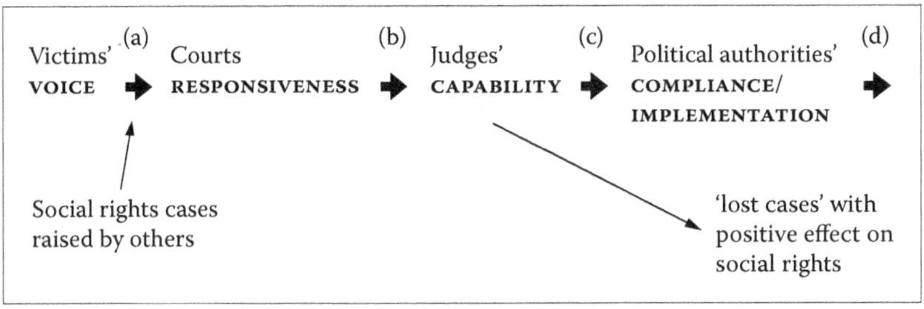

(a) *social rights cases brought to court;* **(b)** *cases accepted by the courts;* **(c)** *judgements giving effect to social rights;* **(d)** *impact on provision for social rights*

The success or failure of social rights litigation depends on (a) the ability of groups whose rights are violated to articulate their claims and *voice* them into the legal system – or have the rights claimed on their behalf; (b) the *responsiveness* of the courts at various levels towards the social claims that are voiced; (c) the *capability* of the judges – that is, their ability to find adequate means to give legal effect to social rights; and (d) whether the social rights judgments that are handed down have authority in the sense that they are accepted, *complied* with and implemented through legislation and policy.

Here focus is on "successful litigation", cases that result in a judgement giving legal effect to the litigants' rights-claims. But even if the case is not decided in favour of the claimants, litigation may have a positive impact. Authorities threatened with court action may settle out of court, and when courts provide a platform for voicing social rights concerns, this may generate or intensify popular debate and create a political momentum. This indirect, political effect is represented in the figure by the downwards-sloping arrow.[9]

As indicated in figure 1, "victims' voice", "court responsiveness", "judges' capability" and the "judgment's authority", represent different stages or junctions in the litigation process. The outcome at each stage is in turn the result of interaction between different factors.

9 Mark Heywood's chapter in this volume, on the Treatment Action Campaign's struggle for an effective HIV/AIDS treatment plan, gives a vivid account of how litigation – and threats of litigation – may form a vital part of a broader social mobilisation strategy.

(1) Voice.

The first stage of the litigation process is the articulation of rights claims by, or on behalf of people whose social rights are violated, and the voicing of these claims into the legal system. Figure 2 indicates factors influencing whether, and how forcefully, social rights claims are voiced.

Figure 2: Factors Affecting Litigants' Voice

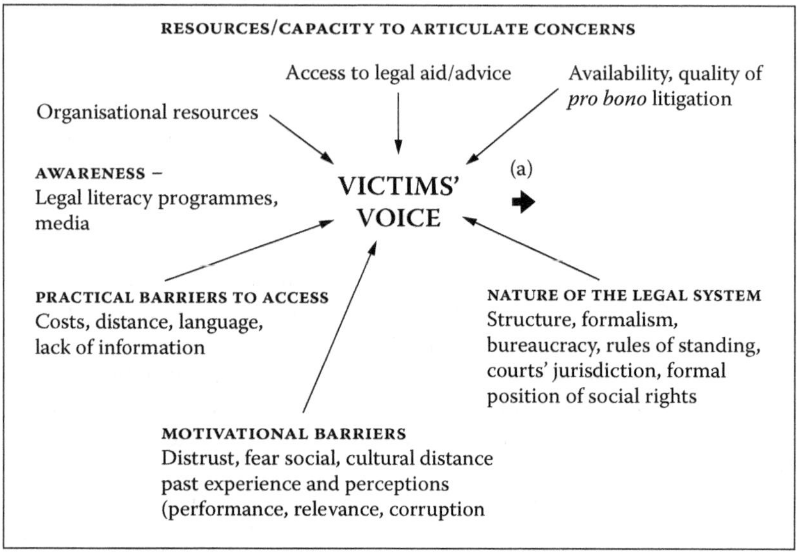

(a) *social rights cases brought*

To be able to voice social rights claims, people whose rights are violated must be (made) aware of their rights, the right-violation and the possibility for redress through the courts. People whose social rights are most at risk often lack such knowledge. Legal literacy programmes, human rights education, and media focus on social rights are essential in providing this.

Once aware that their deprivation constitutes a social rights violation, those affected must have (access to) resources enabling them to effectively sustain their rights-claims and to articulate them in a form that the legal system recognises (Epp 1998). Social rights cases often raise complex legal issues, with few possibilities for lay people to effectively argue their own case. Access to legal expertise, through legal aid or organisations providing free legal assistance, is thus crucial.

Multiple barriers hamper access to the justice system for poor and marginalised groups. Some are motivational and psychological, such as fear and distrust of the courts due to cultural and social distance, or negative past experience. Litigation may also be discouraged by perceptions of poor performance, delays, corruption, bias – or a belief that court decisions are irrelevant. Other barriers are practical, such as the costs of litigating, geographical distance, language barriers, lack of information. Yet other barriers are legal and are related to the structure and nature of the legal system. The status of social rights in legislation and jurisprudence may motivate – or discourage – the voicing of social right claims. So does the degree of formalism and bureaucracy involved. Most systems require detailed formal procedures to be undertaken before starting a case, and time-consuming and costly appeal proceedings to reach the higher courts. The criteria for *locus standi* (who can take a case to court) vary. Particularly important for poor groups is whether an organisation or individual can litigate on behalf of others, and whether cases can be argued on behalf of a group or category of people (class action), or only individual cases are accepted.

(2) Responsiveness

For social rights litigation to succeed, the legal system must also be responsive to the claims that are voiced. They must be recognised as a legitimate matter for the court to decide. As figure 3 indicates, responsiveness is in part a function of "voice" – the manner, in which the claims are articulated, the legal strategies employed by the litigants and the skill with which the case is framed. But the responsiveness of the legal system to social rights claims also depends on other factors.

Figure 3: Factors Conditioning Courts' Responsiveness

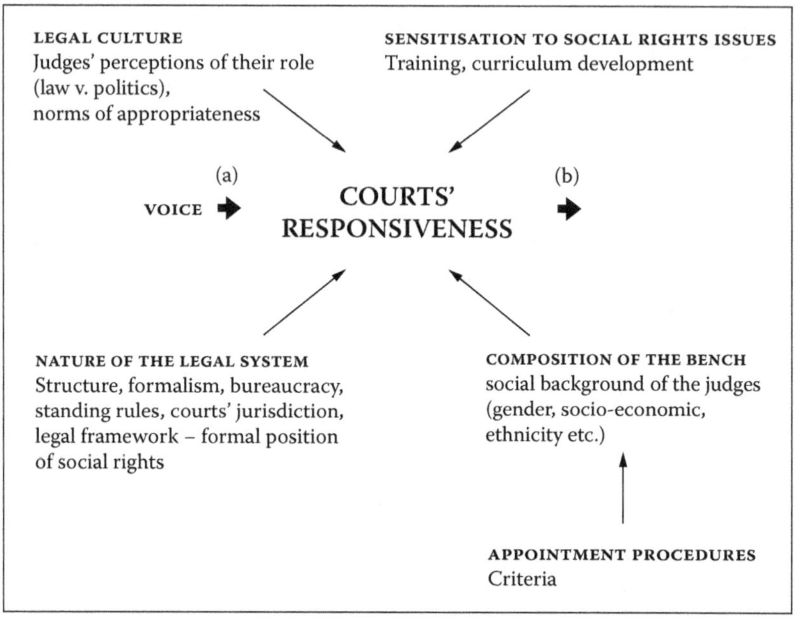

(a) *social rights cases brought;* **(b)** *cases accepted*

Again, the nature of the legal system is crucial, in particular the legal basis for social rights (including the status of international social rights conventions). And, where social rights are formally recognised, are they justiciable rights or "directive principles" outside the scope of the courts' jurisdiction? The courts' responsiveness also depends on the legal culture and prevailing theories of interpretation. This influences the judges' perception of their own role, their norms of appropriateness concerning how they should deal with social rights, whether these are within the proper domain of the courts. Judges' sensitivity – individually and collectively – to the concerns voiced, also matters. This is in turn related to their values and social background, as well as to education and whether they are sensitised towards social rights through ongoing training.

(3) Capability

The third stage of the litigation process regards the judges' capability. That judges are willing to respond to social rights claims is not enough, they must also be able to find adequate legal remedies to repair the violation. This requires professional competence and creativity, access to relevant knowledge and command of the necessary legal remedies. The range of options include "minimal affirmation", merely requiring the state to *respect* a social right in the negative sense of non-interference; courts may rule that the state has a duty to *protect* social rights against encroachment by others; order the state to actively *promote* particular social rights by developing policies to this effect; or they can make concrete orders for state agencies to *fulfil* the individual claimants' social rights. Furthermore, court orders may be *declaratory* (stating that laws or actions are in breech of a social rights obligation, but leaving to the state to devise a remedy); *mandatory* (requiring specific actions to be taken) or *supervisory* (requiring the relevant agency to report back within a set time-frame) (Roux 2004; Liebenberg 2003; Jacob 1996). As indicated in figure 4, court performance depends on the skill and capacity of the judges, and of the jurisprudential resources at their disposal.

Figure 4: Factors Affecting Judges' Capability

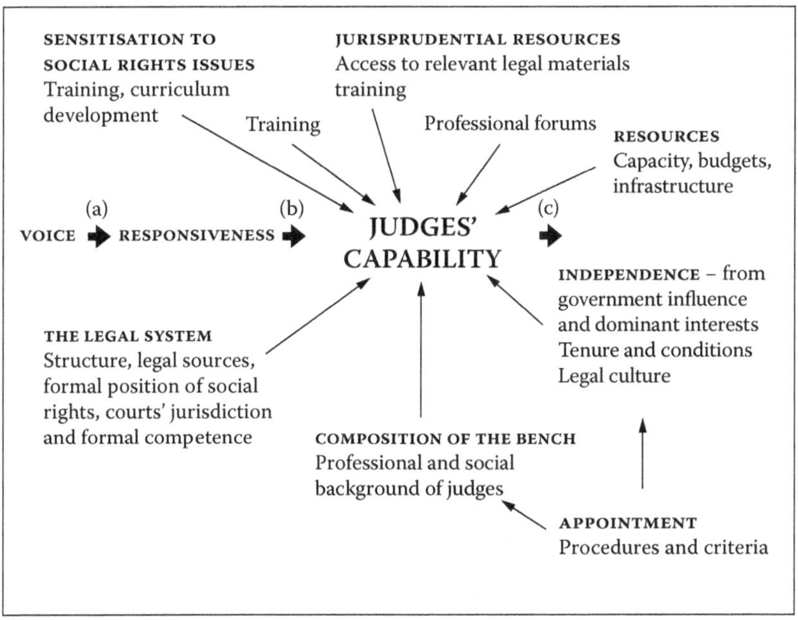

(a) *social rights cases brought;* **(b)** *cases accepted;* **(c)** *social rights judgements*

To develop sophisticated social rights jurisprudence, requires highly skilled judges, research capacity and access to a range of legal materials. Professional fora to exchange ideas and knowledge may contribute positively, and strengthen judges' professionalism and independence. In addition to the professional, jurisprudential resources, courts' capability and capacity to deliver social rights judgments depend on their independence from the state and dominant social interests, and on the financial resources at their disposal.

(4) Compliance

The fourth stage is compliance. For litigation to succeed in improving the actual social rights situation, the judgments must be complied with by the relevant authorities and political action taken to implement the ruling. Compliance is again the outcome of a range of factors, as shown in figure 5.

Figure 5: Factors Affecting Compliance with Social Rights Judgments

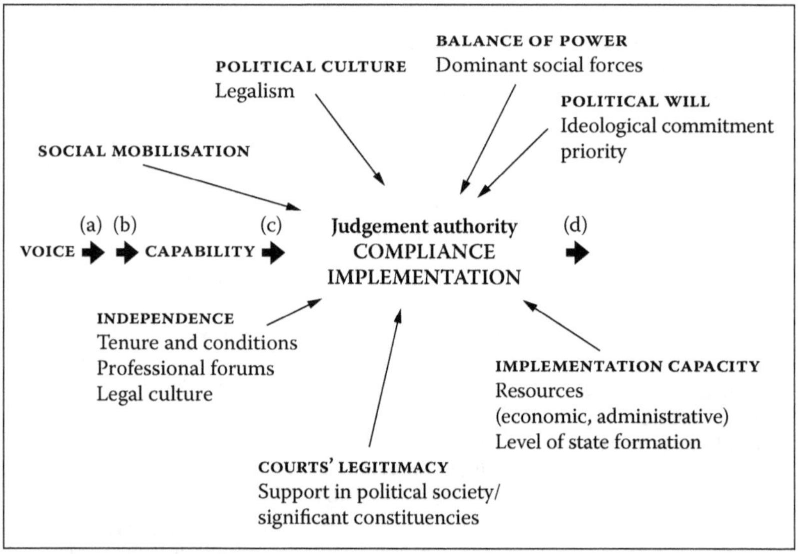

(a) *social rights cases brought;* **(b)** *cases accepted;* **(c)** *social rights judgements;* **(d)** *effects on social rights provision*

The authority of the judgement itself is important. This stems partly from the courts' professionalism, independence and legitimacy. Several aspects of the political context are crucial for compliance with social rights judgments: the prevailing political culture; the balance of power between the parties, and, perhaps most important, the political will to follow up and give priority to social rights issues. Lastly, implementation of court rulings also depends on the state's capacity – financial, institutional and administrative.

Ultimately, the proof of success is whether the situation changes for people on the ground with regard to the relevant right. This is not included in this framework, since it is notoriously difficult to establish a causal link between particular legal actions and the overall social development in a field. The situation with regard to a particular social right (say, housing) – is influenced by a wide range of factors (climate changes, violence and unrest, economic depression, unemployment etc.). To determine the effect of a particular ruling is thus difficult, beyond monitoring direct compliance and trace "ripple effects" in law, policies and implementation.

5. Conditions for Social Rights Litigation in South Africa

Turning to the analysis of social rights litigation in South Africa, I use the framework outlined above to guide the discussion. I start by examining factors influencing whether and how social rights claims are voiced; go on to discuss the courts' responsiveness to such claims; and the judges' capability to give legal effect to social rights; and finally, the factors influencing compliance and implementation of social rights judgements.

A. Voicing Social Rights Claims

I start by examining formal, practical and motivational barriers that hamper the voicing of social rights claims into the South African legal system, then I go on to look at the resources available to potential litigants, before reflecting on how these factors have influenced (potential) litigants' voice.

The structure and nature of the legal system changed quite extensively with the democratic dispensation. South Africa became a constitutional state, and the 1996 Constitution formally recognises social rights as substantive law, with status as justiciable rights. Effort has been taken to simplify the wording of the Constitution – and to some extent legislation – to make it more accessible to ordinary people. Access has been significantly improved through more lenient criteria for standing. Legal aid institutions can now litigate on behalf of a person – or group – whose social rights are violated, and there are possibilities for direct application to the Constitutional Court and direct access from the court of first instance, although this is strictly applied.

While access has been made easier, it is not as open as in some other countries, most notably India, where a newspaper-clipping or a letter to the Supreme Court may suffice to start proceedings (Verma 1997; Brix 2004). In the lawyer-driven South African system, judges cannot take up a case on their own initiative, but can only pronounce on cases placed before them. They can, however, decide which cases not to hear.[10] And they can allow or invite individuals or organisations with particular insights into the issues raised in the case, to address the court as *amicus curiae* (friend of the court), and thus influence the arguments heard. In some landmark cases – most notably in the *Grootboom* case – the judgment relied heavily on submissions from *amicus* rather than the parties' arguments.[11]

As a whole, the South African legal system is quite favourable to social rights litigation. Yet, the system remains quite bureaucratic and formalistic compared to the low threshold of the Indian Supreme Court, and cases are often dismissed on technical grounds.

The nature of the legal system, and experience with, and perceptions of the courts, affect people's motivation to use them as an arena in which to voice their claims. South Africans' attitude towards the courts and the law is marked by ambivalence. As discussed elsewhere in this volume, by Mark Heywood and by Richard Ballard and others, ideologically based scepticism towards the law and the courts is prevalent among South Africa's new social movements. The courts also carry the legacy from the apartheid era when they were part of the white state apparatus enforcing unjust laws (although even then, the picture was nuanced. Human rights oriented judges stretched the law to attain justice and preserve political space, and the courts retained a modicum of legitimacy). Transformation has brought a less pale and male judiciary,

10 But with a light case load, the SA Constitutional Court has limited opportunities to choose the cases they want to decide.

11 In this case the Legal Resources Centre (Geoff Budlender) see (CCT 2000: para 19).

but sitting judges retained their jobs and "hold-over" judges remain on the bench (some occasionally hand down judgments sparking outrage and allegations of racism). The changes in the legal system at the time of the transition – including the new Constitutional Court created to guard the new Constitution – changed perceptions and expectations, not least in the domain of social rights. In the landmark judgment to certify the 1996 Constitution (CCT 1996), the Constitutional Court affirmed its commitment to social rights as rights to be enforced by the courts.

But also the new, transformed judiciary has faced popular dismay. Controversial judgements by the Constitutional Court – abolishing capital punishment, enforcing stricter rights of accused and convicted persons, denouncing discrimination of gays and lesbians – has brought criticism. The Court is considered "soft on crime" and too liberal-minded, eroding traditional norms and values (Rickard 1999; Steinberg 2000). Some fear that efforts to transform the judiciary compromises professional quality. Problems with backlogs, delays, poor performance and perceived bias, particularly in the lower courts, add to the disenchantment. But there are also strong traditions of legalism in South African society, of trusting a judge to hear your case. For many reasons, ambivalence thus continues to characterise South African's attitude towards their courts. This includes social rights cases, as we shall see – but first, a comment on the practical barriers hampering social rights litigation in South Africa.

Costs of lawyers and court fees, transport, income loss; language barriers, and lack of information and knowledge are substantial problems, particularly for the poorest sections of society and people living in the deep rural areas. These problems are shared by poor people virtually everywhere, but in contrast to many other countries, South Africans have significant resources to aid disadvantaged litigants. There are public and private programmes to increase rights awareness, and considerable capacity to assist litigation processes. The public legal aid system (which is limited and problem-ridden), is supplemented by legal NGOs, such as the Legal Resources Centre, the Centre for Applied Legal Studies, and the Community Law Centre, who provide legal assistance. While the demand for legal services is greater than the supply, and access is poor outside the urban centres, these organisations have played a crucial role in facilitating social rights litigation by taking on test cases. They have substantial research capacity and get the most senior advocates in the country to argue cases pro bono. The availability of top legal expertise has been an extremely important resource in the successful social rights cases. Ironically, this extraordinary availability of legal expertise can be seen as part of the apartheid legacy. During the anti-apartheid struggle, legal academia and NGOs played a central role, and attracted many of the brightest legal minds in the country. So far, the organisations have succeeded in retaining and recruiting well-qualified people – and some who have gone on to work as advocates etc., continue to do volunteer work. The question is whether and how this can be sustained in the long run – and replicated in other contexts.

On balance, conditions for victims of social rights violations to voice their claims into the legal system are reasonably favourable in South Africa – but to what extent have social rights claims been voiced? Contrary to what might be expected, given South Africa's status as a showcase for socio-economic rights litigation – not many significant social rights cases have been taken through the legal system. In 1999 a newspaper article complained that

> ... for whatever reason, few cases have been heard [in the South African courts] that have had the potential to affect the lives of those millions who remain disadvantaged. The much-proclaimed range of socio-economic rights has never been employed in litigation. The radical provision, which makes private legal relationships subject to the provisions of the Constitution, has been all but forgotten. Most cases involve crooks, corporations and other wealthy litigants (*Mail & Guardian* 1999).

While this has changed somewhat, and significant social rights cases have worked their way through the legal system, social rights claims have been more a trickle than a flood. To understand why, it may be useful to look at how notable social rights cases have been received and decided by the courts.

B. The Responsiveness of South African Courts to Social Rights Claims

The first case involving a constitutional social right came before the South African Constitutional Court in November 1997. The *Soobramoney* case concerned the right to emergency health services, but was decided primarily on semantic grounds, rather than on the substantial content of the right. Chronic renal failure requiring regular dialysis did not qualify as "emergency". The judgment disappointed proponents of social rights litigation, not only because the litigant lost his case, but due to statements regarding the justiciability of social rights. The view of the Court seemed to be that matters with significant budgetary implications belong in the political domain, rather than under its jurisdiction, thus distancing itself from a more radical Indian judgment on the right to emergency health services (Supreme Court of India 1996). In the South African legal community *Soobramoney* was taken to indicate political deference, discouraging further social rights litigation. Or signalling that for such cases to succeed very careful framing and skilful argument would be required.

Three years later, in October 2000, the Court handed down judgment in the first case actually decided on the grounds of the social rights clauses in the Constitution. The *Grootboom* case concerned the right to housing and in particular the right of children to shelter. The applicants, living under appalling conditions in an informal settlement, had moved onto private land from which they were forcibly evicted. Camping on a nearby sports field, they applied for an order requiring the government to provide them with basic shelter. The Constitutional Court (unlike the High Court[12]) did not recognise a directly enforceable claim to housing on the part of the litigants, but ruled that the state is obliged to implement a reasonable policy for those who are destitute. The judgment thus establishes socio-economic rights as justiciable rights, and defines an active role for the Court in assessing social policies and their implementation at various levels of government.

The *Grootboom* judgment was acclaimed among international academics for its creative and politically astute reasoning – carving out space for itself in the policy process without usurping the space for political decision-making (Sunstein 2001). For prospective litigants it was, however, discouraging that the Constitutional Court limited its role to that of policing the policy-making process rather than recognising an enforceable individual right to shelter, or defining a minimum core of the right to be given absolute priority (Roux 2002; 2004; Bilchitz 2003; Liebenberg 2002).

---

12 The High Court stated that section 28(1)(c) of the Constitution gave all children a right to claim shelter on demand from the state, irrespective of the availability of resources. Furthermore, since it was in the best interest of the children not to be separated from their parents, the state was obliged to provide rudimentary shelter for these families (High Court of South Africa 2000).

The third notable socio-economic rights case heard was politically controversial, but more straightforward in legal terms. The issue in *Minister of Health and Others v. Treatment Action Campaign and Others (TAC)* (CCT 2002), was whether the state was obliged, under the right of access to health care (section 27(1) and (2) of the 1996 Constitution) to provide the anti-retroviral drug, nevirapine to HIV-positive pregnant women and their newborn infants. The court found that, where feasible, the state was obliged to provide for all to be included in the existing "pilot" policy. From a legal perspective this is less invasive than to direct government to formulate new policy. The expansion of the programme was also inexpensive, as the medicine would be supplied, free of change for 5 years.

The *TAC* judgment is more radical than *Grootboom* in the sense that it is mandatory and closer to acknowledging an individual, enforceable right. As clearly shown by Heywood in this volume, it also represented a huge political victory, and marked a turning point in the government's position on HIV/AIDS (see also Heywood 2003). But, as in the *Grootboom* case, the research undertaken was formidable. The litigants outperformed the political authorities in their own terrain.

After *Grootboom* other cases have built onto and developed South African jurisprudence on the right to housing. Particularly notable is the Constitutional Court judgment in the *Kyalami Ridge* case (CCT 2001) and the *Modderklip* judgment from the Supreme Court of Appeal (2003).

The *Kyalami Ridge* case arose when, after a flood in Alexandra Township, the government sought to establish a temporary transit camp on state-owned land. Nearby residents asked the High Court to restrain the Minister of Public Works from establishing the camp, which was not supported by legislation, contravened existing regulations and was undertaken without the required consultation. The High Court had found in favour of the Residents Association, but the Constitutional Court underscored the government's constitutional obligation to provide access to adequate housing, including temporary relief for people living in intolerable conditions or in crisis due to natural disasters or threats of demolition. As the camp was intended to give effect to this constitutional obligation, the government's decision was held to be lawful (Christmas (2004).

In the *Modderklip* judgment, the Supreme Court of Appeal consolidated the protection to vulnerable occupiers, ruling that the state's responsibility towards people in desperate need includes the obligation to ensure humane evictions, which entails making available alternative accommodation. Balancing the rights of the occupiers against those of the landowners, the court underscored that the latter should not be prejudiced by the State's failure to fulfil its obligations. It thus ordered that the landowner was entitled to damages from the state in terms of existing expropriation legislation, while occupiers were entitled to occupy the land until alternative land was made available (Christmas 2004).

Lastly, the judgment in the *Khosa/Mahlaule* case concerns the right of access to social assistance for permanent residents (here Mozambican citizens) (CCT 2003). The issue was a decision to exclude non-citizens from the programs. The majority of the court decided that the litigants, and all similarly situated, had a right to access social assistance, and remedied the legislation by reading in the words "or permanent resident" after "South Africa citizen." The Constitutional Court's approach in this case is less cautious than in previous judgments. In the context of significant public xenophobia, it ruled to protect long-term permanent residents from the degradation of poverty – a decision with potentially grave budgetary implications. "This decision must thus be regarded as a positive portent for expanding access to socio-economic rights through constitutional litigation in the future" (Sloth-Nielsen 2004).

To sum up, it seems that a main factor in "stemming the tide" of social rights cases has been the signals sent by the Constitutional Court that it takes a lot to succeed with such claims – although the most recent judgments, providing classes of litigants with a legally enforceable rights, may increase prospective social rights litigants' expectations.

What explains the South African courts' reluctance to give effect to individual's social rights claims? According to the framework, courts' responses to such claims are in part a consequence of the manner in which they are voiced, but also depend on the legal basis for social rights; the legal culture; and the judges' sensitivity to social rights issues.

In international terms and compared to the pre-1994 situation, South African courts have a sound legal basis for adjudicating on socio-economic rights. The social and economic rights – to housing, health services, food, water, social security and education – were included in the Constitution to enable it to serve as an instrument for principled social transformation, and not a shield for protecting the status quo and the vested interests of the privileged. This ambition is also reflected in the provisions enabling affirmative action and horizontal application of rights (Sections 9 and 8).

For most of the social rights, the State's responsibility is, limited to "take reasonable legislative and other measures within its available resources to achieve the progressive realisation of these rights" (Sections 26(2), 27(2)). The exceptions, which apparently give rise to directly enforceable claims, are the right not to be evicted (Section 26(3)); not to be refused emergency medical treatment (Section 27(3)); the rights of prisoners to adequate nutrition and medical treatment (Section 35(2)) and the rights of children (defined as those under 18 years of age) to basic nutrition, shelter, basic health care and social services (Section 28). The "bite" is, somewhat reduced by a general limitations clause permitting limitation of rights "in terms of laws of general application to the extent that limitation is reasonable and justifiable in an open and democratic society" (Section 36).[13] Nevertheless, the formal constitutional basis for courts to adjudicate social rights issues is comparatively strong in South Africa – much stronger than in India, the country that pioneered social rights litigation. And when certifying the 1996 Constitution the South African Constitutional Court explicitly stated that social rights are justiciable, not merely political aspirations (CCT 1996). The relatively cautious response to social rights thus cannot be ascribed to the legal basis.

According to the theoretical framework, courts' responsiveness to social rights issues also depends on the judges' sensitivity to the concerns voiced, which in turn is determined by the composition of the bench – the judges' social and ideological background, their legal education and training. In South Africa, diversity on the bench has been a priority. This is reflected in the system and criteria for judicial appointment, and prospective judges are questioned on their commitment to constitutional values and social transformation. The judges' sensitivity to social rights issues vary, but ongoing training aims to sensitise and educate judges and magistrates towards human rights.

A cautious approach to social rights may also stem from the legal culture, the prevailing theories of constitutional interpretation and whether social rights are regarded within the proper domain of the courts. This in turn influences the judges' norms of appropriateness regarding how to deal with social rights. Generally, the South African legal culture is influenced by the common-law tradition, with deference to

13 Limitation clauses are common in modern democracies (see Article 19(1) of the German Basic Law and Article 1 of the Canadian Charter of Rights and Freedom).

political authority as a central democratic virtue. However, the injustice of apartheid law led many lawyers towards a constitutionalist perspective, where democracy is defined partly by commitment and adherence to basic human rights – including social rights. Post-1994 South African judges – particularly the first Constitutional Court bench, deciding the early, difficult cases – seemed genuinely committed to social rights, and saw social transformation as an important part of their mandate.[14] However, as reflected in Justice Sachs' chapter in this volume, they were also deeply concerned with the boundary between law and politics. To establish their legitimacy as a legal institution vis-à-vis the political authorities, they had to strike a balance – neither give up on social rights, nor meddle unduly in policy issues. This priority informs their social rights jurisprudence and motivates a cautious approach.

C. *The Capability of South African Judges to Adjudicate on Social Rights*

The third crucial stage of the litigation process is when the judge(s), accepting the validity of a social rights claim, gives it effect in a judgement. For the litigation to be successful, judges must be capable of identifying and applying legal strategies that effectively protect or advance the relevant rights.

As noted earlier, courts have several strategies at their disposal, they may require rights to be *respected*; *protected* against encroachment by others; that the state actively *promotes* rights; or acts to *fulfil* individual claimants' concrete social rights. Court orders may be *declaratory*, merely pointing out breeches in social rights obligations; *mandatory*, requiring specific actions to be undertaken; or *supervisory*, ordering agencies to report on the implementation. The Constitutional Court judgments – particularly *Soobramoney* and *Grootboom*, but also to some extent *TAC* – have been criticised for being too deferential with regard to not intruding on the political domain, and too cautious in their legal remedies. Interestingly, both in *Grootboom* and *TAC*, the High Court went further than the Constitutional Court. In *Grootboom*, the Cape High Court recognised an enforceable right of destitute children (and their guardians) to have shelter provided by the political authorities, while the Constitutional Court handed down a purely declaratory order requiring new policy to be made. In the *TAC* case, the Constitutional

14 Personal interviews with Constitutional Court judges 1997-2003.

Court formulated a mandatory judgment, requiring the state to step up distribution of nevirapine to HIV positive mothers and their newborns but stopping short of the High Court's order, demanding that the state report back on progress within a set time-frame (Heywood 2003; Sachs in this volume). Recently, the Supreme Court of Appeal judgment in the *Modderklip* case and even more so the Constitutional Court in *Khosa/ Mahlaule* have gone further in acknowledging individual social rights claims of vulnerable groups.

Which strategy a judge or bench opts for depends partly on the nature of the case, how it is argued (the impact of "voice"); and on how the judge perceives the issue at stake in terms of facts and law (the impact of "responsiveness"). More systemic factors influencing the repertoire of strategies available to a judge include his or her professional skills, training, access to legal material and research assistance, and opportunities to participate in professional fora.

While this might be decisive for judges' professional ability to find the most adequate means to enforce the right, the capability to actually go for what is best on professional grounds – against the will of powerful state (or private) actors – also depends on the independence of the judiciary as a collective and of the individual judge.[15]

The South African Constitutional Court has excellent conditions for developing a broad repertoire of legal strategies: highly qualified judges, an excellent library, ample research assistance, and authority to draw on diverse sources of law, including international law and case material from foreign jurisdictions. They hear cases as one bench and represent between them a wealth of legal and other experience – and with a light case load they have the time to deliberate and reflect on suitable remedies for each particular case, as well as on the wider jurisprudential implications. In this respect, hardly any court, anywhere, has better conditions for developing sound judicial strategies for giving effect to social rights.

But do South African judges have sufficient independence to act on their professional judgement? Institutional mechanisms to guard

15 Judicial independence is the ability of judges to decide cases on the basis of their interpretation of the law and the facts of the case, without interference (actual or threatened) by government or other agents, and the ability of the courts to make their decisions "stick" (Gloppen *et al.* 2004). The growing literature on judicial accountability includes Russell and O'Brien (2001); Burbank and Friedman (2002); and Sajâo and Bentch (2004).

against undue political influence are in place (constitutionally protected independence, secure tenure and remuneration, a circumscribed role for the executive in the appointment process, transparent nomination by the judicial service commission). However, the concern for legitimacy vis-à-vis the political authorities, may restrain the freedom of the judiciary to act contrary to government interests – particularly in a political context with a dominant ruling party. Those appointed to the Constitutional Court have also generally been ideologically close to the ANC government.

But the Court also needs to generate legitimacy in other important constituencies (within the legal community, nationally and internationally, with the political opposition and in civil society), and this may induce it to look for opportunities to demonstrate its independence. For the Constitutional Court the relationship with the legal community is particularly important. As a novel institution and comprising members with scant judicial experience it was paramount to establish itself as a sound and respected institution on professional legal grounds. Justice Sachs in his chapter talks of the challenge the court faced in the *Grootboom* case of finding "a secure jurisprudential foundation for responding to their situation", and how their social rights jurisprudence has been guided by relying on dignity as the core value of the Constitution. To earn respect for their legal craftsmanship seems to have been a main consideration, tying the court somewhat closer to conventional legal reasoning than the ideological disposition of the individuals on the bench might suggest.[16]

Judges rarely admit to taking strategic considerations into account, but on the basis of the Constitutional Court's position vis-à-vis political society, we might expect judgments that generally affirm and support the political position of the government, but that contain limited and highly visible challenges to state policies. And so far, this is what has been forthcoming (Roux 2002, 2004).

D. South African Social Rights Jurisprudence: Authority, Compliance and Implementation

As noted earlier, compliance can be seen in terms of whether the relevant authorities (verbally) accept the rulings as authoritative; comply

16 For an analysis of the Constitutional Court's negotiation of its relations to various constituencies, see Gloppen (2000).

with the terms of court order and to what extent the ruling has implications for subsequent legislation, policies and administrative action – including ways in which other bodies with a mandate in this field, such as human rights commissions, relate to the judgement (Liebenberg 2003).

The South African government has generally accepted adverse judgments, but with regard to the main social rights judgements, there has been noticeable foot-dragging, as Heywood's article in this volume testifies to. (See also Pillay 2002; Liebenberg 2002; 2003; Roux 2004; Heywood 2003). With regard to the *Grootboom* judgement,

> The SA Human Rights Commission (SAHRC) has been monitoring the situation (...) it took one year for the local administration (the City of Cape Town) and the Western Cape provincial administration to finally decide where 'the locus of responsibility' lay with regard to the implementation of the *Grootboom* judgment. Even after this one-year period of inaction, the effort by these two administrations to implement *Grootboom* is limited to putting together a plan to deal with the permanent resettlement of the Wallacedene Community. There is a clear lack of understanding that the judgment requires systemic changes to national, provincial and local housing programmes to cater for people in desperate and crisis situations. (Pillay 2002)

Also regarding the voluntary settlement to provide the litigants with temporary accommodation, compliance was slow and partial (Pillay 2002).

Concerning the *TAC* case, government representatives made statements indicating that they were not prepared to let the courts dictate their policies. But once the "defeat" was clear, they turned – at least in terms of rhetoric – and committed to changing their policies. However, monitoring of compliance has shown that implementation has been slow and uneven between the provinces. (Heywood 2003). Mpumalanga province failed to take steps to implement the judgement, despite having the capacity to do so, and the Treatment Action Campaign decided to instigate contempt of court proceeding – which seemed to have an effect (Heywood 2003).

This illustrates a point briefly discussed earlier, namely that litigation should not be viewed on it own. In the *TAC* case, litigation was part of a larger process of social mobilisation, and the case was effectively won on the streets before the verdict was handed down. This does not mean that litigation was irrelevant. On the contrary, it provided a focal point and platform for the struggle.

But what explains this failure to promptly implement the judgments? As we have seen, this can in part be ascribed to the nature of the judgments themselves. They rarely place concrete demands on the authorities regarding concrete measures to be undertaken, nor set timeframes within which this should be done.

Lack of capacity – financial, institutional and administrative – is another aspect, but political and normative factors are probably as important. Political factors include the balance of power between political forces, political will and whether the rulings are at cross purposes with the governments' broader policy goals.[17]

Lack of political will seems to be a factor. In the *TAC* case, this was related to personal idiosyncrasies in the political leadership, profoundly politicising HIV/AIDS policy. This is reinforced by the power structure, differences in political culture and diverging views on the nature of South African constitutionalism.

The uneven balance of power in South Africa, with the ANC as the dominant political party, presents particular challenges. On the one hand, the space for contestation offered by the courts, and their role as guardians of democratic ideals and constitutional rights is particularly important when there is a lack of other forces able to sanction the government when it acts in breech of its mandate. This accountability function is central to the Constitutional Court's *ration d'etre* and its legitimacy with the domestic oppositions as well as internationally. On the other hand, if the Court is perceived to repeatedly undermine the government's legitimate policy aspirations, this may jeopardize its legitimacy with the ruling party, expose the counter-majoritarian dilemma inherent in strong constitutionalism, and make the Court vulnerable to infringement of its authority.

There is a marked normative ambivalence in South Africa – and within the current ANC leadership – concerning the proper role of law in relation to politics. There is broad commitment to the Constitution, but the liberal understanding of courts as a check on power, competes with other understandings, where the role of law primarily is to facilitate policy-implementation (Gloppen 2000). This brings us back to the initial discussion, on the disagreements over the proper locus for social

17 For a discussion of capacity and capacity development in relation to social rights realisation, see Engh (2004).

rights – do they belong in the Constitution as anything other than a statement of aspirations? Competing understandings of constitutionalism in South African political society may be a partial explanation for the lack of commitment to implement judgements seen to trespass on the political domain.

Despite disappointments, it is important to also remember the achievements gained – the judgments have to some extent been implemented and reflected in policies and legislation, and they remain important yardsticks that other institutions, such as the Human Rights Commission, use in their work to further social rights. And they continue to be important foci for social mobilisation around social rights issues.

6. Assessing Social Rights Litigation as a Strategy in Fulfilling Rights

Has this analysis brought us closer to understanding the potential and limitations of litigation as a strategy in fulfilling social rights? What is clear is that social rights cannot be achieved by litigation alone. The impact of litigation is bound to be limited, even under the favourable conditions prevailing in South Africa in the past decade – where the ideological commitment to constitutionalism and social rights is strong, both in civil society and within the judiciary, and where the ideal of social transformation and progressive realisation of social rights has also been prominent in political society.

While not sufficient, social rights litigation can clearly be useful to improve the social rights condition in society. But it should not be regarded as the main avenue. The central purpose of social rights – as other rights – is first and foremost to commit and direct the people's elected representatives in their work to carry out their political mandate. Normally, prospects for success might be greater by political mobilisation. But as illustrated by Heywood's account of TAC's experience in this volume, litigation may be effective as an alternative or complementary strategy where there are blockages in the political system so that the voice of those deprived of their rights does not get through.

Social rights litigation can play a constructive role – and has done so in South Africa as well as in other parts of the world. But it is demanding. For litigants to succeed, several conditions must be present, and not all of them are easy to reform at will. With regard to some of the factors that the analysis has identified as significant post-apartheid

South Africa has been in a unique position. One factor is the Constitution itself (although the nature of the text is less unique than the interpretation given it by the courts). The quality of the judiciary and in particular the first bench of the Constitutional Court has been crucial. Likewise the availability of resources for social rights litigation, both financial and in terms of quality of the legal expertise made available. These factors are difficult to replicate elsewhere. And they might also be difficult to sustain in South Africa in the future.

References

Baumgartner, M.P. (1996) "The Sociology of Law" In D. Patterson (Ed.) *A Companion to Philosophy of Law and Legal Theory.* Blackwell, Oxford, 406-420.

Bilchitz, D. (2003) "Placing Basic Needs at the Centre of Socio-Economic Rights Jurisprudence". *ESR Review* 4.

Brix, M.K. (2004) "The Impact of Judicial Activism in India". MA thesis. University of Bergen, Faculty of Law, Bergen.

Burbank, S.B. and B. Friedman (2002) *Judicial Independence at the Crossroads: An Interdisciplinary Approach.* Sage Publications, Thousand Oaks, Calif.

Christmas, A. (2004) "Property Rights of Landowners v. Socio-Economic Rights of Occupiers". *ESR Review* 5.

Dugard, J. (2000) "The Role of Human Rights Treaty Standards in Domestic Law: the Southern African Experience". In P. Alston and J. Crawford (Eds.): *The Future of UN Human Rights Treaty Monitoring.* Cambridge University Press, Cambridge.

Ely, J.H. (1980) *Democracy and Distrust: A Theory of Judicial Review.* Harvard University Press, Cambridge, Mass.

Engh, I. (2004) "Developing Capacity to Realise Socio-Economic Rights: The Example of HIV/Aids and The Right to Food in South Africa." *ESR Review* 5.

Epp, C. (1998) *The Rights Revolution.* The University of Chicago Press, Chicago.

Fuller, L.L. (1978) "The Forms and Limits of Adjudication." 92 *Harvard Law Review*, 1978, pp. 353-394.

Gloppen, S. (2000) *South African Constitutionalism 1994-2000: The Difficult Balancing Act of the Constitutional Court* (Doctoral Thesis, University of Bergen).

Gloppen, S., R. Gargarella and E. Skaar (Eds.) (2004) *Democratization and the Judiciary: The Accountability Function of Courts in New Democracies.* Frank Cass, London.

Hart, H.L.A.(1961) *The Concept of Law.* Claredon Press, Oxford.

Heywood, Mark (2003) "Contempt or compliance? The TAC Case After the Constitutional Court Judgment." *ESR Review* 4.

Hunt, A. (1993) *Explorations in Law and Society. Towards a Constitutive Theory of Law.* Routledge, New York.

Jacob, Herbert *et al.* (Eds.) (1996) *Courts, Law, and Politics in Comparative Perspective.* Yale University Press, New Haven.

Leiter, Brian (1996) "Legal Realism." In Dennis Patterson (Ed.) *A Companion to Philosophy of Law and Legal Theory.* Blackwell, Oxford, 261-279.

Liebenberg, Sandra (2002) "South Africa's Evolving Jurisprudence on Socio-Economic Rights: An Effective Tool in Challenging Poverty?" Vol. 6 No. 2 Law Democracy and Development, 159.

Liebenberg, Sandra (2003) "Making A Difference: Human Rights and Development-Reflecting the South African Experience". Research paper presented at the Nobel Symposium on the Right to Development and Human Rights in Development held in Oslo, Norway, 13-15 October 2003.

Mail & Guardian (1999) "Constitutional Court Rates a Mere Pass." *Mail & Guardian*, February 25.

Pillay, Karisha (2002) "Implementing Grootboom: Supervision Needed." *ESR Review* 3.

Rickard, Carmel (1999) "Judges Agree Criminal Justice System is in Trouble." *Sunday Times*, 25 April.

Roux, Theunis (2002) "Understanding Grootboom – A Response to Cass R. Sunstein." 12 *Constitutional Forum.*

Roux, Theunis (2004) "Legitimating Transformation: Political Resource Allocation in the South African Constitutional Court." In S. Gloppen *et al.* (Eds.) *Democratization and the Judiciary.* Frank Cass, London.

RSA (1996). *Constitution of the Republic of South Africa* Act 108 of 1996 at <http://www.concourt.gov.sa/constitution/index.html>.

Russell, Peter H. and David M. O'Brien, (Eds.) (2001) *Judicial Independence in the Age of Democracy: Critical Perspectives from Around the World.* University Press of Virginia, Charlottesville, VA.

Sajâo, Andrâas. and Lorri R. Bentch (2004). *Judicial Integrity*. Martinus Nijhoff Publishers, Leiden.

Seip, Jens Arup (2004) *Fra embetsmannsstat til ettpartistat.* Universitetsforlaget, Oslo.

Sloth-Nielsen, Julia (2004) "Extending Access to Social Assistance to Permanent Residents." *ESR Review* 5.

Steinberg, J. (2000) "Rights, Crime and the Courts." *Business Day*, 19 April.

Sunstein, Cass R.(2001) "Social and Economic Rights? Lessons from South Africa." 11 *Constitutional Forum*.

United Nations (1996) "International Covenant on Economic, Social and Cultural Rights." (CESCR), United Nation's General Assembly Resolution 2200A (XXI), adopted 16 December 1966 at <http://www.unhchr.ch/html/menu3/b/a_cescr.htm>.

Verma, Ajay (1997) "The experience in India." p 149 in Roger Blanpain (Ed.) *Law in Motion*. Kluwer Law International, The Hague.

Cases

Constitutional Court of South Africa (1996) *Certification of the Constitution of the Republic of South Africa* 1996, (CCT 23/96).

Constitutional Court of South Africa (1997) *Soobramoney versus Minister of Health* (KwaZulu-Natal), (CCT 32/97).

Constitutional Court of South Africa (2001) *Government of the Republic of South Africa and Others v. Grootboom and others,* (CCT11/00). 2001(1) SA 46.

Constitutional Court of South Africa (2001) *Minister of Public Works and Others v Kyalami Ridge Environmental Association and Others* 2001. (7) BCLR 652 (CC).

Constitutional Court of South Africa (2002) *Minister of Health and Others v. Treatment Action Campaign and Others* (No 1) (CCT 9/02), 2002 (5) SA 721 (CC), 2002 10 BCLR 1033.

Constitutional Court of South Africa (2002) *Minister of Health and Others v. Treatment Action Campaign and Others* (No. 2). (CCT 9/02), 2002 (5) SA 721 (CC).

Constitutional Court of South Africa (2003) *Khosa and Others v Minister of Social Development and Another* (CCT 12/03); *Mahlaule and Others v*

Minister of Social Development and Another (CCT 13/03). (Combined judgment referred to as *Khosa/Mahlaule*).

High Court of South Africa (2000) *Grootboom v Oostenberg Municipality and Others* 2000 (3) BCLR 277(C).

Supreme Court of Appeal of South Africa (2003) *Modder East Squatters, Greater Benoni City Council v Modderklip Boerdery* (Pty) Ltd, (SCA 187/03); *President of the RSA and others v Modderklip Boerdery* (Pty) Ltd, (SCA 213/03) (jointly referred to as *Modderklip*).

Supreme Court of India (1996) *Paschim Banga khet Mazdoor Samity versus State of West Bengal* 1996 SOL Case No. 169.

8. Shaping, Making and Breaking the Law in the Campaign for a National HIV/AIDS Treatment Plan

*Mark Heywood**

"One reason we have a strong Bill of Rights today was the painful lesson of those who ran Quatro: that even people with an honourable record of defending a good cause can exercise power in an abusive and inhuman way."

(Judge Albie Sachs quoted in Callinicos, 2004)

1. Introduction

On November 19th 2003 the South Africa Cabinet announced its decision to implement an Operational Plan to use antiretroviral medicines (ARVs) to treat advanced HIV infection (AIDS). It published a 257 page document that set out the components of a plan to provide ARV treatment to 1.4 million people within 5 years, promised substantial improvements to the infrastructure of the health service, and envisaged additional expenditure on HIV/AIDS of up to R12bn over the next 5 years (Department of Health 2003).

In August 2003, when the Cabinet decision to develop a plan was announced, *ANC Today*, the ANC's weekly electronic newsletter, described the decision as "consistent with the approach taken since the ANC took office in 1994."[1] The plan was said to be the natural extension of the government's existing policy towards HIV/AIDS, albeit one where "favourable conditions" had made it possible to introduce

* Head: AIDS Law Project, Centre for Applied Legal Studies (CALS), University of the Witwatersrand. Treasurer, Treatment Action Campaign (TAC).

1 *ANC Today*, 15 August 2003, "Consistency at the Core of Enhanced Treatment Plan."

Peris Jones and Kristian Stokke (eds.), Democratising Development, *ISBN 90 04 14821 3, pp. 181-212.*

an ARV treatment component.[2] In reality it was a sharp rupture with a policy that had stubbornly and unconstitutionally resisted providing ARV treatment (ART) to people with AIDS.

It is generally accepted (even by government) that the change in policy took place as a result of a sustained campaign by the Treatment Action Campaign (TAC) that, for almost five years, had used a combination of legal action and advocacy for the constitutionally entrenched human rights to life, dignity and access to health care services to mobilise in South African society and internationally around the rights of people living with HIV/AIDS to care and treatment.

This chapter analyses this campaign.[3] It describes why and how TAC framed its demands not only as human rights but simultaneously as enforceable (and justiciable) constitutional rights. It describes how there have been three discernible components to the TAC's community mobilisation for a national treatment plan (NTP). To some degree each component has revolved around the law: *Shaping, making and breaking the law*. In so doing it illustrates how the Bill of Rights in the Constitution of the Republic of SA (Act 108 of 1996) can be invoked to provide human rights campaigners with legal and moral legitimacy for their demands. It also confirms how utilising the law can be of practical value in the adjudication of disputes with both government and the private health sector.

2. Making the Law: The Legal Right of "Access to Health Care Services"

One of the greatest tragedies to affect the new South Africa has been the advance of the HIV epidemic. By 2005, over five million people in South Africa were infected with HIV and an estimated 1.49 million people had died of AIDS. According to official statistics the total number of annual deaths from all causes has risen to nearly 500,000 – an increase of over 200,000 per year (Department of Health, 2004; Statistics South Africa, 2004 and 2005).

---

2 *Cabinet Statement on Treatment Plan for HIV/AIDS*, issued by the Government Communication and Information Service, 19 November 2003.

3 This chapter does not deal with the politics of AIDS denialism in South Africa, which is the contextual backdrop that explains why such intense conflict developed over AIDS policy. Here the reader is referred to Heywood, 2004.

South Africa should have been in a strong position to control the HIV epidemic. The successful fight to end apartheid created unity amongst the poor. It also created a range of mass organisations, including the ANC, that could have been mobilised behind HIV prevention.

South Africa had a tradition of human rights activism around health that predated AIDS. But unfortunately for a combination of reasons (Heywood 2004; 2005) the opportunity to stem the epidemic was missed.

TAC was founded in late 1998 – almost 15 years after the start of the epidemic. Since then its campaigns have been multifaceted and its growth well documented (See Mbali in this volume). But in the context of a discussion on campaigns to realise socio-economic rights three things are important to keep in mind: firstly, TAC has argued that people with HIV and AIDS have a *right* to the medicines that will save their lives, in particular ARVs. Secondly, TAC has argued that the right created a positive *duty* for government to adopt and implement a national HIV/AIDS Treatment Plan. Thirdly, although not explored here, AIDS denialism has been the political backdrop that has made a conflict over a rights issue whose realisation could just as easily been a demonstration of democratic purpose by the ANC government.

But in the first two years after it was established TAC's main preoccupation was not primarily with the government's duty to progressively realise the right of everyone of "access to health care services".[4] Instead it was concerned with campaigns that aimed to enforce the principle of the human right to essential medicines in the context of incursions on this right as a result of profiteering by multinational pharmaceutical companies. Campaigns against pharmaceutical companies involved both making and breaking the law and TAC combined legal action with public demonstrations against companies which were profiteering from health needs. For example in 1999 TAC Chairperson Zackie Achmat broke what were considered to be unjust patent laws, by defiantly importing 5,000 pills of a generic version of Fluconazole from Thailand, despite the fact that the drug was held under patent by Pfizer. In January 2000 this action was repeated but this time with generic ARVs, patented by GlaxoSmithKline and Boehringer Ingelheim, which were unlawfully imported from Brazil. On both occasions the companies, aware that TAC held a moral high ground, declined to defend their patents. Then in early 2001 TAC battled the Pharmaceutical Manufacturers As-

4 *Constitution of the Republic of South Africa*, Sec. 27(1) and (2).

sociation (PMA) in support of the Medicines and Related Substances Amendment Act, a law passed by the SA government in 1997 that aimed to make medicines more available and affordable. The implementation of this law had been blocked for three years by a legal challenge from the PMA. In March 2001 the decision of the Pretoria High Court to admit TAC as an *amicus curiae* in this case, took place at the same time as the largest demonstrations ever seen in South Africa or internationally on the right of access to medicines for people with HIV (ALP 2003; Heywood 2001).

These early campaigns created popular support for the idea that access to health care services (including medicines) is a human right. They also built a broad consensus in both South Africa and internationally around the idea that ordinary people, and particularly people with HIV/AIDS, are justified in taking actions to defend this right. This consensus stretched across class lines and came to apply both to the government's duties, as well as those of the private health sector.

However, as TAC notched up victories against the pharmaceutical companies, it became more obvious that the purpose of fighting for cheaper medicines was obviously to permit their systematic use within the health service in SA. The victories against the PMA and Pfizer, and the sudden drastic reduction in key medicine prices, would be meaningless if not taken advantage of by government – and it was this failure to look a gift horse in the mouth that led TAC into its confrontation with government.

Fortunately, during the same time that TAC was building a social movement around the right to health, constitutional jurisprudence was establishing a number of key principles of law around government's duties in relation to the "socio-economic rights." The judgments of the Constitutional Court in *Soobramoney* (1997) and *Grootboom* (2000) laid down important principles about government's rights and responsibilities in relation to health and housing.

In this context the judgment of the Constitutional Court handed down on 5 July 2002 in the *TAC* case (Heywood, 2003), arguably provided the last corner in a triangle of judgments that helped TAC to link its call for a treatment plan to the government's positive obligations in respect of the right of access to health care services. Geoff Budlender, TAC's attorney and then the head of the Constitutional Litigation Unit at the Legal Resources Centre (LRC) summed up these principles as follows:

> Everyone has the right to have access to health care services. The State must take reasonable legislative and other measures, within its available resources, to achieve the progressive realisation of this right.
>
> The Constitution requires the State to devise a comprehensive and workable plan to meet its obligations in terms of the right of everyone to have access to health care services. The national framework must be designed so that these obligations can be met. The programme must be capable of facilitating the realisation of the right. The State must create the conditions for access for people at all economic levels of our society. Those whose needs are the most urgent and whose ability to enjoy all rights is therefore in peril, must not be ignored by the measures aimed at achieving realisation of the right. If the measures, though statistically successful, fail to respond to the needs of those most desperate, they may not pass the test. (Budlender 2003[5])

Despite Budlender's argument sceptics will still argue that the Achilles heel of campaigns for socio-economic rights that rely on the law is the Constitution's proviso that socio-economic rights need only be fulfilled within the State's "available resources" as well as questions about whether the State has the administrative capacity to deliver profound socio-economic change (Chanock 2001; Pieterse 2004). They might add that the Constitution does not define "available resources" (leaving this to the government) and that the Constitution's protection of property rights (including intellectual property) in fact limits the resources it can command. In this vein it would be argued that *Soobramoney* suggested that Courts would not second-guess government departments when they appear to make rational decisions about the allocation of resources. However even in this most cautious area of jurisprudence there is considerable room for argument. For example, in the affidavits it drew up to support its admission as *amicus curiae* in the *PMA* case TAC argued that the right of "access to health care services" justified limitations on intellectual property rights. Similarly, in a complaint to the Competition Commission made in 2002 (ALP 2002) it argued that excessive pricing of medicines harmed the State's ability to meet its duty of making health care affordable. This argument was also made in the campaign for a NTP where TAC commissioned actuarial research to show that ARVs were affordable "within available resources" and would provide significant cost savings. TAC also argued that whilst government's available resources

5 Footnotes in original omitted.

might be reflected in the allocations to health made in the budget there were other ways to reduce the cost of providing health care, for example by issuing compulsory licenses that would drastically reduce the price of ARVs.[6] Finally TAC argued that the resources needed to buy and supply ARVs had to be measured against the social benefits of savings in human life, illness prevented and death delayed.[7]

3. Shaping the Law (1): Establishing the Reasonableness of Rights

Advocacy for human rights should precede legal action and litigation should not be the first resort of health activists. A case that seeks to enforce constitutional rights, in this case of access to health care services, begins long before the first legal papers are filed. In addition to public education and advocacy it is necessary to patiently create and accumulate incontrovertible evidence (scientific, economic etc) that can, if necessary, be used in litigation.

Although TAC frequently threatens litigation (as a demonstration of its confidence in its claims) the initial phase of activism concentrates primarily on attempts at engagement with and persuasion of opponents. One of the most important components of successful litigation is a paper-trail of correspondence and memoranda that demonstrates unremitting efforts to persuade government on a matter of policy.

Thus TAC's first call for a National Treatment Plan was made in a Memorandum handed to the Minister of Health at the end of the "Global March to Save Lives" in July 2000; repeated in a Memorandum marking the opening of Parliament on 12 February 2001 and made frequently thereafter. Litigation and other strategies were only considered when requests for meetings were ignored and there was no engagement by government with TAC's proposals.

Successful political and legal advocacy also depends upon establishing a well-researched case for the demand. Recognising this TAC

6 "Draft a Treatment Plan and Prepare to Declare HIV/AIDS a Public Health Emergency! Apply for Voluntary Licences for HIV/AIDS Drugs!" TAC Memo to the President, Minister of Health and Members of Parliament, 14 March 2001.

7 As evidence TAC drew attention to the AIDS programme of the Brazilian government, which had commenced ARV treatment in 1996, and was able to demonstrate benefits in improved HIV prevention, reduced illness and death.

brought activists together with researchers and health experts and in early 2001 set up a Research Committee which conceptualised a rationale and outline for the NTP.[8] Workshops were held with practitioners and academics in health economics, the clinical care of HIV and TB and public health systems and out of this process a draft Plan emerged.[9] In late 2001 a larger consultative meeting to develop consolidated guidelines on ARV use was hosted by TAC which involved HIV clinicians from the private and public health sectors, rural and urban treatment programmes being run by NGOs, activists and academics on the use of anti-retroviral medicines. Senior officials from the Ministry of Health were invited but did not attend. This expert conference drafted *The Bredell Consensus Statement on the Imperative to Expand Access to Anti-Retroviral treatment for Adults and Children with HIV/AIDS in South Africa*, which – in the face of government protestations that it lacked the infrastructure for ARV treatment – declared that:

> The capacity and infrastructure to use anti-retrovirals safely and effectively and to treat tens of thousands of people with AIDS already exists within the private health sector, parts of the public sector, and within some non-governmental organizations. These provide a foundation to devise and implement a national treatment plan, while simultaneously identifying needs and gaps in under-resourced settings to promote equity.[10]

Almost as soon as the ink had dried on the *Bredell Consensus* it was used by TAC as a new advocacy tool in its armoury. For example, it was published as a newspaper advertisement and distributed to delegates at the first National Health Summit held by government in November 2001. At the summit the former Director General of the Health De-

---

8 Integrated Framework for a National HIV/AIDS Treatment and Prevention Plan, Unpublished "Discussion document issued by the TAC Science and Research Committee" August 2001, TAC Archives.

9 Committees and Main Points of Special Consultative Meeting, TAC Archives.

10 See <www.tac.org.za>. The Bredell Consensus was endorsed by many individuals and organisations and published as an advertisement in *Business Day* on 21 November 2001. It is noteworthy that despite Cabinet's claim in 2003 that "favourable conditions" permitted the introduction of ARVs there is little in the government plan that was not foreshadowed in the Bredell Consensus.

partment, Dr Olive Shisana, called for the use of ARVs in pilot projects and a resolution was taken at the summit to "increase pilot research to provide solid evidence to guide government's policy on treating AIDS related illnesses, using anti-retroviral drugs and effective support and prevention programmes."[11] Predictably, this resolution was not acted on by the Ministry of Health.

4. Shaping the Law (2): Building a Campaign for the Right of Access to Medicines

During 2001, the conceptualisation of the NTP was undertaken by a small number of TAC leaders, engaging with the research community. In 2002, by contrast, TAC began a major political mobilisation of civil society to call for its adoption and implementation: TAC branches began to discuss the NTP, pamphlets to explain its main proposals were developed and meetings were held with allies, such as COSATU, to build support for the demand.

In June 2002, a National HIV/AIDS Treatment Congress was held jointly by TAC and COSATU. The Congress aimed to popularise and educate people about the NTP, be as broadly representative of society as possible and develop resolutions that could be tabled with government.

Despite being in the conflict with both government and the ANC, particularly over prevention of mother to child transmission (MTCT), the TAC leadership understood that the eventual success of the campaign depended on winning over both with an explanation about why a plan was necessary. Therefore both the ANC and senior officials of the Health Department were invited to the Congress.[12] Dr Ayanda Ntsaluba, then the Director General of the Department of Health, accepted the invitation but withdrew at the last minute. Dr Nono Simelela, then

11 Advertisement in the *Sowetan*, 26 November 2001. The Summit took place several days before the first hearing of the TAC case in the Pretoria High Court. At the Summit last ditch efforts were made in private meetings between the Director General of the Health Department and TAC to discuss the possibility of settling the MTCT case. But no resolution could be found.

12 In March 2002 TAC met with Kgalema Motlanthe, the Secretary General of the ANC, and offered to postpone the Congress if this would make it possible for "both the ANC and the government to participate meaningfully in the event." But the ANC failed to respond to the offer. TAC Archives, letters sent by TAC on 24 March 2002 and 14 May 2002 to the ANC.

the head of the government's HIV/AIDS unit, attended briefly. The impression was that senior government officials had decided to snub the conference. However, at short notice the Member of the Executive Committee (MEC) for Health from KwaZulu Natal, Dr Zweli Mkhize, arrived and was given a platform to speak to the whole Congress. Significantly, his speech agreed with the need for an ARV treatment plan but also called for partnerships to tackle HIV related stigma and prevent new infections.

The Treatment Congress was attended by over 600 health workers, academics and people with HIV. It was addressed by the Archbishop of Cape Town, Njongonkulu Ndungane, the President of the Medical Research Council (MRC), Malegepuru Makgoba, and Pregs Govender, an ANC MP. It received extensive media coverage and displayed civil society's determination to confront HIV and desire for better leadership from government.[13]

5. Shaping the Law (3): Using NEDLAC to Negotiate a "Framework Agreement" on a National Treatment Plan

The Treatment Congress passed resolutions on HIV prevention, treatment and the quality of health care services. But in the face of the continued refusal by the Minister of Health to countenance the idea of an NTP, or to meet with TAC, it resolved to refer its resolutions instead to the National Economic, Development and Labour Council (NEDLAC).

NEDLAC is a statutory negotiating forum between representatives of government, organised labour, organised business and community organisations. Amongst its objectives are to "seek to reach consensus and conclude agreements on matters pertaining to social and economic policy" and to "encourage and promote the formulation of co-ordinated policy on social and economic matters."[14] The social and economic implications of AIDS are well understood. But prior to this NEDLAC had not intended to deal with matters of health and had historically con-

13 It also demonstrated how solidarity encourages openness and disclosure about HIV. For example, one of the most moving moments occurred when Theo Steele, COSATU's campaigns co-ordinator, revealed to the Congress that her daughter was living with HIV, surprising even her closest comrades in COSATU.

14 National Economic, Development and Labour Council Act, 35 of 1994, s 5(a) and (e).

centrated mainly on narrower labour and employment issues. However, Ebrahim Patel, the General Secretary of the Southern African Clothing and Textile Workers Union (SACTWU), persuaded TAC leaders about the potential advantages of taking the call for an NTP formally into NEDLAC. In particular he pointed to the benefits that would come from formal discussions with business and labour leaders. Going the NEDLAC route also meant moving the issue of HIV/AIDS beyond the exclusive control of the Minister of Health – but still keeping government, in this case the Ministry of Labour, in the talks.

TAC forwarded the Treatment Congress resolutions to NEDLAC in July 2002. In response the NEDLAC Executive Committee agreed to set up a special negotiating team to develop an agreement on HIV/AIDS. At its first meeting on 3 October 2002 the government negotiating team, led by Advocate Rams Ramashia, then Director General of the Department of Labour, agreed to enter into discussions over a "framework for a treatment plan". Each of the sectors was invited to make written submissions on "the key principles which unite the parties" and "targets, timeframes and resources for treatment."[15]

Albeit a commitment with little immediate consequence, this was a major breakthrough in the TAC campaign: for the first time government had implicitly conceded that there could be a National Treatment Plan. Over the next two months the government's negotiators acted in good faith and through a series of meetings a draft plan began to emerge. The biggest difficulty, however, remained divisions within government on its attitude to AIDS. Outside of the NEDLAC process the Minister of Health maintained her opposition. This was felt on a number of occasions when the government representatives to NEDLAC overstepped an invisible and unstable line on AIDS policy that might be described as "the Manto line". Proposals that were agreed to by government in one meeting were retracted in the next.

But despite these predictable fault lines the process established a new momentum for the campaign and developed as a new source of pressure on government. It led directly to a number of important concessions. Ironically some of these seemed to have been intended to stall the NEDLAC process. The setting up of a joint Task Team of the Ministry of Health and Treasury to research the cost of ARV treatment, for example, emerged directly from the NEDLAC process. The purpose of

15 NEDLAC HIV/AIDS Treatment Action Plan Task Team, Minutes of the Teleconference on 3 October 2002.

the Task Team was to "provide a picture of the cost implications of an expanded response to the impact of HIV/AIDS on all sectors of South African society."[16] In late 2002 and early 2003 the need to "wait for the Task Team's recommendations" was given by government as an excuse to justify delays in a decision by the Cabinet on the use of ARVs. The irony however lies in the fact that the outcomes of its research and recommendations (which were leaked to TAC early in 2003) would eventually make it impossible for government to continue to resist the adoption of a treatment plan. Had it done so TAC would have gone to the Constitutional Court with the government's own evidence that a Plan was affordable and necessary.

By November 2002 the Task Team had drafted a "Framework Agreement for a National HIV/AIDS Prevention and Treatment Plan". In the process of drafting this agreement points of contention were placed in square brackets "[]" and taken back to principals for further consideration and approval. Subsequent to each occasion when the Government negotiators overstepped "the Manto line" the negotiations were marked by backward movement or paralysis. But gradually the square brackets fell away from most of the proposals until, predictably, all that remained were brackets placed by government around every reference to ARV treatment.

Originally the NEDLAC Executive Committee had intended to launch the HIV/AIDS agreement by December 1st 2002, World AIDS Day. A meeting to finalise the draft took place on November 29th 2002. Because of the lies that were later told about the process it is important to point out that in addition to senior trade union and business representatives this meeting was attended by four senior government representatives, the Director General of the Department of Labour, the Director General of the Department of Health, the Chief Director of the HIV/AIDS Unit and the Deputy Director General of the Labour Department. At this meeting there was agreement on all parts of the draft except for the bracketed references to ARVs. As a way around this problem the government negotiators proposed that all the references to ARV treatment be referred back to the Task Team for finalisation after a Cabinet decision on the use of ARV treatment, which they predicted would occur by March or April 2003. This proposal was accepted by all

16 Lend a Hand in the Campaign of Hope Against HIV/AIDS, An Update on Cabinet's statement of 17 April 2002 on fighting HIV/AIDS, 9 October 2002.

the parties. But once again it appears not to have been acceptable to the Minister of Health. Once again "the Manto line" had been transgressed.

On the eve of World AIDS Day the draft agreement was leaked to the *Sunday Independent*, who ran it on the front page under the headline "Drugs for all brings hope on World AIDS day".[17] In the article Phillip Dexter, Director of NEDLAC, reportedly said "It looks like we have an agreement. It's subject to some modification, such as the detailed wording, but the principles are all agreed". However the government's response was to contradict Dexter by denying the nature and content of the negotiations.[18]

In early 2003 Ministers repeatedly denied that "an agreement" had been reached at NEDLAC.[19] To contradict this TAC published the text that had been agreed to by all the people at the November 29th meeting in *Business Day*, South Africa's biggest daily business newspaper.[20] A political leadership that was not in denial about HIV would have seen the draft "Framework agreement" as an opportunity, not a threat. Had it been accepted and used effectively, it might have been a way to synchronise and cohere the HIV prevention and treatment programmes of business, labour and government – taking away the presumption that the primary duty to manage the AIDS epidemic belongs with government. It would undoubtedly have strengthened the country's response to HIV. For example in relation to Voluntary Counselling and Testing (VCT) all the parties agreed:

> to work together to ensure affordable access for and capacity that will enable at least 2 million South African to be voluntarily counselled and tested in the public and private sectors within the first 18 months of this agreement, at least half of who will be tested in public sector facilities. It is agreed that the testing programme will be based on the principles of informed consent, and pre and post test counselling.[21]

---

17 L. Altenroxel, *Sunday Independent*, 1 December 2003.

18 Statement by Government on NEDLAC's HIV/AIDS Task Team, 1 December 2002: "Government has refuted a media report this morning, that an agreement has been reached at the NEDLAC, that could see anti-retrovirals being made available in the public sector some time next year."

19 SA Government denies Agreement on AIDS policy, *Mail and Guardian*, 19 February 2003.

20 *Business Day*, 14 February 2003.

21 NEDLAC draft Framework Agreement, paragraph 5.1.

But government made sure this did not happen.

From TAC's perspective the NEDLAC process is further evidence of the space that exists in post-apartheid South Africa to advance social campaigns through strategic use of statutory and human rights institutions. At the time groups such as the Landless People's Movement criticised this step and claimed that nothing was achieved by TAC at NEDLAC. But in reality there were very concrete outcomes. Amongst these were the growing involvement of the labour movement in the NTP campaign; the drawing in of organised business; the setting up of the Health and Treasury Task team; and the way in which the NEDLAC negotiations narrowed the issues of dispute down to the use of ARVs – eventually limiting the space that was left for the AIDS denialist faction within government to continue to resist providing treatment to people living with HIV/AIDS. It is also important to note that the NEDLAC process did not demobilise TAC's rank and file, who followed the negotiations carefully, organised campaigns of letter-writing to support the negotiations and developed a sense of ownership in one of South Africa's new democratic institutions.

6. Preparing to Break the Law

In early January 2003, TAC resumed its demand that the NEDLAC agreement be signed and implemented. A mass march was prepared for the opening of Parliament on February 14th 2003. The decision to march on the day of President Mbeki's State of the Nation address marked a shift away from negotiations and persuasion that had characterised the campaign in 2002. A more confrontational approach was needed because of the growing urgency for access to treatment for thousands of people now becoming sick with HIV- related illnesses – including many TAC volunteers. But it was also possible because TAC was now armed with the tools that it had created in the campaigns of the previous two years: in particular, the NEDLAC draft Agreement, the Bredell Consensus and the judgement of the Constitutional Court in the TAC case. A march on the opening of Parliament was intended to contest the speech of the President: it was meant to be an explicit reminder from the *sans culottes* that the picture drawn of the state of the nation would be incomplete if it continued to ignore the needs of people with HIV/AIDS.

TAC undertook its largest ever mobilisation for the march. It catalysed a new mood of defiance among people with HIV by developing a poster with the slogan "Stand Up for Our Lives" alongside a photograph of Nelson Mandela wearing an "HIV-Positive" t-shirt.[22] A "Treatment Train" from Johannesburg brought over 600 people, many of them living with HIV, packed into second class carriages, running workshops in the train's canteen, decamping on station platforms in the Free State and Karoo as the train wound its way to Cape Town. In the months that followed the march several of the train's passengers died of AIDS related illnesses, and for some, such as Edward Mabunda, a person with a growing reputation as TAC's poet, going on the train, despite being ill, was a last determined effort to be seen and heard as a person with AIDS.

Both the march and Mandela poster caused anger in the leadership of the ANC. Unsuccessful pressure was put on COSATU and others not to support the march. But despite this the march became a mass demonstration of poor people visibly asserting the rights that come with democratic citizenship. In the history of the AIDS epidemic it was the largest protest to call for access to treatment in a developing country. Over 15,000 people, led by people with HIV, religious leaders, trade union leaders and doctors, marched to the gates of Parliament. The marchers were met by representatives of the Presidency, the ANC and Parliament's Health and Finance Portfolio committees. But despite a statement by Barbara Hogan, then the chairperson of the Finance committee, that "a march of this size could not be ignored by the ANC" – it was.

Outside Parliament a referendum by a show of hands was held to test support for a civil disobedience campaign should TAC's demands for the finalisation of the NEDLAC agreement not be met. Most marchers raised their hands in support of civil disobedience. Consequently TAC was propelled into a carefully designed campaign of law breaking.

22 On 12 February 2003, 2 days before the march, the Nelson Mandela Foundation issued a press statement distancing itself from the TAC poster. The press statement said: "Permission was granted to the TAC to make use of Mr Mandela's pictures for their advertising campaign. However, it was never anticipated that it would include the call for a march to Parliament on the day of the opening of Parliament. Although Mr Mandela supports the TAC in their call for treatment the march is not endorsed by the Nelson Mandela Foundation or Mr Mandela personally." In reality, TAC had obtained the Foundation's permission, but – understanding the political pressure probably being brought on Mandela by the ANC leaders – decided to quietly defend the posters' use, but not to publish the evidence that permission had been sought and obtained. A press statement issued by TAC (12 February) apologized for the "apparent misunderstanding" over the photo's use.

7. Breaking the Law: The Civil Disobedience Campaign

At a National Executive Committee meeting in September 2002 TAC had decided in principle to launch a "Civil Disobedience" campaign to demand a NTP. However, shortly after the NEC, TAC was invited to meet Jacob Zuma, the Deputy President. The most important outcome of the meeting, which took place on 15 October 2002,[23] was a joint press statement recognising "that the NEDLAC process ... on a framework agreement for a national treatment plan was important. All parties committed to the NEDLAC process and agreed that the Framework Agreement would be presented to the South African National AIDS Council (SANAC)."[24]

Zuma also publicly endorsed the principle of an NTP albeit with a caution that the "slowness of government" might not make it feasible to have the plan in place by December 1st 2002, as demanded by TAC. In response to this meeting the TAC Executive resolved: "to postpone civil disobedience until the end of February, 2003" but to "... increase mobilisation efforts for a treatment plan."[25] The suspension of civil disobedience depended upon progress at NEDLAC. Thus, when the NEDLAC process broke down the civil disobedience campaign became unavoidable.

The idea of a civil disobedience campaign against the ANC government was not understood or liked by TAC's allies who worried that it challenged the legitimacy of the government. Extensive canvassing of COSATU and faith-based organisations failed to secure their outright

23 The meeting was also attended by Dr A. Ntsaluba, then the DG of the Health Department. The Minister of Health did not attend.

24 Statement on the Meeting between Deputy President Zuma and the TAC, 16 October 2002, available at <www.tac.org.za>. SANAC was established in 2000. According to its terms of reference it is the "highest advisory body to the Cabinet" on HIV/AIDS policy. It is composed of Cabinet Ministers and representatives of different "sectors" of civil society. Unfortunately, however, instead of appointing independent representatives with the necessary expertise, the Minister of Health mainly selected sector representatives who had neither expertise nor links with the sectors they came from. This predetermined that SANAC would be impotent and most of the time was either by-passed on all the controversial issues of HIV/AIDS policy, or convened only at times when a rubber-stamp was needed.

25 The Way Forward to an HIV/AIDS Treatment Plan, TAC NEC Statement, 24 October 2002, available at <www.tac.org.za>.

support. But, as Zackie Achmat, the Chairperson of TAC, frequently explained, deliberately courting arrest was a tacit recognition of the State and its laws. The act of protest lay in behaving or threatening to behave unlawfully (TAC 2003).

But for TAC's volunteers and people living with HIV/AIDS civil disobedience was now regarded as fully justifiable and was seen as a vehicle to demonstrate growing anger, impatience and disgust. Workshops held to prepare for civil disobedience actions were well attended, and many volunteers wanted to go even further than what had been proposed by the TAC leadership. In addition the growing number of deaths of TAC activists before and during the campaign strengthened the feeling about why civil disobedience had become necessary. This feeling was reinforced by the deaths of well-known TAC leaders such as Edward Mabunda, Charlene Wilson and Kebareng Moketsi. The funerals of Wilson and Mabunda resembled the political funerals of UDF and ANC activists in the 1980s. Wilson was laid to rest in her HIV positive T-shirt at a service attended by many people from Esterhuis who previously had shunned and stigmatised her. Mabunda's coffin was draped in an ANC flag with a TAC T-shirt laid on top of it. Both Mabunda and Wilson were memorialised in large posters with the slogan "Why Civil Disobedience is Necessary."[26]

However, it is important to stress that a civil disobedience campaign is not just about the acts of law breaking, but about the appropriation of a moral right to demonstrate the anger and indignity that scars the lives of oppressed people. TAC's right to engage in civil disobedience hinged on two primary claims: firstly, that 600 people were dying daily of AIDS, and, secondly, that the failure to avail treatment to prevent many of these deaths left the Minister of Health guilty of the charge of culpable homicide. Here it is important to note how TAC

26 Mabunda was an ANC activist from the poverty stricken township of Winterveld, North of Pretoria. He died on April 9th, a day after recording a message to TAC activists calling on them to join the civil disobedience campaign. Charlene Wilson, a TAC leader from the "coloured" community of Esterhuis outside Pretoria died on April 14th. Wilson had been open about having HIV as a direct challenge to her community, where stereotypes and racial prejudices about HIV were rife. During 2002 she had begun anti-retroviral treatment. However, in late March she became ill and – in the absence of HIV specialist services in the public health system – endured the symptoms of an undiagnosed ARV related side-effect, lactic acidosis, to the point where its damage became irreversible.

continued to link its activities to moral claims whilst simultaneously evoking criminal law and constitutional rights to assert its position on the consequences of the political crisis on AIDS.

In a civil disobedience campaign images of this anger are meant to help tip the generally quiescent into action thus building the pressure on the oppressor. In TAC's campaign one of the moments that best expressed the mood of anger occurred when TAC protestors shouted down the Minister of Health at a conference in Cape Town. A widely published photograph of this demonstration captured Zackie Achmat in an angry confrontation with the Minister of Health. This image worried even supporters of the TAC. But it illustrated that there had been a departure from relatively polite exchanges with people such as the Minister of Health to allegations of culpable homicide, the breaking of certain laws and the courting of arrest.

Another of the signifiers of the new mood was a TAC poster bearing portraits of the Minister of Health and the Minister of Trade and Industry, Alec Erwin, which declared in large bold text "WANTED – for failing to stop 600 deaths a day".[27]

The poster's charge of culpable homicide was not an empty one. As part of the campaign a criminal docket had been drafted that alleged that:

> In their capacity as Ministers ... both accused had the legal and power to prevent 70% of AIDS related deaths during this period through developing a treatment and prevention plan, providing medicines and using their legal powers to reduce the price of essential medicines.

The docket (TAC 2003) recounted the history of TAC's efforts over the previous years to persuade government to carry out positive duties required by the Constitution, duties which if fulfilled would have saved the lives of thousands of people with HIV.

The Civil Disobedience campaign started on March 20th 2003, the day before South Africa's Human Rights Day, a day that is commemo-

27 Internally in TAC there was a difficult discussion about whether the poster should accuse the ministers of "causing" rather than "failing to stop" HIV related deaths. The latter was chosen. But, however phrased, the poster represented a development in the way in which it directly laid responsibility for HIV-related deaths at the doors of individual government ministers.

rated to remember those killed in the Sharpeville massacre in 1961. The decision to launch the campaign a day before Sharpeville Day allowed civil disobedience to be linked to the governmental duty to protect and respect life, evoked by Sharpeville, without intruding or appearing to opportunistically capitalise on the day itself. On March 20th, 600 TAC volunteers symbolising the 600 people who die daily of AIDS marched to police stations at Sharpeville, Cape Town and Durban to lay charges of culpable homicide against the two Ministers on behalf of friends or family members who had died. In Cape Town TAC volunteers occupied the Caledon police station and refused to leave. In Durban police assaulted and injured demonstrators by using a water cannon. In Sharpeville a peaceful march, led by people with HIV, went from the Methodist church to the police station.[28]

In the following month TAC organised a series of other protests and sit-ins at the Human Rights Commission (SAHRC), the Commission on Gender Equality (CGE) and the Department of Trade and Industry. TAC protestors also arrived at a cocktail party hosted by the Minister of Health for Dr Richard Feacham, the CEO of the Global Fund to Fight AIDS, TB and Malaria (GFATM). Betraying the rising tensions caused by the campaign the Minister used her speech at the cocktail party to launch an impromptu attack on leaders of the TAC and clumsily tried to deflect the real issues by accusing a white man of masterminding the protests. For example, she described a TAC demonstration at the SAHRC as follows:

> They come with two buses and go to the Commissions where they wait for a white man to tell them what to do ... Our Africans say 'Let us wait for a white man to deploy us ... to say to us ... you must toyi toyi here.'[29]

These accusations bounced back badly on their author. They reflected on her own racist attitude to the motives of white people as well as a

---

28 One of the people who laid charges was Kebareng Moketsi from Alexandra in Johannesburg. She died of AIDS on 2 April 2003. A picture taken of Kebareng in the Methodist Church in Sharpeville, sitting silently with other volunteers, holding the "Wanted" poster is one of the most poignant images of the campaign. Kebareng's death was commemorated in an article in *The Star* on 8 April 2003: M. Heywood "The poor are dead, my lords, dying every day".

29 "The Madness of Queen Manto" *Mail and Guardian*, April 11- 16 2003.

contemptuous view of black people, whose protest was depicted as being orchestrated by external others. But as Zackie Achmat pointed out at the time: "Ironically, this tactic has been used before to undermine the struggle of black people. Those of us who lived during that period will remember that every strike, community action or social mobilization was depicted as 'white communist' or liberal manipulation" (Achmat 2003).

TAC also called for international demonstrations against the SA government. Although these obviously would not involve breaking the law, the act of civil disobedience lay in the SA government – for the first time – finding itself the target of moral censure. In response to TAC's call, demonstrators in cities of Europe, the United States and Asia visited South African embassies and held protests, depositing symbols commemorating the deaths of people with HIV/AIDS, ranging from empty shoes at the embassy in Washington to paper cranes in Tokyo. This was deeply embarrassing to the SA government.

A measure of the groundswell created by the campaign can be seen in individual acts of protest, including an incident where a business class air-line passenger asked not to be seated next to the Minister of Health because he held her responsible for not preventing the deaths of people with AIDS in South Africa. According to a newspaper report this caused the Minister to swear at the passenger.[30]

8. Shaping Policy: Back to Negotiations

The Civil Disobedience campaign lasted for only one month. But it generated news in SA and internationally despite commencing a day after US President George Bush had launched the unlawful invasion of Iraq. It succeeded in highlighting the AIDS crisis and sparked intense media discussion about whether TAC's new strategy was justified. Although some commentators in the media were hostile and chose to focus on issues of race rather than rights (Qunta, 2003) most commentators were sympathetic. For example, political analyst Stephen Friedman wrote that:

> Disobedience inspired by HIV/AIDS policy indicts our democracy, not the impatience of the protestors. Do the activists and the HIV and AIDS sufferers for whom they seek to speak indeed have a say in the policy on

30 "Manto swore at me on flight, claims passenger" SA Press Association, 30 April 2003.

> this issue – and therefore a democratic opportunity which they are spurning?[31]

In view of the fact that the campaign involved only a few thousand people, and that the demonstrations it organised were not threatening to the state, its impact was enormous. Once more, it is evidence of the power of mobilising around a moral issue and being unflinching in demanding that this issue be addressed. The campaign created a political crisis for the SA government which forced it to meet with TAC and be seen to consider its demands. Thus, a day after an illegal demonstration to the National Department of Health in Pretoria on April 24th, another meeting between TAC and Zuma was hastily arranged – on the premise that the SA National AIDS Council (SANAC) had mandated him to meet with TAC to "understand" the Civil Disobedience campaign.

The meeting took place at the Union Buildings on April 25th 2003.[32] Zuma received the TAC delegation respectfully and listened to their grievances. He asked that TAC consider suspending civil disobedience, in return for a pledge to "resume the NEDLAC talks" and a promise that TAC's calls for a NTP would be discussed at the next meeting of the SANAC.

The TAC delegation questioned the benefit of meeting with SANAC – which Zuma admitted had no power to bind Cabinet even if it took a resolution in support of the use of ARV treatment and a NTP. Nevertheless, TAC leaders recognised that by suspending civil disobedience TAC would show that it was reasonable and flexible; meeting SANAC would permit a public airing of the issues and maintain pressure on the government; and the door to reaching an agreement would be reopened.

At a meeting of the TAC NEC on April 29th (in which COSATU Secretary General, Zwelinzima Vavi, and the Archbishop of Cape Town, Njongonkulu Ndungane participated), it was decided overwhelmingly that the campaign should be suspended.

This decision was criticised within and outside of TAC, particularly by other "social movements" who regarded it as a "sell-out."[33] Internally there were justifiable criticisms that there had been insufficient consul-

---

31 *Business Day*, 25 March 2003.

32 The TAC's delegation was Zackie Achmat, Louisa Hobson (the mother of Charlene Wilson), Prudence Mabele (a young woman with HIV), Pholokgolo Ramothwala and Mark Heywood.

33 "Government Cosies up to TAC," *Mail and Guardian*, 2 May 2003.

tation beyond the NEC; that TAC's volunteers had already accepted the risk of imprisonment; and that the offers of the Deputy President were insufficient. For example, at report-back to support groups of people with HIV/AIDS in Gauteng Province, which was attended by over 300 people, many visibly ill, the suspension was fiercely questioned with one delegate complaining that "you can suspend civil disobedience, but you cannot suspend our pain". Meetings like this tested the ability of TAC's leadership to persuade volunteers of the merits of going back to talks with government officials, and of member's understanding of decision-making processes within TAC. Nonetheless, this meeting and many others eventually approved the decision on the condition that it was a suspension of the campaign that would be reviewed if a commitment to an NTP was not achieved quickly.

The meeting with SANAC took place on June 14th 2003.[34] Six Ministers, a number of sector representatives and the TAC delegation were present.[35] At the outset it appeared as if the Minister of Health was intent on derailing the meeting as she made outbursts about "the body language" of members of TAC and called on TAC to "make an apology to the President". She also invited leaders of the National Association of People Living with HIV/AIDS (NAPWA) into the meeting, despite the fact that they were not members of SANAC.[36] But these provocations were ignored.

The agenda of the SANAC meeting included a discussion about the organisation of TAC[37] and debate about TAC's call for the right of access

---

34 The meeting had originally been scheduled for May 8 and 9, but was postponed because of the death of veteran ANC leader, Water Sisulu.

35 The TAC delegation was Zackie Achmat, Prudence Mabele, Sipho Mthati, Mark Heywood, Pholokgolo Ramothwala. In addition to the Deputy President, the Ministers present were: Dr E. Pahad, the Minister in the Office of the Presidency; Dr B. Ngubane, Minister of Arts and Culture; Dr Manto Tshabalala Msimang; Ms T. Didiza, Minister of Land Affairs; and Mr M.B.M. Mphalwa the deputy Minister of Finance.

36 TAC's relationship with NAPWA is not examined in this chapter. However it is relevant to point out that NAPWA has been the only organisation to support the government's stance on AIDS. In return the Department of Health overlooked frequent accusations of mismanagement, corruption and intimidation made against the leaders of NAPWA.

37 In order to satisfy continued questions about its funding and activities TAC made its annual reports, constitution and financial statements available to SANAC at the meeting.

to ARV treatment and the need for a NTP.[38] However, the efforts of TAC to persuade SANAC to take a resolution on these issues failed because of the timidity of the civil society members of SANAC who appeared to be unwilling to take a position contrary to the Minister of Health. Nonetheless progress was made. In a joint press statement issued by SANAC and TAC after the meeting a commitment was made to the finalisation of the NEDLAC process and to urgency in Cabinet taking a decision on the Joint Health and Treasury Task Team report.[39]

In terms of tangible concessions the SANAC meeting appeared to achieve very little. However, progressive social activism does not usually make break-throughs with big bangs, but by the incremental whittling away of its opponent's arguments. Throughout this period TAC did everything with one eye to winning public opinion and another on a future court challenge – meetings like that with SANAC contributed to the growing paper trail of evidence of the reasonable steps TAC took to persuade government of its demands.

In the weeks after the meeting with SANAC there was no *volte face* by government and it appeared as if TAC had suspended civil disobedience on a false promise. However, there was another card to play.

In May 2003 a draft of the report of the Health/Treasury Task Team had been given to TAC. The report detailed the affordability and benefits of an ARV programme. In June 2003, TAC had also been given a copy of a presentation that had been made to a meeting of the Health MinMEC by Dr Ntsaluba, on 9th May 2003.[40] The slides were a summary of the findings of the Task Team and showed how ARV treatment would lead to significant reductions in AIDS mortality and a "significant extension in years of healthy life". For example, the Task Team estimated that even if ARV treatment was only provided to 50% of the numbers of people estimated to need it 733,000 deaths would be "deferred" until after 2010 and the number of children that would be orphaned would be reduced by 350,000.

38 The TAC produced a Memorandum to SANAC summarising these discussions after the meeting. See <www.tac.org.za>.

39 Media Statement: Meeting Between the SA National AIDS Council and the TAC, June 14, 2003 (available at <www.tac.org.za>).

40 A. Ntsaluba "Treatment Options to Supplement Comprehensive HIV/AIDS care in the Public Health Sector", 9 May 2003 (made publicly available on <www.tac.org.za>).

Faced with further delays after the SANAC meeting TAC decided to release the report and slide presentation to the media.[41] The publication of the slides by the *Cape Times* led to a furore. TAC was accused of "theatrics,"[42] "mischief" and even of breaking the law concerning official secrets.[43] However of greatest significance was the fact that in a live radio interview on July 15th neither the slides nor their findings were disputed by Ntsaluba.

This was a decisive moment for the campaign – the Task Team's findings were public and not being disputed. Legally and morally a government decision on a plan to make ARV treatment available was inevitable. But even after the leaking of the reports the delays continued and caused a mounting anger among TAC's volunteers. At provincial congresses that were held in six Provinces during June and July 2003 resolutions were passed unanimously to renew civil disobedience and commence litigation for an NTP if a decision was not taken soon. On August 1-3 at TAC's Second National Congress over 400 delegates from TAC's branches voted overwhelmingly to support lifting the suspension of civil disobedience.[44]

The TAC Congress received extensive media coverage which helped to crystallise a mood of more generalised impatience and anger in South Africa. TAC deliberately chose the venue and date of its congress to be days before the first South African National AIDS Conference which began in Durban on the same evening that the TAC Congress ended. At the opening of the conference by the Deputy President and Minister of Health a silent placard protest, organised by TAC, was supported by over half the audience. Then in the following days there were repeated public statements of frustration from the medical and scientific community. The Congress ended with a plenary debate in which Dr Farid Abdullah, the Head of the AIDS programme of the Provincial Government in the Western Cape, wore an "HIV positive" T-shirt. He declared that South Africa had only two options: "a successful ARV programme or an unsuccessful one."

41 J. Smetherham, Will Secret AIDS Report get a State Response? *Cape Times*, 14 July 2003.

42 SAPA, State accuses TAC of "theatrics" over Report, 14 July 2003.

43 "Leaking of details of report is a moral obligation – not 'mischief' and 'theatrics'", TAC Electronic News, 14 July 2003.

44 A full report of the Congress, including the resolutions is available at <www.tac.org.za/SecondNationalCongressReport.pdf>.

This was the context in which on 8 August 2003 – hardly a week after the conference – the Cabinet announced that it had taken a decision to instruct the Department of Health to develop, urgently, a comprehensive plan for the use of ARV drugs in South Africa.[45] Days later a Task Team was established by the Minister of Health to develop an implementation plan for approval by the Cabinet within one month.

TAC welcomed both steps despite the exclusion of TAC and many key people in the scientific and clinical research community from the Minister's Task Team. The Task Team was composed predominantly of officials from the Department of Health. Ironically, the only civil society member was from NAPWA – who had opposed TAC's campaign and been ambivalent about the use of ARVs. The team was also assisted by a specialist team from the Clinton Foundation under the leadership of Dr Ira Magaziner.

TAC was concerned that the composition of the Task Team meant that the Plan that would be developed would not be the best plan for South Africa. There was a risk that it would ignore the experience of providing ARV treatment that had been gained at clinics such as the one run by *Medecins Sans Frontieres* (MSF) in Khayelitsha in Cape Town. The exclusion of TAC also meant that it risked ignoring the lessons of community mobilisation and treatment literacy programmes which TAC was pioneering.

In view of this, TAC decided to develop a "shadow" plan for submission to the team and requested to meet the Chairperson of the Task Team, Dr Antony Mbewu. The meeting took place on September 9th 2003. The manner in which the meeting was held seemed to confirm rumours that the Task Team had been told by the Minister of Health to have nothing to do with TAC. Reminiscent of clandestine meetings that took place in restaurants in the days of the struggle against apartheid, Mbewu met TAC in a Wimpy bar and arrived without so much as a notebook and pen. This lent more importance to trying to distil the experience of ARV programmes in South Africa thus far in a "shadow" report, something which required a wide and intensive consultation with clinicians, researchers and academics. The report (TAC, 2003), which was endorsed by a large number of organisations, was formally presented to members of the Task Team on September 29th 2003.

45 Statement on Special Cabinet Meeting: Enhanced Programme Against HIV and AIDS, 8 August 2003, issued by Government Communications (GCIS).

In early October the official Task Team handed over its report to the Minister of Health – but there then followed another period of delay before it was considered by the Cabinet. Once again people anxiously awaited the approval of the Plan and had to live off rumours as to why there was a delay, including worrying suggestions that Cabinet had rejected the report or referred parts of it back to the Task Team. It was not until 19 November 2003 that Cabinet finally announced that it had approved the Plan, which was then released on the internet marked "confidential."[46]

9. Looking Forwards: The Future Role of Law and Mobilisation in the Second Decade of Democracy

TAC's campaign for an NTP has also been a campaign for Constitutionalism and the keeping of Constitutional promises. With such a modest objective it has largely been situated in the "mainstream" of progressive politics. This has had the advantage of consistently forcing people and organisations (including its allies) into moral and political dilemmas that are easily avoided if an organisation conducts itself in a fashion that allows it to be cast as "ultra-left".

Nonetheless, critics of TAC's NTP campaign are to be found both in the ANC and some of the "social movements".[47] The former accuse TAC of having an "academic desire to test the limits of our constitution and the law in general in pursuit of their subjective goals as lobby groups."[48] The latter argue that cabinet's adoption of the NTP in late 2003 did not lead to its rapid implementation.

---

46 Cabinet Statement on Treatment Plan for HIV/AIDS, issued by GCIS, 19 November 2003. In a 2004 sequel government lawyers attempted to use the marking of the publicly released plan as "confidential" as a justification for not releasing to TAC detailed implementation schedules. This was rejected by the Pretoria High Court.

47 The term "social movement" is not very helpful because it is a "catch-all" that lacks definition and precision. As recent research in SA has revealed social movements use very different tactics and also differ in the extent to which they are really rooted in their constituencies. See: *Development Update* 5:2, November 2004, Mobilising for Change, The Rise of the New Social Movements in South Africa.

48 *ANC Today*, Volume 4, No 4, 4-11 November 2004, "TAC Court Case: Constant Legal Threats Don't Help HIV and AIDS Fight."

It is admitted that throughout 2004 TAC had to continue to campaign for the implementation of the NTP and combine mobilisation with threats of and actual litigation to move the programme forward.[49] But despite this, the fact that a major shift in government policy was influenced by TAC, cannot be denied. It has been admitted even by the Minister of Health who, in mid 2004, told the Public Protector that:

> Government's cautious approach to the use of ARVs, not withstanding their wide use in many developed and developing countries, was accelerated by the judgment of the Constitutional Court in the *TAC* matter. (Public Protector 2004)

In a similar vein claims that the campaign has brought about only short-term and superficial benefits for people with HIV also flounder on the evidence. By April 2005 35,000 people were receiving life-saving ARVs through the public health service. In addition government has made budgetary allocations of R12bn for HIV/AIDS prevention and treatment over the next three years and the Operational Plan proposes to recruit 14,000 additional health care workers over the next five years.

This is the evidence that TAC has proved convincingly that expressing poor people's needs as human rights demands and taking advantage of the Constitution and other legal instruments to pursue these demands has great redistributive potential.

Since it was founded in 1998 TAC has demonstrated consistently that using human rights law (and law for human rights) is able to catalyse (rather than subvert) political and community mobilisation. In fact, the NTP campaign shows that strategic and political use of law, as long as it is backed up by research, education and mobilisation, creates a space where poor people can contest the policies and practices of both government and pharmaceutical companies – and can make gains.

49 In March 2004 TAC prepared legal papers to compel the Minister of Health to use interim measures to procure anti-retroviral medicines before the conclusion of the tender process. Litigation was avoided after the Minister, who had initially refused to use such measures, permitted Provincial governments to buy medicines. In February 2005 the Ministry of Health awarded tenders for ARVs worth R3bn. In November 2004 a case between TAC and the Minister of Health was heard in court over TAC's application for access to implementation schedules for the Plan. Judgment in TAC's favour was handed down on December 14 2004 and is available on the TAC website.

These gains are more than just short-term reforms given away at the peak of campaigns. They are concessions, extracted under pressure, that can erode aspects of the very structure of inequality. The events described in this chapter, therefore, contradict pseudo-Marxist arguments that using the law to make claims on behalf of the poor, demobilises "the masses" and automatically legitimates a political and economic system that keeps poor people in thrall (A. Hunt 1993).[50] In a post-apartheid era, the campaign for an NTP repeats what Chanock described in relation to the Legal Resources Centre's use of the law against apartheid as avoiding "an impatient discarding of legal forms" through "an effort to realize the promise of law on an entirely new scale, [which] might create a far broader consciousness of the possibilities of "legal rights." (Chanock 2001)

Implicit in TAC's approach is a recognition that whilst historically the law in South Africa has been the subject of multiple appropriations by the dominant white classes, it can also – and should – now be appropriated by poor people in their quest for a better life.

For this end, the Constitution dictated that the democratic government create an array of laws and statutory institutions to protect and underpin human rights, including the right to health. As this chapter has shown, the TAC campaign has consistently utilised these institutions and laws. Consequently its approach to law and the State has been different to that of other "social movements" such as COSATU, the Landless People's Movement (LPM) and the Anti-Privatisation Forum (APF). The APF and LPM have rarely used the Constitution which they regard as a "sell-out" of the poor. Despite a grudging recognition that there may be benefits to using the law (Centre for Civil Society Research Report, 16, 2004), they have concentrated their campaigns on protesting the "neo-liberal and capitalist policies" of the ANC government which they argue impact negatively on poor people. But although full of sound and fury, in reality they are more like the mad King Lear cast out on the heath threatening to devastate his enemies, but in reality powerless. By contrast TAC's use of human rights argument in a variety of spheres and its engagement with "reformist" institutions such as the National Economic Development and Labour Council (NEDLAC), the

50 Hunt for example says that: "The most pervasive ideological effect of law is to be found in the fact that legal rules and their application give effect to existing social relations. The rules of law affirm the existing social and economic relations that exist within capitalist society."

Competition Commission and even the Advertising Standards Authority has made it possible to invade some of the "internal" spaces of governance in order to pursue human rights claims. It has also helped to stimulate a discussion about the methods of struggle that are available to enable pro poor and human rights organisations, including South Africa's powerful trade union movement, to achieve their objectives. For example, at COSATU's Conference on Ten Years of Democracy held in March 2005, Zwelinzima Vavi the General Secretary stated in his keynote address that:

> Given the fact that the Constitution is the product of our struggles, and the judiciary itself is a terrain of contestation, we need to ask whether it has been correct to limit engagement with that institution to the extent that we have. In relation to broader social matters conservative forces, including business, have largely occupied this space. (Z. Vavi 2005)

In South Africa defining and mobilising struggles of the poor as primarily moral contests, rather than as ideological ones, has proved to be a strategy with great potential for mitigating social crises and forcing the reallocation of resources by both private capital and the State to address the needs of the poor. Indeed, it might be argued that this is *currently* the only way to contest pro-poor struggles given that the political ideology of the poor (still described as "socialism," but rarely defined) still faces a crisis of theory and thus of legitimacy. Simply denouncing the obvious evil (neo-liberalism, capitalism or corrupt government), without a plan or the capacity to provide a viable alternative, may provide satisfaction to the organisation doing the denouncing, but is more likely to leave the poor without reform or lasting relief.

The HIV epidemic is a global crisis which predominantly affects the poor. However, it is important to realise that the HIV pandemic, in common with the history of most epidemics of communicable disease, is a reflection and a result of social inequalities and the deprivation of billions of people of their fundamental human rights. Therefore the campaign for access to treatment for people with HIV/AIDS is not a narrow one, but one that requires challenging the roots of inequality and poverty. The question is how to do this?

The TAC's approach, as demonstrated in the campaign for an NTP as well as in campaigns against profiteering from medicine, has been to make the issue one of public morality that will not go away. There is a recognition that, although the political ideology of the poor is in crisis, past campaigns and conflicts have left today's social movements with tools of great efficacy. Utilising the Constitution and other laws does not make TAC guilty of worship of the law or legality, but is an example of working within the State to contest for resources and priorities.

Organisations of the poor do not need to constantly re-start or re-tool the struggle. SA's Constitution, and other progressive legal documents internationally, including the International Human Rights Covenants, should not be "impatiently discarded", but used to legitimate and invigorate new struggles. As illustrated with reference to Vavi, in SA there appears to be a growing recognition of this as more organisations of, or acting on behalf of, poor people are taking advantage of the Constitution. In late 2004, for example, important judgments of the Constitutional Court were made changing the customary law of succession so that it does not discriminate against women and girls (Bhe 2004) and on the duties of the State to take reasonable steps to protect rail commuters from criminal violence (RCAG 2004). The criticism is that unless these legal challenges are accompanied by education and mobilisation their impact on the practice of government and on people's enforcement of individual rights remains limited.

These statements about the value inherent in the Bill of Rights are not made naively. Of course, the evolving politics of SA – and the extent to which the existing democratic space is protected from executive interference – will impact on the value of using the law to continue the process of social transformation. The Constitution is not set in stone and cannot be totally insulated from the vagaries of politics: it can be changed by a two-thirds majority. Similarly, recognition of the separation of powers and the independence of the judiciary was a political decision – that can be nibbled away at. Indeed it has been reported that in the context of unpopular court decisions a wing of the ANC, that includes the Minister of Health, actively argue against aspects of the current constitutional dispensation.

It has not been argued in this chapter that use of the law is a panacea for all social problems. Litigation is riddled with risks, some as arbitrary as which judge is allocated to a case. Obviously, the post-apartheid judiciary will reflect the tensions of the society it lives in, as much as its predecessor. Therefore, just as under apartheid there were enthusiastic hanging judges, and those who resisted the compunctions of the executive, so the post-apartheid judiciary will also include some judges who bow to governmental reasoning, and others who hold the government strictly to all the high benchmarks of behaviour and conduct that are set by the Constitution. The bitter intra-judicial disputes which surfaced in early 2005 would seem to be evidence of this. However, it is important to distinguish that there were two strands to these disputes – an overdue reaction against lingering racism within the judiciary together with a marked divergence on political (not racial) lines with regard to government's positive constitutional duties. Both strands were evident in the litigation around pharmacy dispensing fees.

In conclusion therefore it is necessary to restate that public impact litigation is not just about the pressure that is created within a court, on the strength of evidence and argument, but also the pressure that is mobilised around the court. Mobilising a country on a moral issue and expressing that mobilisation through public demonstrations means that a court deciding a conflict does so in the knowledge of the expectations and lives that depend on the outcome. It deepens democracy because it alerts citizens to avenues that exist to challenge inequity. Thus, although TAC was not ultimately forced to make the demand for an NTP a matter for constitutional adjudication, this possibility infused the campaign from first to last. Along the way its moral and political arguments were reinforced by litigation on the issue of prevention of mother to child HIV transmission (MTCT), as well as with successes against multi-national pharmaceutical companies. This approach to the HIV/AIDS issue, as well as to other key human rights issues, has by no means run its course and will have to continue in the second decade of South Africa's democracy.

References

Achmat, Z., Living Non Racialism, *Mail and Guardian*, 2 May 2003.

AIDS Law Project (ALP), *The Price of Life, Hazel Tau and Others vs GlaxoSmithKline and Boehringer Ingelheim, A Report on the Excessive Pricing Complaint to South Africa's Competition Commission*, July 2003.

Budlender, G., The Right of Access to Health Care Services: Access to Medicines and the State's Positive Obligations to Develop and Implement an Enabling Framework, paper presented to AIDS Law Project Seminar on "Rethinking Patent Law in the Context of a Right of Access to Essential Medicines," March 2003.

Callinicos, L., Oliver Tambo, *Beyond the Engeli Mountains*, David Philip, 2004.

Centre for Civil Society Research Report, 16, *"Nothing for Mahala" The Forced Installation of Prepaid Water meters in Stretford, Extension 4, Orange Farm*, April 2004.

Chanock, M., *The Making of South African Legal Culture 1902-1936 Fear, Favour and Prejudice*, Cambridge University Press, 2001.

Constitutional Court, judgments in:

- *Soobramoney* v *Minister of Health, KwaZulu-Natal* 1997 (12) BCLR 1696 (CC).
- *Government of the Republic of South Africa and others* v *Grootboom and others* 2001 (1) SA 46, 2000 (11) BCLR 1169 (CC).
- *Minister of Health and Others* v *Treatment Acton Campaign and others (No 2)* 2002 (5) SA 717, 2002 (10) BCLR 1033 (CC).
- *Bhe* v *Magistrate, Khayelitsha and Others*, CCT 49/03.
- *Rail Commuters Action Group and others* v *Transnet ltd t/a Metrorail*, CCT 56/03.

Department of Health, *Operational Plan for Comprehensive HIV and AIDS Care, Management and Treatment for South Africa*, Department of Health, November 2003.

Department of Health, *National HIV and Syphilis Antenatal Seroprevalence Survey in South Africa*, 2003.

Development Update 5:2, November 2004, Mobilising for Change, the Rise of the New Social Movements in South Africa.

Heywood, M., "Debunking 'Conglomo-talk': A Case Study of the Amicus Curiae as an instrument for advocacy, investigation and mobilization," *Law Democracy and Development*, 5, 2001(2).

Heywood, M., "Preventing Mother to Child HIV Transmission in SA: Background, Strategies and Outcomes of the TAC Campaign Against the Minister of Health," *South African Journal on Human Rights*, 19, part 2, 2003.

Heywood, M., "The Price of Denial," *Development Update*, 5:3, December 2004.

Heywood, M., "The Achilles Heel? The Impact of HIV/AIDS on Democracy in South Africa," forthcoming in *HIV/AIDS in South Africa*, eds. Karim and Karim, Cambridge University Press, 2005.

Hunt, A., *Explorations in Law and Society, Towards a Constitutive Theory of Law*, Routledge, 1993.

National Economic Development and Labour Council (NEDLAC), draft Framework Agreement on a Plan for HIV Prevention and Treatment in South Africa, December 2002.

Pieterse, M., "Coming to Terms with Judicial Enforcement of Socio-Economic Rights," *South African Journal on Human Rights*, 20, 2004.

Public Protector. Report on An Investigation Into Allegations Of Impropriety In Connection With The Approval By The Cabinet Of An Operational Plan For Comprehensive HIV And AIDS Care, Management And Treatment For South Africa, Designed By The National Department Of Health, October 2004.

Qunta, C., "White Males' Rage is Blacks' Burden," *Business Day*, 23 May 2003.

Statistics South Africa, Mid-Year Population Estimates 2004.

Statistics South Africa, Report on *Mortality and Causes of Death in South Africa* over a 6-year period 1997-2003, February 2005.

TAC, *The Bredell Consensus Statement on the Imperative to Expand Access to Anti-Retroviral treatment for Adults and Children with HIV/AIDS in South Africa,* November 2001.

TAC, *Dying for Treatment,* TAC Briefing Document on the Civil Disobedience Campaign, March 2003.

TAC, People's Docket, People *v* Mantombazana Tshabalala Msimang and Alexander Erwin, March 2003.

TAC, A People Centred ARV Programme – Proposals for the Roll Out of an Anti-retroviral programme to Strengthen a People's Health Service, Civil Society Submission on the Operational Plan, 19 September 2003.

Vavi, Z., "Labour, Socio-economic Transformation and the State – Reflections on South Africa's Ten Years of Democracy", Address to the COSATU Conference celebrating ten years of democracy and freedom, March 2005.

9. The Treatment Action Campaign and the History of Rights-Based, Patient-Driven HIV/AIDS Activism in South Africa

Mandisa Mbali

1. Introduction

Over five million South Africans today are HIV positive.[1] In the post-apartheid era, the AIDS policy-making process has been characterised by a well-documented conflict between AIDS activists aligned with the Treatment Action Campaign (TAC) and the government over official denialism and inadequate access to HIV treatment.[2] Contemporary AIDS activists aligned to the TAC have framed their struggle for HIV treatment access in terms of the human rights of people living with HIV/AIDS. They insist that access to such life-saving combination antiretroviral drug treatment for all HIV positive people is a human right, in as much as it fulfils their rights to life and the socio-economic right to access to health care. As a result of the TAC's campaign, in September 2003 the South African Cabinet instructed the health ministry to develop a comprehensive HIV treatment and prevention plan. The government has since begun to roll-out HIV treatment at public health care facilities across South Africa. TAC is now seen by many commentators as perhaps the most successful example of civil society pushing for South African – and indeed international – government policy to reflect socio-economic and health rights in the post-apartheid era.[3]

---

1 A figure extrapolated from the Department of Health's 2004 annual antenatal clinic survey.

2 I have documented and traced the possible reasons for this disagreement extensively elsewhere. M. Mbali, "HIV/AIDS policy-making in post-apartheid South Africa", In Habib, A., Daniel, J. and Southall, R. (eds.), *State of the Nation: South Africa 2003-2004*, (Cape Town: Human Sciences Research Council Press, 2003).

3 For instance Friedman and Mottiar recently argued that TAC is a "success-

Peris Jones and Kristian Stokke (eds.), Democratising Development, *ISBN 90 04 14821 3, pp. 213-243.*

What receives less attention is the way in which the history of HIV/AIDS activism in late apartheid and transition South Africa fundamentally shaped TAC's strategies, tactics and use of rights-based rhetoric. This Report explores two ways in which the history of AIDS activism in the 1980s and 1990s shaped TAC's politics. Firstly, it examines the influence of "patient driven," anti-apartheid, gay rights[4] activism on TAC. Secondly, it looks at how the early openness of gay rights activists living with HIV has shaped TAC's work against HIV-related stigma and its creation of a large and visible constituency of HIV positive people demanding their rights.

In asserting these continuities, it is not this chapter's aim to underplay the discontinuities between anti-apartheid, gay rights activism in the 1980s and early 1990s and TAC's militant AIDS activism in post-apartheid South Africa. Conservative gay AIDS activists affiliated to Gay Activists of South Africa (GASA) tried and failed to gain access to the apartheid government's AIDS committees during the 1980s. In the early 1990s, anti-apartheid gay AIDS activists used transition-era negotiating spaces such as the National Aids Convention of South Africa (NACOSA) to further their aims. However, the post-apartheid era brought much greater scope for AIDS activism as it brought with it a free press and the Constitutional Court, which were used to maximum potential by TAC activists, especially in advocating HIV treatment access for all, as the second and third sections of this chapter argue. In using these democratic institutions, TAC defended and extended "first generation" political rights.

story" as a social movement and that TAC shows that "It remains possible to use the rights guaranteed and the institutions created by liberal democracy to win advances for the poor and weak." Steven Friedman and Shauna Mottiar, "A moral to the tale: The Treatment Action Campaign and the politics of HIV/AIDS" (2004:28). Available at <www.ukzn.ac.za/ccs>. Heywood's chapter in this same volume cautions that it is too early for TAC to proclaim "victory" in its struggle for a roll-out.

4 I am using this term to describe the movement for equal rights for gay, lesbian, bisexual, transgender and intersex (GLBTI) people. Some queer theorists prefer to use terms such as "queer activism" or the acronym GLBTI. I will use the term "gay rights movement" for ease of reading and because it is the only term used in all archival and oral sources I consulted throughout the period under discussion.

It should also be noted that South African AIDS activists used rights-based discourses to attain different goals in different periods. Whereas during the early 1990s the focus was on confidentiality, by the late 1990s openness was used to push for access to treatment. This suggests that activist uses of rights-based discourse are contested and changing. Despite these historical legacies of AIDS activism of the late 1980s and early 1990s, TAC's formation in 1998 was based much more upon distinctly post-apartheid democratic cultures and institutions. Similarly, TAC's success in pushing for wider access to HIV treatment using the language of socio-economic rights poses wider theoretical questions about the potential power and meaning of discourses of human rights, when used by new social movements to fight for socio-economic justice in post-apartheid South Africa.

2. Theorising Human Rights and Civil Society

In considering the history behind TAC's emergence as a rights-based, civil society movement, there are a few relevant theoretical debates on human rights and civil society which need to be briefly highlighted. Although activists in TAC talk about human rights as if they are absolute, true and universal, human rights are instead contested, constructed and given different meanings in different contexts.

In the international context, human rights have been central in discourses against unfair discrimination against people living with HIV since at least the early 1990s.[5] As TAC's lobbying and advocacy successes show, human rights remain one of the most important ways of asserting political and normative claims in contemporary post-apartheid South Africa. Moreover, South Africa's Constitution is revered as being one of the most progressive in the world for its inclusion of socio-economic rights, and the rights to gender equality and non-discrimination

5 Jonathan Mann famously invoked human rights-based discourse to argue against AIDS-related stigma and discrimination, see: Jonathan Mann, "Medicine and public health, ethics and human rights" in (eds.) Gruskin, S., Grodan, M.A. and Annas, G. *Health and Human Rights – A Reader.* (New York: Routledge, 1999). In a similar tradition Paul Farmer has more recently invoked human rights discourse to argue for access to HIV and multi-drug resistant tuberculosis treatment for poor people in poor countries such as Haiti. Paul Farmer, *Pathologies of Power: Health Human Rights and the New War on the Poor* (Berkeley: University of California Press, 2003).

on the grounds of sexual orientation. However, human rights discourse is not without its critics and the interpretation of human rights, or constitutional law depends very much on the socio-economic, political and historical context in which they are interpreted and invoked.[6]

As I have argued elsewhere, Jürgen Habermas's understanding of civil society as constituting and protecting the public sphere and rights–based discourse, in his book *Between Facts and Norms,* is a useful way of understanding organisations such as TAC.[7] TAC is an example of Habermas's idea that communication in civil society sustains the public sphere itself and, simultaneously, the maintenance of this public sphere entails the ongoing defence and extension by civil society of the right to freedoms of speech, expression and opinion.[8] Differently put, in fighting for "second generation" socio-economic rights such as the right to access to health care, TAC has defended and extended "first generation", political rights such as the right to freedom of speech and opinion and the right to peaceful demonstration.

Despite the power of the invocation of rights-based discourse by civil society in post-apartheid South Africa, it has not been immune to post-structuralist and post modern critiques. Such critiques of rights-based discourse have argued that in a Derridean sense the law is part of the myth of modernity.[9] Fitzpatrick has argued that "Myth is the mute ground which enables "us" to have a unified law and which brings together law's contradictory existences into a patterned coherence".[10]

As I shall try to demonstrate in the following sections of this Report, as fabricated, contested and context bound as it is, rights-based

6 For instance, Marxist critics of civil society have framed it as the realm of individual egoism and self- interest, as "bourgeois society" which limits the power of the state and protects the right to private property. Ashenden, S., "Chapter 5: Questions of Criticism: Habermas and Foucault on Civil Society and Resistance". In Ashenden, S., Owen, D., (eds.) *Foucault contra Habermas: Recasting the Dialogue between Genealogy and Critical Theory.* (London: Sage, 1999), pp. 143-46.

7 M. Mbali, "Researcher/activist engagements with AIDS policy-making after the death of objectivity", Available at <www.ukzn.ac.za/ccs>.

8 J. Habermas, *Between Facts and Norms.* Transl. Rehg, W. (Cambridge: MIT Press, 1996), pp. 367-69.

9 P. Fitzpatrick, "Introduction", *Inside and Outside the Law: Anthropological Studies of Authority and Ambiguity* (London: Routledge, 1996), pp. 10-12.

10 *Ibid.*, p. 2.

discourse can be made and remade over time by activists in changing political and historical circumstances. In terms of this, the next section of this chapter will demonstrate how gay rights, anti-apartheid activists invoked human rights discourse in the late apartheid and transition eras to fight racism in gay rights organisations and homophobia in anti-apartheid organisations, government policy and institutions and broader society. Some of these activists later became prominent in AIDS activist organisations such as TAC and applied political lessons they had learnt in their experiences in earlier anti-apartheid and gay rights struggles to their work in groups such as TAC. In contemporary South Africa, TAC shows that rights-based discourse can be a useful political strategy to articulate normative claims of civil society at particular social, political and historical moments, even if it is essentialised for rhetorical force.[11]

3. The Legacy of 1980s Anti-Apartheid, Gay Rights Activism

> Two South African Airways stewards have died after apparently becoming the first South African victims of a rare disease which is believed to affect mainly homosexuals and drug addicts.
>
> *"'Homosexual" disease kills SAA Staff,' Argus 4th January 1983*[12]

In historically contextualising TAC as a patient-driven, rights-based activist movement, it is worthwhile revisiting the earliest years of the epidemic in South Africa, over two decades ago. In the earliest years of the epidemic, there were only a handful of white gay men dying of AIDS and a public panic was created by the arrival of a new and poorly understood disease, which was then commonly phrased as the "homosexual plague." AIDS emerged in South Africa in 1982, one year after the American Centres for Disease Control announced the emergence of the

11 Here, I am drawing on Marie Benedict Dembour's arguments against an outright rejection of strategic essentialisation of human rights discourse to realise normative political goals. See: Benedict-Dembour, "Human rights talk".

12 South African History Archive (SAHA), Gay Association of South Africa (GASA), Gay Association of South Africa, Gay Association of South Africa /Gay Association of South Africa 6010 (GASA/GASA 6010) Box, Media Scrap Books, "Scrap Book Kept by Leon Eksteen who died in August 1986. He was the 5th Capetonian to die of AIDS." Leon Eksteen.

new disease amongst young gay men in New York and San Francisco in its Weekly Morbidity and Mortality Report.[13] In South Africa, as in the United States, shocking headlines announced that the 'homosexual' disease or the "gay plague" had arrived in South Africa.[14] Illustrative of the fundamental crisis that the AIDS epidemic represented for gay men in South Africa in the period, by the mid-1980s it was estimated that ten to fifteen percent of gay men in Johannesburg were infected.[15]

The early location of HIV/AIDS activism in the gay rights movement has had significant implications for the formation of the TAC. It provides a partial explanation of why the movement is led by gay rights activist Zackie Achmat and why gay rights activist Edwin Cameron has been one of the most passionate advocates of wider HIV treatment access and non-discrimination on the grounds of HIV status. Furthermore, the emergence of anti-apartheid, gay rights activism situated in universal rights-based discourse, provided the basis for such gay rights activists to form broad-based, human rights-focussed alliances such as TAC in the post-apartheid era.

As Howard Philips has argued, HIV/AIDS occupies a unique position in South Africa's epidemic history as the years of relatively good health following infection before the onset of "full-blown" AIDS have enabled a much higher degree of activism than around other infectious diseases in South Africa's epidemic history.[16] Even in its early years the HIV/AIDS epidemic created a large number of relatively fit and active young people, some of whom were articulate, well-educated and schooled in the art of political mobilisation in the gay rights and anti-apartheid movements. In the post-apartheid era, TAC is in many senses

13 Paula Treichler has offered an excellent account of the homophobic panic generated by the emergence of AIDS in the US. Triechler has argued that AIDS is an epidemic of signification, where multiple stories have been generated focusing on the text of the body of the male homosexual. See: Paula Treichler, *How to Have a Theory in an Epidemic: Cultural Chronicles of AIDS*, (Durham and London: Duke University Press, 1999), pp. 19-26.

14 SAHA, GASA, GASA/GASA 6010 Box, Media Scrap Books, "Scrap Book Kept by Leon Eksteen", Leon Eksteen, "'Gay' plague: More victims?" *Sunday Times*, January 9 1983, p. 3.

15 Ruben Sher, "HIV infection in South Africa 1982-1989 – A review", *South African Medical Journal*, 76, (1989), pp. 314-318.

16 Howard Philips, "AIDS in the context of South Africa's epidemic history", *South African Historical Journal*, 45, (2001), p. 22.

driven by people living with HIV/AIDS and can therefore be framed as what I will call "patient activism."[17] As I will argue in this section of the chapter, this patient activism by people living with HIV/AIDS is rooted in traditions of AIDS activism in gay rights activism, established in the 1980s and early 1990s.

Early gay AIDS activism can be framed as patient activism on the basis of the fact that a significant and growing number of gay men were identified as HIV-infected or as having AIDS during the period. Moreover, even uninfected gay men who participated in gay organisations were fairly likely to have known other gay men infected with HIV, not least through social support networks established for members of gay organisations who were HIV positive. Also they were concerned about both the issue of AIDS itself and the media-induced homophobic panic inspired by the epidemic in its first years. Representations of the epidemic as a "gay plague," which depicted it as a phenomenon that resulted from an "innate pathology" in gay sexuality and the material discrimination that resulted from these representations catalysed anti-discrimination patient activism by gay AIDS activists.

There is evidence of representation of the epidemic as a "gay plague" in the South African media in the early 1980s and that this sparked some resistance by gay activists. Gay activists at GASA, some of whom were dying of AIDS at the time, were reading and compiling media scrapbooks which have been preserved at the Gay and Lesbian Archive at the South African History Archive at the University of the Witwatersrand. Some gay activists were also responding, albeit in a relatively muted and non-militant sense, to the dominant discriminatory representation of AIDS as stemming from some innate pathological characteristic of "homosexuals." For instance, some of the headlines gathered in these scrapbooks depicted "AIDS carriers" as sexual predators who lied about their infection and wilfully infected others[18] and as menaces to public health who were unfit to even serve food on airlines. A *Sunday Times* article decrying the arrival of the "gay" plague announced in horrified tones

17 I am drawing here on the work of social medical historians such as Roy Porter who have argued for medical histories to be written from patients' perspectives. See Roy Porter, "The Patient's View: Doing Medical History from Below", *Theory and Society*, 14 (1985), p. 175.

18 SAHA, GASA, GASA/GASA 6010 Box, Media Scrap Books, "Scrap Book Kept by Leon Eksteen", Leon Eksteen, Chris Erasmus. "'Concealment' by AIDS victims", Unknown newspaper, undated.

that "Seven months before he became the first South African to die of the newly discovered disease – Ralph Kretzen, a self-confessed homosexual – still handled food on overseas flights."[19]

In South Africa, as elsewhere, in the early 1980s, gay men faced the brunt of early AIDS-related institutionalised discrimination, and its impact on gay activism has been seldom documented and discussed in accounts of South Africa's history, in general, or its history of AIDS, in particular.[20] For instance, posters went up in Natal urging "gays" and "moffies"[21] or people who had had sex with "gays" and "moffies" not to give blood to prevent transmission of AIDS.[22] This discrimination was informed by the dominant late apartheid, public health constructions in the *South African Medical Journal* (SAMJ) and the Durban Medical Officer of Health's Annual Reports, of gay men, black prostitutes and foreigners as abnormal "disease carriers", as pathological types, not individuals with complex life histories who were operating in complex socio-cultural contexts, as I have demonstrated elsewhere.[23]

---

19 "'Gay' plague: More victims?", *Sunday Times*, 9 January 1983, p. 3.

20 With a few notable exceptions where the issue is very briefly discussed, as a part of broader discussions: Grundlingh, Gevisser's and Philips have all separately discussed the stereotyping of AIDS as a gay plague. I hope to build on these accounts by showing the real suffering and material discrimination this caused and how the effects of such representation catalysed activism. Howard Philips, "AIDS in the Context of South Africa's Epidemic History", *South African History Journal*, 45 (2001). Mark Gevisser, "Another fight for freedom", In Cameron, E. and Gevisser, M. (eds.) *Defiant Desire: Gay and Lesbian Lives in South Africa* (Johannesburg: Raven Press, 1994). Louis Grundlingh, "Government responses to HIV/AIDS in South Africa as Reported in the Media", *South African Historical Journal*, 41, (2001).

21 A derogatory and prejudiced South African term for gay men. For more on the historical origins and genealogy of the term see Shaun de Waal, "Etymological note: On 'moffie' ", In: Cameron, E. and Gevisser, M. (eds.) *Defiant Desire: Gay and Lesbian Lives in South Africa* (Johannesburg: Raven Press, 1994), p. xx.

22 A discriminatory practice that continues today. SAHA, GASA, GASA/GASA 6010 Box, Media Scrap Books, "Scrap Book Kept by Leon Eksteen", Leon Eksteen. Shaun Harris "Row brew over 'moffie' posters", Unknown newspaper. SAHA, GASA, GASA/GASA 6010 Box, Media Scrap Books, Vol. 8.5, "Gays angry over blood transfusion poster" *The Citizen*, 29 January 1986, p. 15.

23 Mandisa Mbali, *'A long illness': Towards a History of Government, NGO and Medical Discourses around AIDS Policy-making*, (Unpublished Bach-

It has been widely discussed how AIDS was frequently represented internationally, in the early phases of the epidemic, as "just desserts" for the "sin" of "homosexuality", in line with the conservative view of homosexuality as "evil."[24] In South Africa, the discrimination against people living with AIDS in the early years even included some private hospitals refusing to admit AIDS patients.[25]

As histories of the epidemic in the West have shown, there were similar AIDS-related discrimination and relative apathy on the part of governments to the problem in Europe and North America in the early 1980s.[26] However, in the United States, AIDS-related discrimination, especially the refusal to spend sufficiently on developing HIV treatment, catalysed much more radical action. Some of this influenced TAC's activism. In particular, the radical group AIDS Coalition to Unleash Power (ACT UP) was formed in the late 1980s and it targeted the US government, pharmaceutical companies and AIDS researchers, for failing to develop effective HIV treatment in the first decade of the epidemic.[27] ACT UP loudly heckled to interrupt speeches, staged "lie-ins" where they would "play dead"

elor of Arts Honours Thesis, University of Natal, Durban, 2001), pp. 2-16. It is also important to remember that at that time, *SAMJ* was the mouthpiece of the Medical Association of South Africa, which had an accommodationist relationship to the apartheid government and refused to publish pieces documenting doctors' collusion in human rights-violations. Baldwin Ragaven, Laurel de Gruchy, Jeanelle and London, Leslie, *An Ambulance of the Wrong Colour: Health Professionals, Human Rights and Ethics in South Africa* (Cape Town: University of Cape Town Press, 1999), pp. 158-159.

24 In these early years, even mainstream medical science toyed with the idea that there was something innate in "the gay lifestyle", which made gays vulnerable to AIDS. Not, as Watney has argued at the time, a lack of access to accurate AIDS prevention information in the period. Paula Triechler, "AIDS, Homophobia and Biomedical Discourse", pp. 21-23. Simon Watney, *Policing Desire: Pornography, AIDS and the Media* (Minneapolis: University of Minnesota Press, 1987).

25 SAHA, GASA, GASA/GASA 6010 Box, Media Scrap Books, Vol. 8.5, Cas St Leger, "AIDS patients turned away", *Sunday Times Metro, July 6, 1986.*

26 Watney, *Policing Desire.* Alan M. Brandt, *No Magic Bullet: A Social History of Venereal Disease in the United States Since 1880* (New York and Oxford: Oxford University Press, 1987).

27 Ronald Bayer and Gerald M. Oppenheimer, *AIDS Doctors: Voices from the Epidemic* (Oxford and New York: Oxford University Press, 2000), pp. 138-140.

and developed powerful political slogans such as "Silence=Death." ACT UP activists even asked more moderate AIDS pressure groups: "WHAT ARE YOU DOING TO SAVE MY FUCKING LIFE!"[28]

There was no such placard waving on the part of GASA, South Africa's main gay organisation during the early 1980s. GASA actively eschewed militancy, in a context where gay and lesbian sexual activity was criminalised and political repression against state opponents perfectly legal. In this context, the relatively quiescent response by GASA to AIDS related discrimination targeted at gay people can be explained by the nature of gay political organisation at the time, which was dominated by conservative white men. GASA believed in a different, "apolitical" model of organisation, which mainly focussed on providing social support.[29] As has been documented by historians of South African gay organisations, it aimed to provide its members with total confidentiality and actively eschewed "militancy" and demonstrations.[30] As Mark Gevisser has argued, "For GASA's architects being apolitical meant two things: firstly remaining non-aligned in broader South African politics, and secondly, following a moderate, non-confrontational and accommodationist strategy."[31]

The reasons for GASA's conservatism can be explained by its history and its membership. GASA was formed in 1982 by the merging of three gay organisations in Johannesburg and it became a nation-wide organisation soon after its founding. Its membership, which numbered over a thousand by 1983, was mostly middle class, white, gay men and its focus was on developing social support for such gay men.[32]

---

28 Centre for Health Policy (CHP), University of Witwatersrand, Resource Room, "What Are You Doing to Save My Fucking Life", Larry Kramer, *TAC: HIV & AIDS Treament Action Campaign: A Reading Package for Treatment Action Campaign Volunteers: HIV/AIDS: An Activists' Guide to Treatment Rights and Literacy: Building a movement to secure the rights and dignity and access to treatment for people with HIV and AIDS.*

29 I am not arguing that such social support wasn't vital for lesbians and gays in a heterosexist and heteronormative South Africa, simply that it wasn't accompanied by militant political resistance to homophobia and heterosexism. This social support through identifying and feeling a sense of belonging to a particular oppressed group is a vital pre-requisite to gay political organisation.

30 Gevisser, "A different fight for freedom", pp. 50-51.

31 Gevisser, *Ibid.*, p. 51.

32 Geviser, *Ibid.*, p. 48.

GASA did try to inform its membership about the threat of AIDS. It published basic information about AIDS and its transmission in its newsletter "Link/Skakel." However, the depiction of the level of the threat posed by AIDS was not universally high across different branches in different regions of the country. As Gevisser has argued, whilst in Johannesburg GASA played down the threat posed by the epidemic in the early 1980s, GASA in Cape Town was, by contrast, a "shrill voice in the dark" providing a range of AIDS prevention and care services;[33] and it used its newsletter to decry homophobic AIDS-related discrimination.

Fundamentally, however, with its accommodationist and nonmilitant strategy, GASA's answer to this crisis was not to wave banners and toyi-toyi. It was to meet with the late apartheid government's National Department of Health and Population Development's National AIDS Advisory Group. For GASA, recognition by the minister of health of GASA as the "official mouthpiece of the gay community" with which the National AIDS Advisory Group was to liase was seen as "a positive development".[34] However, consultation did not translate into representation on policy-making bodies, as GASA was actively excluded from the government's AIDS Advisory Group, which provided expert guidance on its AIDS policy, despite representing the majority of people living with HIV/AIDS in the 1980s.[35]

While AIDS was taken seriously by gay rights organisations, there was the overshadowing issue of apartheid and issues of institutionalised racism and legal segregation. The organisation's racism and "apoliticism" on apartheid were highlighted by its manner of dealing with the 1984 arrest and incarceration of one of its members, Simon Nkoli. Nkoli was detained for anti-apartheid activity with other United Democratic Front (UDF) activists who were tried in the Delmas Treason Trial. Nkoli became a *cause celebre* for anti-apartheid gay rights activists around the world. As a result of their efforts, GASA was suspended from the International Lesbian and Gay Association (ILGA) for its "apolitical" stance and refusal to condemn apartheid, which crystallised in its refusal to support Nkoli.[36]

33 Gevisser, *Ibid.*, p. 59.

34 *Ibid.*, p. 11.

35 South African History Archive, University of the Witwatersrand, NAMDA, NPPHCN Funding/Finances Box, NPPHCN Discussion Papers File, "AIDS in South Africa: Experiences and Responses". August 1990. A paper prepared for the ANC presentation to Congressman McDermitt.

36 Gevisser, "A different fight for freedom", p. 56.

In the years when GASA was trying to respond to AIDS, the political divide in GASA between a handful of militant anti-apartheid activists such as Nkoli, Edwin Cameron, Sheila Lapinsky and Peter Busse[37] and accommodationist non-militant apolitical activists would become so great that GASA ceased to exist as a national movement. Speaking of this period, Achmat has argued that there was "a moral failure of the white lesbian and gay community with very few exceptions ... to speak out against apartheid and racism."[38] This splintering process incapacitated gay rights activists from formulating any unified strategy to respond to homophobic AIDS-related discrimination and the obvious shortcomings of late apartheid AIDS policy.[39] Yet simultaneously, these conflicts created new kinds of radical, more militant gay rights activism, which was located explicitly in human rights-based, anti-apartheid politics, a development essential for the later involvement of some of these activists in the TAC.

There is strong archival evidence that racism existed in the organisation and that issues around racism within the organisation caused divisions comparatively early on in its history. In 1984, the more progressive Western Cape Branch (GASA 6010) denounced racism within GASA in 1984 its newsletter "The 6010th position" in an article entitled "No Room for Racism". Significantly, the article argued that gay rights were inseparable from human rights in general and *for all*.[40]

There are ongoing racial, class and gender-based cleavages in the gay rights movement and in the communities it represents today, which is by no means socially or culturally unified or uniform. Indeed there remains a great deal of racism and sexism and classism in these communities, which pose ongoing challenges to the movement.[41] Still, the

37 Busse was later a founder member of the National Association of People Living with HIV/AIDS, which was formed in the mid-1990s.

38 Zackie Achmat "Appendix to Edwin Cameron's Address to the HIVOS Symposium on *Homosexualities, HIV/AIDS and HIV – Why?*", 21 October 2004.

39 These shortcomings will not be discussed here, as I have already discussed them at length in my BA Honours short thesis. M. Mbali, *"A Long Illness"*

40 SAHA, GASA, Gay Groups Minutes Etc Box, File A, "No Room for Racism." *The 6010th Position, 1* (1984).

41 Teresa Dirsuweit, "The problem of identities: The lesbian, gay, bisexual, transgender and intersex social movement in South Africa" (2004), CCS Research Report for the Globalisation, Marginalisation and Contempo-

importance of even a small handful of gay rights and anti-apartheid activists having located gay rights within wider discourses of universal human rights and in broader progressive movements such as the UDF in the mid-1980s must not be understated.

There were several legacies of their early location of gay rights within wider human rights discourses of the anti-apartheid movement. It would later politically enable the National Coalition for Gay and Lesbian Equality (NGCLE) to succeed in lobbying for the enshrinement of non-discrimination on the grounds of sexual orientation into the country's post-apartheid Constitution. The Equality Project would also later manage to obtain thirty-five pieces of legislative reform, based upon this strategy of invoking wider human rights discourse.[42] These successes may have enabled gay activists to turn their attentions to wider struggles such as TAC's and to apply lessons on the power of invoking human rights discourse in a broader-based movement like TAC campaigning for wider access to HIV treatment.

Significantly, the move by Simon Nkoli into AIDS activism and his early openness about his HIV status and his subsequent death from AIDS over a decade later, became a catalyst for the formation of the TAC. This was the case as anti-apartheid gay rights and head of the NGCLE, Achmat, promised to carry forward Nkoli's struggle for openness and the protection of the rights of people living with HIV, especially their right to treatment access.

An instance of the new anti-apartheid, gay rights activism was the work of Cameron in the 1980s. He would go on to be an important activist and human rights lawyer (and later a judge) in defending the rights of people living with HIV/AIDS. In the early to mid-1980s, he was a trade union lawyer who was very active in advocating for law reform to ensure non-discrimination on the grounds of sexual orientation and defending anti-apartheid gay rights activists (such as Ivan Tomms) when they were imprisoned for anti-apartheid activity. In a 1986 keynote speech, Cameron argued that white gay people in South Africa were "living a dream" and merely looking after their own interests while ignoring both the discrimination and oppression that they faced as gay people and the overwhelming racist oppression that black South Africans faced.[43]

rary Social Movements in South Africa Project. Available at <www.ukzn.ac.za/ccs>.

42 Dirsuweit, "The problem of identities", p. 8.

43 Gevisser, "A different fight for freedom", p. 60.

GASA's refusal to support Nkoli during his detention, which revealed its "apolitical" and "accommodationist" nature, precipitated the collapse of GASA as a national organisation. In its place several explicitly militant, anti-apartheid, gay rights political organisations were formed, which were not only focussed on fighting homophobia, but were also directly opposed to both GASA and its tacit support of apartheid such as The Rand Gay Organisation and the Gay and Lesbian Organisation of the Witwatersrand (GLOW) and the Organisation of Gay and Lesbian Activists (OLGA).[44]

It was a messy fracturing in which GASA Rand asked GLOW to prove the liberation movement was indeed against homophobia. Nor did Nkoli and his gay comrades find the liberation movement free of homophobia. Nkoli's fellow detainees at first asked not to be imprisoned and tried with him because of his sexual orientation. However, gay rights activists like Nkoli believed in fighting against homophobia in the liberation movement from within and that his involvement in the liberation movement could win credibility for the gay rights within the liberation movement: he thought that gay activists had to "stand up and fight" for their rights in the liberation movement, even if it meant courting "unpopularity" with other anti-apartheid comrades.[45] It has been documented elsewhere how gay "anti-apartheid comrades" in OLGA and GLOW, such as Nkoli, fought against this homophobia and to get the outlawing of discrimination on the grounds of sexual orientation included in the ANC's Bill of Rights, which formed the blueprint for the country's democratic post apartheid Constitution.[46]

This history could help to illustrate why TAC activists such as Achmat from an anti-apartheid gay rights background have come to see gay rights as closely related to a broader struggle for the realisation of social justice and human rights for all. Also, a case could be made that Achmat's notion of campaigning for treatment access from within the ANC as a "loyal, card carrying ANC member" may relate to the tradition established in the late 1980s and 1990s typified by Nkoli of anti-apartheid

44 Gordon Isaacs and Brian McKendrick, *Male Homosexuality in South Africa: Identity Formation, Culture and Crisis.* (Cape Town: Oxford University Press, 1992), p. 94. Gevisser, "A different fight for freedom", p. 57.

45 Nkoli, "Wardrobes", p. 256.

46 Gevisser, "A different fight for freedom", pp. 70-71.

gay rights activists lobbying for gay rights from within ANC and UDF structures.[47]

4. The Origins of a TAC's "Campaign for Openness" in the Early 1990s

> On Friday night at Simon [Nkoli]'s funeral I made a call for ten people with HIV/AIDS, their families, friends and allies to start a symbolic fast for access to treatment on 10 December 1998 ... Openness and Treatment are two pivotal issues ... A campaign for 'Openness' is in reality a call for activism and the assertion of identity. People with HIV/AIDS are on our own (whether in or out of the closet)- while we should seek love, compassion and care - we should also demand treatment.
>
> *A letter from Zackie Achmat to HIV/AIDS activists, 1998.*[48]

In one of his first letters to AIDS activists calling for the formation of TAC quoted above, written when he was the head of the NCGLE, Achmat called for TAC's campaign for treatment to be based on HIV positive activists being open about their HIV status. Openness about HIV status has been a cornerstone of TAC's political strategy as a social movement.

Despite the fact that the first few HIV positive AIDS activists publicly revealed their status to fight AIDS-related discrimination in the early 1990s, Achmat's call for openness was a bold step even in the late 1990s. However, the full political potential of this strategy of disclosure to push for human rights-based AIDS policy was not fully realised when the first activists disclosed their status in the early 1990s and would only become apparent when it was adopted *en masse* in the post-apartheid

---

47 For more on this and the activist debates it has generated see Annie Devenish and Mandisa Mbali "A critical review of Zackie Achmat's Wolpe Memorial Lecture, March 2004", Available at <www.ukzn.ac.za/ccs>.

48 Centre for Health Policy (CHP), University of Witwatersrand, Resource Room, "A Letter from Zackie Achmat", Zackie Achmat, *TAC: HIV &AIDS Treatment Action Campaign: A Reading Package for Treatment Action Campaign Volunteers: HIV/AIDS: An Activists' Guide to Treatment Rights and Literacy: Building a movement to secure the rights and dignity and access to treatment for people with HIV and AIDS.* Zackie Achmat, "A Letter from Zackie Achmat."

era by TAC. From a mere handful of openly HIV positive white gay activists in the early 1990s, in the first years of the twenty-first century, AIDS activists' would heed Achmat's call and TAC's protests would come to consist of a human sea of thousands of HIV positive and HIV negative activists wearing t-shirts proudly proclaiming "HIV POSITIVE." Yet as I have begun to argue above, the seeds of TAC's militant patient activism of the late 1990s grew largely from anti-apartheid, gay rights activism in the late apartheid and transition eras. The transformation of HIV/AIDS from an unspeakable and invisible epidemic in the early 1990s to one which affects a highly politically vocal and visible constituency in the early 2000s has been absolutely fundamental to the success of TAC as a political movement. Whereas human rights-focussed AIDS activists in the early 1990s were largely focussing their efforts on pushing for wider respect for patients' rights to confidentiality, in the late 1990s, human rights-focussed AIDS activists in TAC were using openness to push for the socio-economic right to access to health care. This clearly points to the changing and contested nature of human rights discourse. Similarly, AIDS activists' strategic use of spaces for political negotiation of AIDS policy provided to them in the transition period, such as NACOSA, suggests how civil society contributes to the creation and extension of democratic public spaces.

Openness about HIV status was and remains a significant and courageous step because of HIV/AIDS-related stigma. This stigma has been articulated with pre-existing racist, homophobic and sexist readings of disease and sexuality.[49] As with many other previous epidemics, both internationally and in South Africa, outsiders and minorities have been unfairly blamed for the spread of AIDS.[50]

Just over a decade ago, in the early 1990s, the continuation of AIDS-related stigma and prejudice convinced many people that AIDS was the "Other" racial or sexual group's problem and led to widespread, sustained social acceptance of unfair AIDS-related discrimination. Moreover, in such an environment, the first gay, HIV positive, patient activists

49 I demonstrated the history of such stigmatising discourses in the apartheid era in my BA Hons thesis: Mandisa Mbali, " 'A Long Illness': Towards a History of Government, Medical and NGO Discourses around AIDS Policy-making." Available at <www.ukzn.ac.za/ccs>.

50 Howard Philips, "AIDS in the Context of South Africa's Epidemic History: Preliminary Historical Thoughts", *South African Historical Journal*, 45 (2001), pp. 14-16.

to speak out against AIDS faced stigma, largely linked to their sexual orientation, and were far from universally accepted: whilst stigma did not prevent people from talking publicly about AIDS in the abstracted third person as something which affects "them", it was largely "unspeakable" for HIV positive people to speak about their HIV status in the first person, in a public political context.

In terms of early patient activism, the Maputo Conference on Health in Southern Africa, and NACOSA process it catalysed, provided the first political forums for gay, HIV positive, AIDS activists such as Shaun Mellors and Peter Busse, to publicly declare their HIV status. They disclosed their HIV status publicly at such national forums to push for an anti-discriminatory framing of AIDS policy in line with the human rights-based approach outlined in the AIDS Consortium's *Charter of Rights for People Living with AIDS and HIV*.

In the early 1990s, the first handful of gay AIDS activists got the ANC to denounce AIDS-related homophobia. This was a shift which was in line with the success of anti-apartheid gay rights activists getting non-discrimination into the ANC's Bill of Rights, which influenced South Africa's post-apartheid democratic Constitution. The origins of the first-person, patient-driven AIDS activism, which has driven TAC's campaign based on the discourse of socio-economic rights is a significant, under-documented and unique phenomenon in South Africa's epidemic history. To speak about HIV infection and risk of contracting the virus in the first person remained controversial in the early 1990s and there was by no means universal support amongst NACOSA participants for the first white, gay activists who openly revealed their HIV status. This was at least partially due to widespread homophobia in the liberation movement, which has been noted above.

AIDS was an "invisible epidemic" in the early 1990s, which, due to stigma, was largely unspeakable publicly in the first person. The epidemic's invisibility was assured by stigma and discrimination that had led to activist demands for the protection of the right to doctor-patient confidentiality. Doctors were professionally and ethically obliged to maintain secrecy on the patient's condition. However, this right may have been interpreted by patients as *necessity* to maintain secrecy, as opposed to the *right* of the patient to decide on whether to publicly disclose their HIV status. Illustrative of the contradictions and dilemmas posed to activists in this period, is AIDS activist Cameron, who was working flat out and very publicly for human rights-based policy and legislation (largely to uphold confidentiality). Yet Cameron was terrified to reveal his own HIV positive status (which had been diagnosed in 1986) and only did so in 1999.

That being said, the reasons why gay men remained virtually the only patient voice in the early 1990s are suggested by several factors in the period. Firstly, the epidemic affected the gay community early and hard.[51] As discussed above, AIDS was first represented as a "gay plague" and homophobic AIDS related discrimination swiftly followed such representations. Although this representation receded as it became clear it would mainly affect heterosexuals, the memories of the early "gay plague" representations remained.[52] Also, there was a well-developed, militant, gay, anti-discrimination, AIDS activist movement established in the United States by the late 1980s which inspired South African anti-apartheid gay activists organising against AIDS-related discrimination. While South African gay AIDS activism would not reach such a fever pitch until the late 1990s, freed from the shackles of GASA's moderation and "apoliticism", gay rights activism including AIDS activism became more measurably militant and outspoken. Early openly HIV positive AIDS activists pushed for equal rights and fair treatment in all contexts including the workplace, in the health sector, through litigation, use of the media and lobbying and relevant forums such as NACOSA.

Cameron, who had fought against *both* regressive amendments to criminal law discriminating against gay people *and* against racism in gay organisations in the 1980s, turned his brilliant legal and political mind to fighting AIDS-related discrimination in the 1990s. By 1992, he was based at the University of Witwatersrand's Centre for Applied Legal Studies (where AIDS Law Project, a close ally of TAC's is based today), and played a key role in founding The AIDS Consortium Project.[53] Several anti-apartheid organisations, which had played a vital role in pushing for

51 *Ibid.*, p. 3.

52 Edwin Cameron, "Address to the HIVOS Symposium on *Homosexualities, HIV/AIDS and HIV-Why?*", 21st October 2004. In his address, Cameron went on to argue that many anti-apartheid, gay activists threw themselves into fighting the epidemic in the 1990s as if it were solely "straight epidemic", thereby ignoring the need to struggle for prevention services and programmes designed for, and cognizant of the specific vulnerabilities of, gay, lesbian, bisexual, transgender and intersex people.

53 Centre for Health Policy (CHP) Resource Room, University of the Witwatersrand, "The AIDS Consortium Project: Bulletin: Issue 1, August 1992. Centre for Applied Legal Studies, University of the Witwatersrand", p. 1.

AIDS policy to be rights-based, were involved in the AIDS Consortium. The AIDS Consortium was central in lobbying for AIDS policy to protect the rights of people living with HIV as it was formed after meetings between several organisations were convened to discuss the drafting of a *Charter of Rights for People with AIDS and HIV.*[54] The organisation aimed to facilitate contact and information sharing on AIDS between member organisations. However, most significantly, it aimed to be an effective lobbying and advocacy tool; by analysing and sharing information on AIDS policy from a rights-based perspective, it hoped to help affiliated AIDS organisations quickly present a united front on AIDS policy.

This was by no means the extent of rights-based AIDS activism in the period. Cameron's major case involving AIDS-related discrimination in the early 1990s was acting as the plaintiff's advocate in legal action for breach of doctor-patient confidentiality, which was pursued by a man named Barry McGeary. There was an important principle at stake in this case: the right to doctor-patient confidentiality. The violation of this internationally-recognised principle was indicative of the broader systemic ethical bankruptcy of apartheid medicine because, as literature on apartheid medicine has shown, it was far from sacrosanct in all cases. For instance, during the apartheid era, political prisoners were granted scant right to privacy when consulting with physicians, in some cases information on their medical status could be used to determine methods of torture and purposeful maltreatment.[55]

McGeary was a patient infected with HIV, which was then heavily stigmatised and widely misunderstood disease, who lived in Brakpan. His right to confidentiality was violated by his doctor, who in 1991, without his consent, told two other people of his HIV status.[56] That same

54 *Ibid.*, p. 1.

55 The right to doctor-patient confidentiality dates back to the Hippocratic Oath and is designed to ensure that the patient trusts the doctor and that the patient suffers no adverse consequences merely as a result of consulting with their doctor. Indeed, the violation of this right under apartheid was one of the most grievous violations of detainee-patients dignity by health professionals: Laurel Ragaven-Baldwin, Jeanelle de Gruchy and Leslie London, *An ambulance of the wrong colour: Health professionals, human rights and ethics in South Africa* (Cape Town, University of Cape Town Press, 1999), pp. 54-69.

56 SAHA, the Edwin Cameron Archive (Cameron), Box A, File B.1: Press Clippings-Local, "AIDS in the new constitution", *Springs Advertiser,* 27 May 1994.

year, he decided to sue his doctor for violating his medical confidentiality as, according to his lawyer Mervyn Joseph, "... he felt control had been removed from his hands."[57] Cameron handled McGeary's case as his advocate, which Cameron eventually won, although his client, McGeary, died of AIDS before the completion of the trial.

The case is significant as it highlighted issues of confidentiality, discrimination and stigma. Seen in the light of the subsequent tragic HIV prevalence figures and AIDS related mortality, which I would argue was partially caused by the earlier secrecy surrounding an individual's positive HIV status in the early 1990s, it also highlights a painful choice for AIDS activists living with HIV in the period: whether to make personal sacrifices by openly declaring their status to tackle stigma and promote HIV prevention and make themselves vulnerable to AIDS-related discrimination, or whether to reinforce the right to privacy and confidentiality in the face of stigma. The latter decision had the important implication of keeping the epidemic politically and socially invisible and, therefore, a marginal and poorly understood issue.

Issues of confidentiality, secrecy and "truth-telling" around AIDS were also forced onto the agenda in the early 1990s, as doctors began writing letters to editors of newspapers arguing for AIDS to be made a notifiable disease to prevent occupational exposure: that is, an infectious disease where doctors would have to notify the authorities when patients were found to be HIV positive.[58] On the other hand, the earliest proposals for notification met with some resistance on the grounds of existence of the "window period" of the earliest months of infection, where HIV infection may not be detectable and against the breaching of doctor-patient confidentiality in the case of such a stigmatised disease.[59]

Early AIDS activists, whose work was focused on protecting the rights of people living with HIV, thought that the discrimination sur-

57 SAHA, Cameron, Box A, File B.1: Press Clippings-Local, Charmain Naidoo, "World watches as AIDS case drags on", *Sunday Times*, 7 February 1993, p. 4.

58 SAHA, Cameron, Box A, File B.1: Press Clippings-Local, I B Copeley, "Killer Aids should be a notifiable disease", *Sunday Star*, 30 December 1990.

59 SAHA, Cameron, Box A, File B.1: Press Clippings-Local, "Medical Ancillary." "Doctors' puzzling prejudice against Aids", *Sunday Star*, 6 January 1991.

rounding AIDS meant that it had to be kept private and confidential, something certainly underscored by the McGeary case and debates over notification brewing at that time. However, this further fed into the secrecy around AIDS and contributed to what I will call the publicly "unspeakable" nature of their positive HIV status for the vast majority of people living with HIV in the period. But the fact that their status was for the vast majority "unspeakable" was a product of its time: in the transition period, discrimination against gay and lesbian people remained legal. Moreover, in terms of race, in an analogous sense to the "Sanitation syndrome" documented by Maynard Swanson in Cape Town over a century before, conservative racists were (incorrectly) arguing that racial integration which was taking place in the transition era through casual physical contact could "spread" AIDS.[60] Just as racism remained pervasive amongst white conservatives, sexual conservatism was still alive and well in the early 1990s as debates over gay HIV prevention sexual education material in Cape Town showed.[61]

In October 1992, NACOSA met at NASREC under the theme "South Africa United Against AIDS", which was clearly an outflow of the recommendation of the establishment of a National AIDS Task Force at the 1990 Maputo Conference. The conference was significant as it was the first national gathering on AIDS in South Africa, and it incorporated all the major anti-apartheid organisations and representatives from civil society, business and government.

Significantly, in the history of patient activism, a session, entitled "What is AIDS? Two HIV positive people", was addressed by Shaun Mellors. Mellors was a white HIV positive gay man who clearly had links to the AIDS Consortium and who was one of two HIV positive delegates who addressed the audience. He spoke first-hand about the painful effects of AIDS-related discrimination, including losing his job

60 SAHA, Cameron, Box A, File B.1: Press Clippings-Local, "Aids-the end of denial", *The Star*, Monday 5 November 1990. In a similar vein, Maynard Swanson has shown how in turn of the twentieth century Cape Town, the spread infectious diseases was presented as due to the existence of multiracial slums, which colonial officials used to argue for segregation on "public health" grounds. See: Maynard Swanson, "The Sanitation Syndrome: Bubonic Plague and Urban Native Policy in the Cape Colony, 1900-1909", *Journal of African History*, 18, 3 (1979).

61 SAHA, Cameron, Box A.6: ASET, D. Roberts, "Young at Risk: Warning on teaching the wrong way on Aids", *Weekend Argus*, 20-21 February 1993.

and medical aid benefits and urged the audience to sign the AIDS Charter which had been developed by the AIDS Consortium. His speech received a mixed response. Malcolm Steinburg of the Medical Research Council's AIDS group found that his "moving" account "served to emphasise several complex human rights issues that arise with regard to the management of the HIV-infected person as well as their long term care as AIDS patients."

On the other hand, Professor Alan Flemming of the South African Institute of Medical Research wrote: "The presentation was tearful and most in the audience found it moving: I was an obvious minority, as it was in my opinion an exercise in self-pity, and as the first speech from the floor diverted attention to the lesser problem (homosexual transmission) and away from the consequences of heterosexual and vertical transmission."[62]

However, this reading of the speech is contingent on an understanding of the epidemic as only being important in terms of narrow concepts of risk groups and modes of transition, not as being important from a human rights perspective and as highlighting the real emotional and social-economic isolation caused by AIDS-related discrimination, in the sense that Steinburg suggested at the time. Moreover, just as anti-apartheid gay rights activists in the 1980s saw racial discrimination as equally wrong as homophobia on the grounds of universal human rights, early openly HIV positive gay rights activists argued against discrimination less from the point of view of their sexual orientation and more from a universal, rights-based perspective: from the point of view that *all* HIV positive people should not be discriminated against on the basis of their HIV status.

A second male heterosexual HIV positive man spoke in Zulu to the crowd but refused to be recorded or filmed:[63] a factor which probably blunted the political impact of the talk. However, both of these early public first person statements on living with HIV, coupled with Barry

62 *Ibid.*, p. 1.

63 *Ibid.*, p. 1. Lynn Dalrymple of the NGO Drama in AIDS Education (DramAidE) who attended that conference mentioned to me in a conversation in Durban on the 4 December 2003 that she remembers this man as having been a Zambian Zulu-speaking HIV positive man who almost a decade later denounced Mbeki's denialism as having made him stop taking his anti-retroviral combination therapy at a Treatment Action Campaign Congress in 2000.

McGeary's court action, were perhaps the first instances of a new and powerful constituency asserting itself: the HIV positive citizen who demanded his/her rights. In post-apartheid South Africa, this constituency would grow and become a powerful political voice against AIDS-related discrimination. As the first few brave openly HIV positive AIDS activists stepped forward, it showed that the right to confidentiality did not have to mean enforced secrecy, nor did people living with HIV have to give all their power to the doctors treating them; they had the right to either hide or reveal their HIV status, showing their agency in forming strategies and tactics to resist AIDS-related discrimination.

Yet this early activism by people living with HIV was by no means the most militant internationally. By the late 1980s, militant AIDS activism by people living with HIV for the development of HIV treatments had reached fever pitch in the United States: with heckling of scientists not seen to be doing enough, accusations of complicity in genocide against people living with HIV and unethical conduct of AZT drug trials and occupation of Federal Drug Administration (FDA) offices.[64] This kind of militant treatment activism would be echoed a decade later in TAC's 2003 civil disobedience campaign, which attempted to place charges of culpable homicide against Health Minister Manto-Tshabalala Msimang and Trade and Industry Minister Alec Erwin.

Just over a decade ago, the NACOSA conference resolved to form a National AIDS Council of South Africa, representing all the groups and regions, a resolution which the AIDS Consortium's Cameron participated in drafting.[65] Whereas the AIDS Consortium would have been a natural candidate to represent AIDS NGOs, there was distrust towards the AIDS Consortium because it was "... perceived to be dominated by male homosexuals and to be concerned with issues more related to gay rights than to an AIDS campaign: several gay men expressed their disapproval of this confusing of two issues and their personal commitment to the campaign in response to the heterosexual epidemic."[66]

64 Ronald Bayer and Gerald M. Oppenheimer, *AIDS Doctors: Voices from the Epidemic. An Oral History.* (Oxford: Oxford University Press, 2000), pp. 138-140.

65 Interview with Salim Abdool Karim, 15 September 2003, University of Natal, Durban.

66 "Report", p. 4.

Despite the homophobic rumblings from some of its delegates, the first NACOSA Conference kick-started a process lasting just under eighteen months through which a broadly consultative National AIDS Plan would be debated. Despite Fleming's description of the existence of hostility towards a kind of "white gay cabal", which some delegates saw as running the AIDS Consortium, and general hostility he picked up towards the Progressive Primary Health Care Network (PPHCN), representatives from both groups were later elected to represent the NGO sector on the NACOSA steering committee.[67] Early AIDS activists tested the democracy and potential of transition era political and legal spaces just as TAC activists would, just under a decade later, test the potential of democratic institutions and legal spaces to deliver on socio-economic rights outlined in the new Constitution which was fashioned in the mid-1990s under a gathering dark cloud of steadily rising new HIV infections.

Yet while a tiny group of gay rights activists were being open about their status to combat AIDS-related discrimination, it was heavily stigmatised among straight African young people who were increasingly becoming infected. Indeed, HIV positive people were routinely counselled that their status was confidential, which may have been interpreted as meaning an enforced secret. Confidentiality was seen by PPHC activists, such as Nikki Schaay, as "hindering" the Community AIDS Workers' work as they could not encourage HIV positive people to draw on their existing support structures:

> Another problem is HIV-positive people or people living with AIDS are discriminated against and often isolated by the community. There is a lot of pain and silence that that person would have to live with ... The issue of confidentiality often hinders our work ... What can we do if we know someone is HIV positive and we know that he/she is unable to tell his/her lover, family or friends? That person needs support...Because of the potential discrimination that that person could face if his/her HIV status was known, and because we respect the individual's confidentiality we feel our work is slowed down.[68]

67 CHP Resource Room, "Update on NACOSA", *AIDS Bulletin,* 2, 1 (1993), p. 1.

68 *Ibid.*, p. 4.

In her 1996 critique of the Kwa-Zulu Natal Health Department's policy of confidentiality (which was in line with the National AIDS Plan devised by NACOSA), Gill Siedel argued that many patients and health workers in the province interpreted their right to confidentiality as meaning "your status is your secret", akin to the secrecy of an individual's vote in the first democratic election, an interpretation which may have reduced prospects of de-stigmatising the disease.[69] The flip side of this interpretation of confidentiality was evident in gay AIDS activists who began revealing their status at an early stage, a political strategy, which enabled them to get anti-discrimination onto the agenda of NACOSA if not (yet) out onto the streets.

5. Out and Open in the Streets: TAC as a Post-Apartheid, Rights-Based and Patient-Driven Movement

> To talk about human rights but not mention treatment and that's basically like saying talk about other rights and [do] not talk about right to life, which is ridiculous.
>
> *Interview with Promise Mthembu*[70]

In earlier sections of this chapter I have tried to show how TAC shares historical continuities with late 1980s and early 1990s anti-apartheid gay rights activism such as the emphasis on universal human rights-based discourse and early openness of such activists about their HIV status. However, it is important to note that despite its roots in early AIDS activism in the late apartheid and transition eras TAC is also fundamentally a *post-apartheid* political creature, which has used entirely new political and legal spaces created in post-apartheid South Africa. There are two main historical developments post 1994, which I wish to point to which have fundamentally contributed to TAC's emergence, agenda and the strategies it adopted: the development of a powerful combination of antiretroviral drug therapy (HIV treatment)[71] and the adoption

69 Gill Siedel, "Confidentiality and Gender Status in KwaZulu-Natal, South Africa: Implications, resistances and challenges", *Health Policy and Planning*, 11, 4, (1996), p. 423.

70 Interview with Promise Mthembu, 19 August 2003, Durban.

71 This is generally referred to in medical circles as Highly Active Anti-retroviral Therapy (HAART), it can also be referred to as ART (antiretroviral

of South Africa's democratic Constitution enshrining socio-economic rights.

As has been discussed above, TAC was formed in 1998 by Achmat, partially in response to the death of a stalwart of the gay liberation movement, Simon Nkoli. Simultaneously, the stoning to death of openly HIV positive AIDS activist Gugu Dlamini for revealing her HIV status mobilised HIV positive activists in the KwaZulu-Natal region, to begin lobbying for equal HIV treatment access, which in turn linked them with TAC simultaneously being formed by anti-apartheid, gay rights activists in Cape Town.[72]

TAC aimed to widen access to anti-retroviral drugs for prevention of mother-to-child-transmission (MTCT), post-exposure prophylaxis following sexual assault and for use in combination drug therapy. TAC is not entirely historically unique. Like the AIDS Consortium in the early 1990s, TAC is a broad-based network, which includes unions, churches, gay rights groups, health-workers and doctors. Also in common with the AIDS Consortium it frames its campaigns in terms of rights-based discourse. TAC has also used similar tactics, such as openness about HIV infection, litigation, and attracting media attention for its campaigns, albeit on a much grander scale involving mass-openness, the international media and the Constitutional Court. This demonstrates further the value of seeing recent events in the context of the history of AIDS activism in the first decade of the epidemic.

TAC's post-apartheid campaign for wider access to HIV treatment was necessitated by two factors blocking access to HIV treatment: pharmaceutical industry profiteering through protection of patent monopolies, and the rejection of the efficacy and safety of HIV treatment by several key figures in government, such as the President and Health Minister, due to their adherence to AIDS denialism.

The new, powerful and very expensive HIV treatment worked by suppressing viral replication and allowing for immune system recovery. This scientific breakthrough, which was announced in 1996, changed HIV from an irrevocable terminal illness to a manageable chronic condition in the wealthy Northern countries. However, the pharmaceutical industry kept the price of these medicines unaffordable in developing

therapy) or ARVs (antiretrovirals). TAC has tended to refer to it simply as "HIV treatment."

72 Interview with Promise Mthembu, 19 August 2003, Durban.

countries in the South with a high HIV prevalence, such as South Africa, through abusing their patent monopolies.

In 2001, the Pharmaceutical Manufacturers Association representing 47 multinational pharmaceutical companies took the South African government to court to block the passing of the *Medicines Act* of 1997, which would have allowed for the production and importation of cheaper generic essential medicines, such as antiretroviral drugs in South Africa. TAC supported the government in the case acting as "friend of the court" and helped to mobilise local and international activist support and global public opinion in favour of the government. Due to international public pressure and the negative perceptions the case generated about the pharmaceutical industry, the case was dropped. TAC subsequently successfully pursued action against industry abuse of patent monopolies to inflate prices at the Competition Commission against GlaxoSmithKline (which produces antiretrovirals such as AZT and 3TC) and Boehringer Ingelheim (which produces Nevirapine).

Wider treatment access was also blocked by the bitter and drawn-out struggle between government and TAC activists over government denialism and HIV treatment access, which lasted from 1999 to 2003. President Thabo Mbeki, supported by Health Minister Manto Tshabala-la-Msimang, questioned HIV as the viral cause of AIDS, the accuracy of HIV tests, and the safety and efficacy of HIV treatment, a set of beliefs that AIDS activists referred to as denialism.[73] This denialism was driven by Mbeki's belief that AIDS was a post-colonial, racist conspiracy to discredit African sexuality.[74] Government endorsement of AIDS denialism, due to its rejection of the safety and efficacy of combination anti-retroviral drug therapy, was in turn a crucial factor blocking equal access to combination anti-HIV drug therapy for people living with HIV.[75]

While TAC may not be the first instance of rights-based, patient-driven AIDS activism in South African history, it is certainly historically unique in terms of its militancy. On the back of its success in forcing the

73 M. Mbali, "HIV/AIDS policy-making in post-apartheid South Africa", In Daniel, J., Habib, A. and Southall, *State of the Nation: South Africa, 2003-2004* (Cape Town: Human Sciences Research Council Press), pp. 318-320.

74 M. Mbali, "AIDS discourses and the South African state: Government denialism and post-apartheid AIDS policy-making", *Transformation* (2004).

75 The other important factor being the pharmaceutical industry's refusal to permit production and importation of cheaper generic drugs. M. Mbali, "HIV/AIDS Policy-making", pp. 321-3.

government to roll out Nevirapine for prevention of MTCT, at its 2002 Congress TAC decided to push government to adopt a National Treatment Plan to roll out anti-retroviral combination drug therapy in the public sector. Through its trade union federation ally, the Congress of South African Trade Unions (COSATU), it forced its Plan onto the negotiating table of National Economic Development and Labour Council (NEDLAC), a major socio-economic policy negotiating forum involving government, labour, business and civil society. When government withdrew from the negotiations in 2003, TAC embarked on a civil disobedience campaign, where its members volunteered to be arrested for non-violent protest.[76]

TAC's militancy in the post-apartheid era, as expressed in its civil disobedience campaign can be partially explained by the fact that medical breakthroughs in treatment and prevention of HIV increased the stakes in fighting AIDS related discrimination. Whereas previous struggles were about confidentiality and equality, in the struggle for treatment life itself was at stake, which meant more radical strategies had to be adopted. In 1999, Cameron, by then a supreme court of appeals judge revealed his HIV positive status to protest at the fact that only a tiny minority of extremely wealthy people living with HIV, such as himself, could afford drugs: he had essentially bought something which he thought should be freely available to all, the right to live.[77]

For many TAC activists, fighting for the right to live through access to treatment made openness worth the risks it entailed. The brave openness of activists like Achmat and Justice Cameron put a 'human face' on the epidemic and made the arguments for treatment access as basic an appeal at an ethical level as "a person dying of starvation asking you for bread".[78] But as Achmat argued from the outset, generation of compassion or pity has not been TAC's number one goal. It is the realisation of the right to life and health for HIV positive people, as equal

76 I have described and discussed all these events elsewhere. See: M. Mbali, "HIV/AIDS Policy-making."

77 Cameron famously revealed both his gay sexual orientation and his HIV positive status during hearings on his appointment to the Supreme Court of Appeals. Given his years of dedicated gay rights and AIDS activism, in hindsight the revelation of neither fact should have come as a particular surprise.

78 This apt characterisation came from my interview with Salim Abdool Karim: Interview with Salim Abdool Karim, 15 September 2003, University of Natal, Durban.

citizens.[79] Similarly, TAC is unique in its ability to use the post-apartheid Constitution, enshrining as it does socio-economic rights, such as the right to access to healthcare, as a powerful legal and political tool. A tool which it successfully used in a 2001 Constitutional Court challenge which forced the government to roll-out Nevirapine to prevent mother-to-child-transmission.[80]

At the time of writing, in November 2004, TAC had successfully forced the government to relent on developing a National Treatment Plan to provide anti-retrovirals in the public sector. Critics such as TAC argue that government appears to lack the political will to provide adequate infrastructure and human resource development required to rapidly roll-out the treatment and make the plan a success. Its most recent "Right to Know Campaign" has also criticised the government for not being transparent about its patient targets and the timetable for the roll-out. Despite the roll-out's ongoing shortcomings, in forcing the government to develop a National Treatment Plan and being the roll-out of HIV treatment, TAC has been one of the most successful post-apartheid social movements.

6. Concluding Remarks

Placing TAC in the longer history of rights-based, patient-driven AIDS activism can help to explain its political nature in several crucial ways. Firstly, the fact that anti-apartheid, gay rights activists played such an important role in early patient driven AIDS activism helps to explain why the movement is led by a former anti-apartheid gay rights activist. TAC's emphasis on universal human rights also mirrors the location of gay rights within universal human rights discourse by anti-apartheid gay rights activists in the late 1980s and early 1990s. Also, the emphasis of TAC activists such as Achmat on fighting for treatment "from within" ANC structures mirrors Nkoli's gay rights strategy in the 1980s

79 For instance, Achmat argued at a public lecture at University of Natal Durban in April 2003 that HIV positive people do not demand pity, they demand rights. He was in turn implicitly arguing for a shift away from early tear-jerking "AIDS testimonials" given by NAPWA activists in the late 1990s towards more militant TAC style activism.

80 For an excellent account of this see G.J. Annas, "The right to health and the Nevirapine case in South Africa", *New England Journal of Medicine,* 348, 2003.

and 1990s of pushing for gay rights from within the UDF and later ANC structures. Similarly, Achmat's call for TAC's campaign to be based on openness was not the first time the strategy had been used. Anti-apartheid gay rights activists living with HIV had first begun to reveal their status at political forums such as NACOSA to push for AIDS policy to be rights-based in the early 1990s.

What is new and specifically *post-apartheid* about TAC are its demands for access to new drug therapies which did not exist until after 1996 and its use of South Africa's new democratic constitution to forward its aims. Furthermore, it is far more militant than any earlier forms of rights-based, patient-driven activism and it has had far greater success in encouraging mass-openness.

As legally, philosophically and politically contingent as rights-based discourses may be, TAC has powerfully deployed this rhetoric to push for policies that have literally saved lives. Human rights-based discourses have also been used differently by AIDS activists over time in South Africa. Whereas they were initially invoked mainly to promote confidentiality, the rights arguments are now used by a movement led by openly HIV positive activists to push for access to treatment. This shows that the invocation of human rights-based discourse by civil society is contested, changing and context bound; which is not to discount its potential as a political strategy. This history of patient-driven, rights-based AIDS activism also demonstrates that in a Habermasian sense communication in civil society sustains and maintains the public sphere and gives meaning and substance to first generation political rights; just as AIDS activists in the transition era tested the lobbying and advocacy potential of new transition-era negotiating spaces such as NACOSA, TAC has taken its fight to new democratic spaces such as the Constitutional Court.

It is unclear whether TAC's success in invoking rights-based discourses in new democratic spaces will be replicated by other new social movements pushing for the realisation of socio-economic rights. For instance, will they be able to marshal the kind of funds and legal support TAC has used in its court challenges if they wish to pursue similar action? What sort of success could new social movements which contradict aspects of the Constitution, such as the Landless Peoples' Movement, which argues for expropriation of land (which contradicts the Constitution's property-rights clause) expect in such court action? Certainly, TAC reveals how socio-economic rights on paper can in certain instances be translated into rights in reality through civil society activism.

A comprehensive oral and archival history of TAC has yet to be written, however, as I have tried to show, there is a longer political history of rights-based, AIDS activism by anti-apartheid gay rights, HIV positive patients, a legacy which has formed the socio-political basis for TAC's patient-driven, contemporary activism for the realisation of the socio-economic right to access to health care. The history of rights-based, patient driven AIDS activism demonstrates that history can be made through the exercise of agency in struggle. However, it remains to be seen whether AIDS activists exercising their agency will continue to successfully push for further rights-based AIDS policy gains, and it also remains to be seen how successfully the roll-out of HIV treatment will proceed.

10. Communal Land Rights and Democracy in Post-Apartheid South Africa

Ben Cousins and Aninka Claassens***

1. Introduction

This chapter explores the connections between communal land rights and democracy in South Africa, with a particular focus on the recently approved but hotly contested Communal Land Rights Act of 2004. Property rights and their redistribution are core elements of government's land reform programme, but what form these rights should take in the former reserves (or "communal areas"), where they should vest, and which local institutions should administer such rights, remain controversial issues. Questions of democratic governance arise, given the central role of local bodies in the realisation of formal rights, and continuing debate over the roles and powers of traditional authorities in local government and land administration. These are the substantive aspects of the politics of communal land rights.

Also relevant to the politics of land rights is the processual dimension. This chapter analyses the highly politicised and polarised process through which the Communal Land Rights Act was drafted and then steered through parliament by government officials and representatives of the ruling party, in the face of widespread opposition to the draft law from a range of community groups, NGOs, and statutory organisations. This experience illustrates clearly how South Africa's new constitution has opened up space for a renewed politics of land rights and the active participation of citizens in policy-making processes, but also points to the limitations of an activism focused primarily on legislative and par-

* Programme for Land and Agrarian Studies, School of Government, University of the Western Cape, P. Bag X15, Bellville 7535, South Africa <bcousins@uwc.ac.za>.

** Consultant <aninka@icon.co.za>.

Peris Jones and Kristian Stokke (eds.), Democratising Development, *ISBN 90 04 14821 3, pp. 245-270.*

liamentary arenas. Discussion of these issues is located within current debates on the character of democracy and citizenship in post-apartheid South Africa.

2. Debating Democracy

Despite global dominance of the liberal, representative version of democracy, with its primary focus on formal institutions and procedures, alternative conceptions that emphasise questions of *substance* continue to resonate. For advocates of participatory democracy, the term is empty if it co-exists comfortably with unequal access to resources and opportunities, and if popular participation in politics is limited to periodic voting for a decision-making elite. This is certainly the case in post-apartheid South Africa, where deep-seated poverty and inequality persist, and the ranks of a large "underclass" of unskilled, unemployed and marginalized people continue to swell (Seekings and Nattrass 2002). The continuing struggle for substantive freedom for the majority means that the limits of liberal democracy are often questioned by activists, dissenting intellectuals and social movements. These groups have made use of the political space created through the founding institutions of the new democracy - the Constitution and the Bill of Rights – to call for a *deepening* of democracy, in part in order to address the developmental challenge more effectively.

Liberal democracy is also sometimes questioned in the context of custom and "traditional" culture. What do citizenship and rights (for example, of equality and non-discrimination) mean in the context of "traditional communities"? This question was at the centre of heated controversies during parliamentary debates on the Traditional Leadership Framework and Governance Act of 2003 and the Communal Land Rights Act of 2004, and in recent constitutional court cases on customary marriage and women's rights. Are customary values and democratic norms inherently conflictual? Can they be married through a "democratization of tradition", guided by the Bill of Rights, or perhaps through a return to "African participatory democracy", as some traditional leaders argue (Holomisa 2003)?

An important distinction is that between *democratic institutions* and *democratic politics.* The former are emphasised in most strains of political science, which stresses the formal or procedural aspects of democracy. Democratic politics, in contrast, refers to "the struggle for power or for access to rulers and collective goods" (Luckham *et al.*, 2000: 10).

In traditions of democratisation that stress citizen participation over institutional form, a key focus is the "deep politics" of society, a politics focused on the lived conditions of socio-economic existence. Following Beetham (1994), a truly democratic politics requires not only political competition, but also the principles of popular control (over government) and political equality (amongst all citizens). These in turn require increasing the scope for citizen participation, maximising accountability and transparency of holders of public office, guaranteeing equal political and civil rights as well as the basic social and economic entitlements that allow them to exercise their rights (Luckham *et al.* 2000:11).

The civic capacity of those citizens to engage in political activity and influence decision-making is clearly of central importance. Electoral participation, although vitally important in a functioning democracy, is not the most important form of political voice, since it has little to do with the key policy issues facing society (Friedman 2004: 2). Elections in South Africa are determined largely by identity (race identity in the main) not by debates about policy choices in relation to poverty and inequality. The key problem, according to Friedman, is neither the indifference of the ruling party nor the lack of a vibrant civil society. Civil society has not become voiceless since 1994, far from it; the HIV/AIDS issue demonstrates clearly how well-organised activist groupings such as the TAC are able to influence government policies. The problem, rather, is that relatively few South African citizens are able to organize themselves to participate in public policy debates with the potential to influence policy.

A key symptom of the problem is the mismatch between the needs and realities of the poor and anti-poverty policies, for example in relation to housing policy and the erroneous assumption that poor people will benefit from the availability of mortgage finance (*ibid.*: 3). Democracy in South Africa is in trouble because "until poor people effectively participate in our democracy, poverty and inequality will not be addressed adequately"(*ibid.*:1). But poverty makes it difficult for the poor to participate in public life since they are concerned above all with day-to-day survival, in informal and dispersed settings that make it hard for them to organise themselves to act collectively. The key challenge is thus one of *enhancing citizen capacity through organisation*, so that the poor, who are in the majority, can directly represent themselves in the policy debate. The policy process around the Communal Land Rights Act of 2004 illustrates both the potential for such organisation and how difficult it is to influence the outcomes of such a process.

3. Constituting Democratic Citizens

More fundamental even than the issue of capacity, however, is the question of political identity and the formation of "democratic citizens". van Lieres suggests that:

> ... any alternative approach to democracy must confront the deeper political problem of how people who are excluded come to develop a sense of their own participation as worthwhile and as binding in a wider context. ... A 'bottom up' approach must be linked to an understanding of politics as processes of contestation over inclusion and exclusion by changing actors who themselves are not always cohesive.... it must be accompanied by a problematisation of the idea that the opening up of political space automatically guarantees democratic self–representation. (van Lieres: pers. comm.)

Comaroff and Comaroff (2004) see emerging forms of identity politics in post-apartheid South Africa as threatening to disrupt the premises of the Constitution and the Bill of Rights. Conflicts over issues such as initiation rituals, inheritance, succession and land rights bring into question the sovereignty of the liberal state, which is contested by traditional authority. While for the liberal, modernist state the generic citizen of post-apartheid South Africa may be "the rights-bearing individual inscribed in the new Constitution", in ethno-polities dominated by traditional leaders, the language is that of "subjects and collective being" (*ibid.*:6). Even though traditional authorities are recognized, as are rights to practice a group's culture or religion, these "may not be exercised in a manner inconsistent with any [other] provision of the Bill of Rights". Does this set up an irreconcilable contradiction between culture ("things African") and the Constitution?

The Comaroffs note an interesting feature of these conflicts between citizenship rights and culture – the increasing resort to courts of law to resolve them. This is because traditional authorities have no choice, even when contesting the sovereignty of the state, but to engage with it in juridical terms, "in the idiom of rights, constitutionalism and due process". This is impacting on the law itself, and is fashioning a new jurisprudence that must deal with cultural difference.

In our view, however, the Comaroffs give undue emphasis to the tensions between citizenship and subjecthood, and exaggerate the prevalence of culture-based conflict in contemporary South Africa. Their notion of a contradiction between the Constitution and "the age-old traditions, customs and cultures observed by millions of black South Africans" seems dangerously essentialist, with echoes of apartheid-era discourses of race and ethnicity. Culture, as their work more generally acknowledges (and indeed emphasises) is much more dynamic, more actively constructed in character and responsive to changing political and economic context and circumstance. Similarly, van Lieres (forthcoming) stresses ethnically based organising by marginal groups to advance their interests (as in the case of land claims by the Khoe-San), but her analysis neglects the large number of cases where members of rural communities pursue land claims with explicit reference to their rights in the Constitution, and narrate their collective efforts to resist dispossession as part of the struggle for a democratic South Africa that would protect their rights, provide them with full citizenship and secure their livelihoods. Parliamentary submissions on the Communal Land Rights Act in November 2003 also bear witness to the centrality of notions of "democratic rights" in local political struggles over land.

The increasing use of litigation in instances where custom and rights seem to contradict each other, may mean that jurisprudence is evolving ways of recognising differences between "free and equal" citizens, as the Comaroffs suggest, but also has effects in the opposite direction: it means that the proponents of "tradition" are having to accommodate notions of gender equality, for example, and make arguments about the accountability of traditional authority in decidedly democratic terms (Holomisa 2004). This can open up political space for local gender activists, and thus for democratic contestations over the "emancipatory possibilities" within tradition (Mamdani 1996).

4. The Politics of Post-apartheid Land Policy

Both in the "struggle years" and since 1994, the land sector has seen diverse discourses, practices and processes invoking democracy in one form or another (Cousins 2004b). Narratives of popular participation, accountability and socio-economic rights have contended with *real politik* considerations of inclusive stakeholder negotiation and bargaining; notions of "continuing struggle" and popular mobilisation have been cut across by emerging discourses of "lobbying and advocacy" to influence government policy. Concerns to build the capacity of rural people to claim their rights and decide on their own futures have had to battle with approaches to project planning that involve token consultation with "beneficiaries". A strong initial emphasis by the new democratic government on wide consultation within relatively transparent policy processes has given way over time to a narrower, more technocratic approach to policy development.

The 1994-1996 period, in the land and other sectors, was characterised by the holding of an enormous number of workshops, conferences and working groups, the drafting of a swathe of policy papers and new laws, and heated debates between diverse interest groups. This was the heyday of "participatory" policy-making. By 1997 and 1998, however, most ministries had produced either Green or White Papers on key policy issues, legislative processes were in full swing, and the emphasis increasingly shifted to implementation. Policy debates continued, but a certain amount of workshop fatigue had set in, and the willingness of government to consider new ideas was in decline.

In May 1999 Thoko Didiza was appointed as Minister of Land Affairs and Agriculture in place of Derek Hanekom. She immediately initiated a review of land reform policy, imposed a moratorium on new redistribution projects, and scrapped a Land Rights Bill on communal tenure reform that was in its final stages of drafting. In February 2000 new strategic directions for land reform were announced, and although some aspects were widely welcomed (such as increasing the pace of land restitution) others proved highly controversial (Turner and Ibsen 2000). In particular, the new emphasis in redistribution policy on de-racialising commercial agriculture and creating opportunities for emergent farmers, rather than on reducing poverty and enhancing the livelihood opportunities of the poor and marginalized, provoked criticism. In addition, the announcement suggested that communal tenure reform would be pursued through the "transfer of state land to tribes", arousing fears that traditional leaders would be the main beneficiaries at the expense of ordinary rural residents. In striking contrast to the earlier period, policy making was undertaken without any significant consultation with NGOs, community groups or other stakeholders, and no public consultation forums were established.

A key arena for the politics of land policy since 1994 has been lawmaking. The legal dimensions have loomed large in part because of the use of law by activists, lawyers and communities as a "weapon of struggle" in resisting forced removals during the 1970s and 1980s. This is also probably one reason for the centrality of rights-based approaches to land reform in South Africa. Opportunities for direct participation in the formulation of land reform laws has often been limited to (i) an "inner circle" of drafters, selected for their legal expertise (but also sympathy with the thrust of legislation as defined by government); and (ii) elected members of parliament. Nevertheless, land sector NGOs and the Legal Resources Centre often played key roles in drafting new land laws in the early years of the new government. Public consultation took place in workshops with stakeholders, meetings to provide information on draft legislation and to solicit responses, and hearings convened by parliament's portfolio committees. In recent years, however, opportunities to contribute to drafting processes have been few and far between and this has contributed to the shift to a more adversarial relationship between civil society and government.

5. Reforming "Communal Tenure"

Debate on land tenure reform in the former reserves, or communal areas, is informed by different understandings of the property regimes currently in place. Some clarification of the key terms is thus required. Calling these tenure systems "communal" is in some respects a misnomer, since it is often taken to imply common ownership of *all* resources and collective production, which is rarely the case. What "communal" generally means is a degree of community control over who is allowed into the group, thereby qualifying for an allocation of land for residence and cropping, as well as rights of access to the common property resources used by the group. Groups often restrict alienation of land to outsiders, and thus seek to maintain the identity, coherence and livelihood security of the group and its members. In these systems allocations of residential and arable land usually result in strong and secure rights for individuals or families, the household being the basic unit of production.

The overall character of communal tenure is that rights to land and natural resources are socially and politically embedded, and as a result are systems of *shared and relative rights*, with *flexible boundaries* between a variety of social units, but nevertheless conferring *high levels of security of tenure.* Relative rights are nested within a hierarchy of social and administrative units or levels. Okoth-Ogendo (2002:2) puts it thus:

> ... the [African] Commons are managed and protected by a social hierarchy. ... the family, the clan and lineage, and the community ... are decision-making levels designed to respond to issues regarding allocation, use and

> management of resources comprised within the Commons on the basis of scale, need, function and process.

Western ideas about property tend to equate it with "ownership", and even more narrowly, with private ownership. Western legal systems often do not recognize non-western systems of property rights, and this has been widely used to discriminate against indigenous land rights holders. One important difference between western and non-western systems of property is the degree of exclusion involved. Key features of private property and the "ownership" model are clearly defined (often surveyed) physical boundaries between areas of land, unambiguous definitions of who has what kinds of rights and who does not, and the exclusion of non-owners. As Peters (1998) points out, this is not necessarily the case with non-western systems, where inclusivity and the "right not to be excluded" are often core features.

6. The Legacy of Colonial and Apartheid Land Policies

By the early 1990s a range of problems afflicted communal tenure systems in rural South Africa, and these persist today, forming the backdrop to contemporary policy debates and struggles. The fundamental legacy of past interventions in systems of communal land rights is the "second-class" status of these rights in law, which provides few protections from arbitrary decisions by those wielding authority over land allocation or land use. Underlying historical rights of occupation have never been adequately recognised in law. Closely linked to the weak legal status of black land rights is the overcrowding and forced overlapping of rights that derives from South Africa's history of conquest, forced removals and evictions. While some accommodation between original residents and new arrivals often took place in the apartheid years, when both groups resisted forced removals, latent tensions over land rights have emerged strongly since the advent of democracy (Claassens 2001).

A consequence of past policies is the partial breakdown of the legitimacy of group systems of land tenure. One manifestation of the malaise is corruption and abuse of authority by chiefs and Tribal Authorities (Levin and Mkhabela 1997; Ntsebeza 1999), sometimes challenged by civic organisations or local residents associations, which can lead to a vacuum in legitimate authority. Tenure insecurity is increased by the near-collapse of land administration systems in the former homelands, where magistrates no longer play a role in land matters. PTOs are not issued in some areas, in others the procedures followed are *ad hoc* and unclear, and registers are often not kept up to date (Turner 1999). In peri-urban areas that are nominally under traditional tenure, as well as in some densely settled rural areas, it is not uncommon to find shack-lords allocating land in return for cash and warlords building a power base through control over land. Discrimination against women in the allocation of land and the holding of rights is a fundamental feature of tenure systems in most of rural South Africa (Meer 1997).

Lack of clarity on land rights is constraining infrastructure and service provision in rural areas, and there are tensions between local government bodies and traditional authorities over the allocation of land for development projects (*e.g.* housing, irrigation schemes, business centres, tourist infrastructure) (Oomen 2000: 66). It constrains effective management of common property resources, which are key to rural livelihoods. Other problems include constraints on investment in smallholder irrigation schemes, poor performance of agricultural projects, under-utilisation of arable land, and tensions over mineral rights or benefits from mining on communal land.

How widespread are these problems? The available evidence suggests that tenure-related problems tend to receive recognition only when the underlying lack of clarity in respect of legal status is brought to the fore by development planning or investment projects on communal land, such as Spatial Development Initiatives (Kepe 2001), or within land reform programmes such as restitution or redistribution. The majority of occupants of communal land have *de facto* tenure security, because existing systems, many of them now informal as a result of the breakdown of administrative systems, work reasonably well on a day-to-day basis. However, there is also evidence that these systems are failing to facilitate efficient use of arable land (*e.g.* through sharecropping or land rental) and that lack of clarity is negatively affecting management of common property resources (Turner 1999).

Tenure insecurity in the communal areas of South Africa thus takes two forms: (a) a relatively small number of high profile cases where conflicts and contestations over land rights and competing jurisdictions are explicit and obvious, and (b) a larger number of chronic, low profile situations where lack of clarity and certainty are constraining land-based livelihoods, but no immediate threat to occupancy and use is evident.

7. The Land Rights Bill of 1999

Between 1994 and 1998 the tenure reform programme of the Department of Land Affairs focused largely on securing the rights of labour tenants and farm workers, as well as creating a new form of legal entity for holding land rights in common Communal Property Associations. Since 1998 the main focus has been reform of communal tenure, both in the former "Coloured" reserves and in the former African "homeland" areas, and drafting of a new law to provide improved security of tenure in communal systems, and thus give effect to the Bill of Rights (sec. 25 (6)):

> A person or community whose tenure of land is legally insecure as a result of past racially discriminatory laws or practices is entitled, to the extent provide by an Act of Parliament, either to tenure which is legally secure or to comparable redress.

Drafting of a Land Rights Bill (LRB) was initiated in early 1998.[1] It attempted to provide full recognition of the underlying land rights of people who occupy areas registered as "state land" in the Deeds Registry. The rights were to be vested in the members of group systems, not in institutions such as legal entities, the chieftaincy or Tribal Authorities. Group systems had to provide "bottom line" protections for their members, consistent with constitutional principles of democracy, equality (including gender equality) and due process. In situations of overlapping and contested rights, transfer would only take place after a rights inquiry.

At first policy was based on a paradigm of transferring ownership from the state to its rightful owners. However, experience in a number of test cases revealed inherent difficulties (Claassens 2000), most notably in relation to defining the unit of ownership in communal areas: should land be transferred to "tribes", or "nations", often consisting of hundreds of thousands of people, or to wards, or to villages, or to groups at Tribal Authority level? Vesting land ownership in the larger group could make it difficult for smaller groups to make meaningful decisions about land within their own localities; conversely, vesting rights at the local level might deny some rights inherent in the larger group. These questions derive from the nested character of land rights in communal systems.[2]

---

1 Both the authors of this chapter were members of the drafting team.

2 See Okoth-Ogendo (2002) and Cousins (2004).

The test cases showed that the prospect of transfer triggers intractable conflicts over boundaries and membership.

As a result of these difficulties, the drafters of the LRB moved towards a paradigm based on statutory rights which are secure but do not convey full ownership. The law would create a category of protected rights, for which the majority of those occupying land in the former "homelands" would qualify. The Minister of Land Affairs would continue to be the nominal owner of the land, but with strictly delimited powers. Protected rights would vest in the individuals who use, occupy or have access to land, but in group systems, these rights would be relative to "group rules". These in turn would require the definition of the boundaries of the group, but:

> ... 'boundaries' must be seen as flexible. In other words, the boundary of the group would be determined with reference to who (which group of people) is affected by the particular decision. Thus, if the decision is about a change in grazing practice then the people affected by the change must be consulted, not the entire 'tribe.' (Claassens 2000:255)

Protected rights, defined by statute, would thus confirm in law the rights of the 2.4 million households (the *de facto* rights holders), occupying and using land in the communal areas of South Africa, without having to first resolve, in each and every case, disputes over the extent of rights.

There is a constitutional imperative for the state to provide tenure security or comparable redress to those whose tenure was made insecure as a result of previous policies, such as forced removals and the overlapping rights that resulted. The LRB attempted to provide a mechanism for unpacking these situations through recognition of legitimate claims, albeit of differential strengths, and allowing for "tenure awards" to protected rights holders who cannot all be accommodated on the same land, commensurate with their rights (Makopi 2000).

8. The Communal Land Rights Bill of 2002

In June 1999 a new Minister of Agriculture and Land Affairs took office, and work on the LRB was stopped. The minister's view was that the LRB was too complex, that it would be too costly to implement, and that it assumed that a nanny state would protect people's rights on their behalf. She was in favour of a law that transferred title of state land to "tribes", that gave a key role in land administration to traditional leaders, and that did not require such high levels of institutional support to rights holders.

Following several false starts a Communal Lands Rights Bill (CLRB) was drafted and its key provisions and overall thrust were discussed at a national land tenure conference in Durban in 2001, attended buy over 800 delegates.[3] This third draft included several provisions that appeared to privilege traditional leaders, for example it allowed "traditional communities" operating under "customary law", as well as authorised representatives (chiefs), to be recognised as "juristic persons" for the transfer of state land in full ownership. This pleased the traditional leader lobby at the conference, but was seen by many other participants as highly problematic, sparking heated debates.

Civil society delegates also saw the processual dimension as highly problematic. The draft Bill was not released in full either before or during the conference; only its general outlines were communicated, and many participants felt that this was not an adequate basis for discussion. Calls were made for a process of wide public consultation to be initiated before further drafting took place, and senior officials at the conference, together with the Minister, committed the department to such consultation. No such consultation processes were initiated, however, and in June 2002 a civil society grouping launched their own consultation project. This was aimed at promoting awareness of the Bill amongst affected communities in five provinces, and assisting community members to express their views on tenure problems and on the reform proposals embodied in the CLRB.

The project was organised jointly by the national office of the National Land Committee (NLC) and the Programme for Land and Agrarian Studies (PLAAS) of the University of the Western Cape. Partners include NLC provincial affiliates, the Trust for Community Outreach and Education, the Legal Resources Centre, the Transkei Land Service Organisation, the Legal Entity Assessment Project, and others. Ten large meetings were held between October 2002 and June 2003, with over 75 communities represented and around 800 people in attendance (Claassens 2003). In each meeting discussions took place over two days, and representatives were elected to draft submissions on the Bill that would be presented to parliament.

3 In addition to the CLRB, the conference discussed the land rights of farm workers and labour tenants, as well as the linkages between land rights and rural development.

In August 2002 the CLRB was published for public comment. The Bill provided for "transfer of title" of communal land from the state to its current occupants. Complex procedures for transfer included a rights inquiry, community meetings, and adoption of community rules on tenure. Registration of these rules would convert the community into a "juristic person" capable of owning land. Once the rules were registered a land administration committee could be elected, made up of community members. Traditional leaders had to be on the committee in an *ex-officio* capacity, but could comprise no more than 25 percent of members. This was controversial: groups such as the Congress of Traditional Leaders of South Africa (Contralesa) argued for the transfer of title to traditional authorities, on the basis that they have always held land rights in trust for their communities, and that they are not inherently undemocratic and unaccountable.[4] This lobby objected vehemently to the "25 percent" rule.

Land NGOs submitted highly critical comments on the Bill to government, and many members of rural communities raised a number of objections (Claassens 2003). One key flaw identified in the bill was the underlying paradigm of a transfer of freehold title, requiring clear boundaries between communities to be drawn. This could open up and exacerbate boundary disputes and ethnic differences. In addition, community representatives, and in particular elected councillors, feared that transferring title would effectively "privatise" communal land. The common law of South Africa holds that ownership of land and infrastructure cannot be separated, and hence government refuses to provide services and infrastructure on privately owned land. The effect of a transfer of title would thus be to insulate poor rural areas from local government development programmes, forcing rural people to choose between ownership rights and development.

Other problems were identified as the long-winded and intricate procedures for transfer of title,[5] and until transfer occurred the status of people's existing rights to occupation and use would remain unclear. In addition, women's land rights were not adequately provided for. Civil

4 Patekile Holomisa, "Resolving communal land rights a vital link in reform process", *Business Day*, 21 May 2003.

5 Over 30 administrative steps were required before title could be transferred to a community, requiring a minimum of 12 months (and the likelihood that bureaucratic slippage would result in delays of at least two years).

society submissions generally approved of the provisions for awards of alternative land as a form of comparable redress for tenure insecurity, citing the need for tenure reform to contribute in a significant manner to land redistribution "beyond the 13%" of land allocated to black South Africans in the past.

9. Amendments and Debates in 2003

In response to mounting civil society criticism, the Bill was amended in several drafts between August 2002 and October 2003. In April 2003 the South African Local Government Association (SALGA), representing all the country's local government bodies, asked for a legal opinion on the powers granted in the Bill to land administration committees. This opinion expressed concerns that a "fourth tier of government" was being created, and indicated that the privatisation of communal land via titling would create difficulties around service provision by local government. In response, a June 2003 draft of the Bill introduced the provision that a "communal general plan" (*i.e.* a land use plan) must be registered with the Surveyor-General prior to any transfer of title. This would allow the Minister to reserve part of the land to the state, for the provision of infrastructure and municipal services, and it was hoped that this would be a solution to the service provision problem.

Other changes resulted from attempts to shorten the Bill, and many provisions were now to be dealt with in separate sets of regulations. Civil society critics pointed out that a critical omission was the absence of community consultation on whether or not they desired a transfer of title, or on the form and content of land rights. The Minister was given sweeping powers of determination in relation to a range of key decisions, including the boundaries of the land to be transferred to "communities". A continuing problem was the lack of clarity on how the different processes set out in the Bill (*e.g.* the drawing up of the communal general plan, the rights enquiry, the drafting of community rules, the making of determinations by the Minister) relate to one another, and in what sequence these different processes were supposed to occur. On the other hand, the Bill still did not recognise the complexity and onerous nature of the land administration tasks (registration, recording, land use and development planning, dispute resolution) to be carried out by local committees, and did not provide for dedicated support to these committees.

In a presentation to the Deputy Minister of Land Affairs and senior officials in July 2003, community members pointed out that women's land rights were not adequately secured by the Bill. For example, it provided for the registration of existing rights, which generally vest in men, without any proviso that women's rights should be asserted or registered. Earlier sections explicitly barring discrimination in community rules had disappeared. Concerns were also expressed that the status of people's land rights prior to transfer and registration remained unclear and hence potentially insecure; this called into doubt the constitutionality of the Bill.

Government drafters paid little heed to these concerns. A thirteenth draft of the Communal Land Rights Bill, similar in all important respects to the June 2003 version, was approved by Cabinet in early October 2003, and published in the government gazette. Notice was given that the Bill would be debated in parliament within a matter of weeks. However, within days another version, containing a highly contentious new provision, was submitted to and approved by Cabinet. This was in relation to the land administration committees that the Bill required all communities to establish, to "represent the community owning communal land", and which would have "ownership and administrative powers conferred on it by the rules of the community."[6] The new clause stated that where a community has a "traditional council", the functions and powers of the land administration committee "must be performed by such a council."[7]

This provision cross-referred to the Traditional Leadership and Governance Framework Bill (TLGFB) then being debated in parliament's portfolio committee on local government. This Bill (adopted by the House of Assembly on 11th November 2003, and now an Act) sets out to clarify the long-unresolved issue of the roles and powers of traditional leaders and their relationship to local government (Murray 2003). The Act provides for the establishment of "traditional councils", sets minimum requirements with which such councils must comply, and lists the functions of traditional leaders and councils. These functions are fairly "soft" (Murray 2003:11), including such roles as "facilitating develop-

6 According to section 25.3 of the Communal Land Rights Bill of 8 October 2003, these had to include allocating new rights to land, registering such rights, maintaining registers and records of rights and transactions, liaising with municipalities, resolving disputes, and other functions.

7 Section 22.2 of Communal Land Rights Bill of 8 October 2003.

ment". However, they include the wider function of "administering the affairs of the traditional community" (including in relation to land).

The final version of the TLGFB required that 40 percent of the members of the traditional councils be elected and that 30 percent be women, and these are seen as "transforming" traditional leadership to bring them into line with the country's democratic dispensation. The Act also contains a provision for a transitional arrangement which deems existing Tribal Authorities, created in terms of the Bantu Authorities Act of 1951, to be traditional councils, and gives these Authorities a year to "transform" (but without any specified sanctions should they fail to do so).

The proposal that land administration committees be traditional councils wherever these existed was greeted with jubilation by the traditional leader lobby, and considerably reduced their unhappiness over the weak and vaguely defined powers conferred on them by the TLGFB. In contrast, the new clause was met with dismay by NGOs and community groups, provoked considerable public controversy, and became one of the key aspects of the Bill that was debated in parliamentary portfolio committee hearings in November 2003.

Civil society groupings saw the new clause as the imposition of structures dominated by un-elected traditional leaders, undermining fundamental democratic rights. According to a press release of the NLC/PLAAS Community Consultation Project, the clause "deprives rural people of the right to choose who will administer their land rights". The statement pointed out that the Bantu Authorities Act, which established Tribal Authorities and gave them considerable power over rural communities, was prime apartheid legislation designed to secure rule from above, and had provoked rural revolts across South Africa in the 1950s (Mbeki 1964). Together with the sweeping powers of determination given to the Minister, this lack of choice over how a land administration committee should be composed gave the Bill an authoritarian character at odds with the strong emphasis on democratisation of decision-making within communal tenure in previous policy documents (such as the 1997 White Paper on Land Policy).

NGOs and community groups were also angry that so little consultation with rural communities had taken place, and that the new clause on traditional councils had been introduced so late in the process. It seemed to them that the Bill was being rushed through parliament at the last possible moment because of wider political dynamics and "deal-making" in the run-up to the general election of April 2004. According to Murray (2003: 15), three issues appeared to underlie government's willingness to accommodate traditional leaders: the need to avoid pre-election violence in KwaZulu-Natal;[8] the fact that traditional leaders are perceived to command votes in rural areas; and the need for government to work with traditional structures in delivering services to rural people, given the real weakness of elected local government in many rural municipalities. Murray speculates that another reason may have to do with culture and identity, since "many South Africans are in search of a political culture that feels less imposed than the one we inherited from our colonial rulers" (*ibid.*:16).

10. Parliamentary Debates

A total of 34 submissions were made to public hearings on the Bill called by the portfolio committee on Agriculture and Land Affairs, in the last two weeks of November 2003. These included 13 submissions by community groups[9] and 12 by NGOs.[10] Other bodies which presented submissions were two statutory bodies (the Commission for Gender Equality and the Human Rights Commission), a committee of parliament itself (the Joint Monitoring Committee on the Status of Women), Cosatu, two academic research institutes,[11] the Coalition of Traditional Leaders, and the railways parastatal Spoornet. Of these, 31 submissions were highly critical of the Bill on a variety of grounds, and were unanimous in calling for its withdrawal and a fresh start. Only three submissions were in favour of the Bill, those by Spoornet, the traditional leader lobby, and

8 Pre-election violence in KwaZulu-Natal had marred both the 1994 and 1999 general elections.

9 The NLC/PLAAS consultation project provided support for community groups and NGOs to prepare their submissions through joint workshops to discuss the Bill and its implications. Different views emerged on some key issues (*e.g.*, the role of chiefs), and broad consensus on others; the project did not attempt to resolve differences and the principle that diverse views could be held was accepted by all participants in these workshops.

10 The NGO grouping included the South African Council of Churches, the Legal Resources Centre and the Women's Legal Centre, in addition to land activist organisations such as the National Land Committee and many of its affiliates.

11 The Programme for Land and Agrarian Studies (PLAAS) from the University of the Western Cape, and the Centre for Applied Legal Studies (CALS) of the University of Witwatersrand.

the Bafokeng Royal Nation (a "community group" represented by their monarchy, and closely aligned to the traditional leader lobby).

The critics argued that the Bill was deeply and fundamentally flawed, and was probably unconstitutional in a number of respects. In addition to the criticisms mentioned above, the following arguments were made:

- The nature and content of the "new order rights" to be created in the Bill are not clearly defined, and instead the Minister of Land Affairs is given wide and sweeping powers to determine these rights on a discretionary basis.
- The Minister is not explicitly required by the Bill to define land rights in a manner consistent with the Bill of Rights, and leaves decisions on equal land rights for women to the discretion of the Minister.
- The wide discretionary powers given to the Minister to make determinations on a range of issues central to the security of people's land rights are probably unconstitutional, insofar as the Bill of Rights requires the law to define clearly the extent of the land rights to be secured. No clear criteria and factors to guide the Minister's decisions are provided, and few opportunities to either participate in making these crucial decisions or to challenge them are provided in the Bill.
- The measures in the Bill for achieving gender equality in relation to land rights are weak and unconvincing and are likely to be overridden by the provision that traditional councils dominated by traditional leaders will allocate land, and can do so on the basis of custom. In addition, many of the "old order rights" which the Bill seeks to secure, such as Permits To Occupy (PTOs), vest exclusively in men, and their upgrading to registered 'new order rights' will be at the expense of the informal use and occupation rights of women.
- The Minister will make determinations on who has land rights, on what these land rights will be, and on the boundaries of the "community" that will have ownership of communal land transferred to it, and will be guided by the report of a land rights enquirer. However, the people whose rights are to be decided in this manner have no right to view or challenge the report that the enquirer sends to the Minister, and no opportunity to agree or disagree with a decision to transfer title. The terms of community participation in the land rights enquiry are not made clear. There are no provisions that

ensure that people will have a real choice over the nature of their tenure system or the content of their land rights.

- Communities are required to adopt community rules to govern land use and administration, that will set out who can hold new order rights, but there is no requirement that the community must agree to the content of these rules, and no procedure for adopting these rules is provided. In addition the Minister may impose a standard set of rules on a community (as adapted by the Minister) should a community fail to adopt a set of rules.
- The constitutional requirement that tenure legislation provide for comparable redress in the event that land rights cannot be secured due to overlapping rights is not met in the Bill, which devotes only two clauses to this issue, and does not define the extent of such redress nor provide any clear basis for doing so. Again, the Minister has wide discretionary powers, and no guidelines are provided to direct Ministerial decisions.
- Democratic and accountable institutions for land administration are not adequately provided for in the Bill.
- The Bill undermines the existing property rights of communities who own communal land historically, or through trusts and Communal Property Associations; many of the latter have had their land restored to them through the restitution component of the land reform programme, and many do not support or recognise traditional leaders that were imposed on them in the apartheid era.
- Despite attempts in the Bill to address the problem of municipal service delivery on communal land transferred from the state into private ownership by communities, the problem will remain where undivided blocks of land are transferred, since in South African law ownership of infrastructure (*e.g.* water pipes) and buildings (*e.g.* schools) attaches to the owner of the underlying land.
- Where land for "development" by local government is excluded from transfer of title, long delays in compiling a communal general plan could result while detailed and long term land use planning is carried out, far in advance of any development actually taking place, and without clear guidelines from the Integrated Development Plan for the area.

In addition to questions of substance, most submissions were highly critical of the non-consultative nature of the process through which the Bill had been developed.

11. Amendments, Public Controversy and Passage of the Act

As the final parliamentary session of 2003 came to a close, the portfolio committee deferred further discussion of the Bill until January 2004. The Department of Land Affairs commissioned legal opinions on the constitutionality of the Bill, and officials began to draft a number of amendments. Before its final passage through parliament, the Bill continued to be dogged by controversy and intense behind-the-scenes lobbying, over issues of both substance and procedure.

Amendments sought to address a number of issues. On the question of women's rights, one amendment provides that "old order rights" are deemed to be held by all spouses in a marriage, not by the husband alone. However, no provision is made for securing the current use and occupation rights of single women (widows or unmarried women), and no requirement that land administration committees allocate land on the same basis as men was inserted.

Other amendments also seek to head off potential challenges on constitutional grounds. Rewording of certain sections attempts to create greater certainty that section 25 (6) of the Bill of Rights (requiring clear definition of the extent and content of "security of tenure") are being given effect to, but may still not be adequate. Amendments were also made in relation to decisions and determinations of the Minister. For example, a land rights enquiry must seek to establish the majority views of a community, and these must inform the making of community rules. However, there is still no requirement that majority consent is necessary for the decision to transfer title, or when a land administration committee is established, or prior to the Minister reserving part of communal land for state use. One amendment states that the Minister may not make a determination on land rights until outstanding disputes have been resolved, but no definition is provided of "dispute" and it is unclear who determines whether or not a dispute exists.

The final version of the law also contains a definition of 'land administration committee' that avoids specifying that it will be a traditional council in all areas where these exist. Section 21 (2) states that "If a community has a recognised traditional council, the powers and duties of the land administration committee of such community may be exercised and performed by such council." However, the word "may" appears to be permissive, enabling a traditional council to exercise the powers of a land administration committee, rather than to create a choice for rights holders. No other provision of the Act allows for such a choice.

Unprecedented public interest in the passage of the Bill saw wide media coverage, editorials calling for it to be scrapped or "substantially amended",[12] angry articles by gender activists,[13] and a statement by the Gender for Gender Equality that it had "taken an executive decision to challenge the bill constitutionally."[14] A constitutional challenges to the law was also mounted in 2005 by the Legal Resources Centre acting on behalf of some of the communities that presented submissions to parliament. The Community Consultation project that sustained community participation in the policy process has, however, come to an end, and land sector NGOs have not attempted to continue to mobilise or organise rural people around these issues. The focus of engagement with these issues has thus shifted to the judicial arena.

12. Conclusion: Communal Land Rights and Democracy in Post-Apartheid South Africa

Informing the politics of tenure reform policy are competing understandings of both land rights and of institutional arrangements for land administration. In relation to land rights, one view is that only land titling (*i.e.* private ownership) provides adequate tenure security – but forms of group title must be made available, as well as individual title, given the strong rural demand for a community-based form of tenure. The strongest demand from the ground, however, is for security of rights of families and individuals, within a system that secures access to common property (Claassens 2003).

Most controversial remains the issue of traditional authority and its role in communal tenure regimes. Political deals may have informed the rapid progress of the Communal Land Rights Bill through parliament, but the long-term prospects for chiefs and headmen are not at

12 "The wrong direction" *Cape Times*, 29 January 2004; "'Land Bill turns back the clock", *This Day*, 30 January 2004.

13 "Parliament gives rural women a raw deal", Pregs Govender, *Sunday Times*, 15 February 2004.

14 "United front to oppose controversial land bill", *Sunday Independent*, 29 February 2004.

all clear. At stake are some of the fundamentals of South Africa's new democracy, as Murray (2003:18) points out:

> It may be possible to marry the idealised notions of an older, different democratic order eulogised as an intrinsic part of an original, untainted, form of pre-colonial traditional leadership with the requirements of a modern, democratic state. But such an amalgamation should not be the product of either short-term horse trading or transparently sectional interests for whom tradition is little more than a shield from the demands of democratic accountability. We must guard against the possibility that a new order revelling in its emancipation from (neo) colonial rule will abrogate its responsibility to its citizens in the name of a new Africanisation. The danger is that settlement with the lobby of traditional leaders will be a smokescreen for the failure to implement democracy where it really matters: at grassroots, in the material conditions of the ordinary existence of women and men.

The African experience of tenure reform has largely been one of ineffective law and policy, in which interventions have failed to bridge the gap between *de facto* realities and *de jure* rights, and tension and conflict over competing jurisdictions persist (Berry 1993). This has arisen partly from inadequate funding or weak state capacity, both underpinned by lack of political will, but another reason is the persistent lack of understanding by policy makers and legislators of the realities of African systems of land rights (Okoth-Ogendo 2002).

It is now widely accepted that freehold title is not a "magic bullet" for increasing security of tenure in Africa and other developing countries (World Bank 2003). This has resulted in acceptance of the core features of communal tenure: rights to land and natural resources are shared and relative, flexible boundaries exist between a variety of social units, and rights are nested within a number of social and administrative units (Okoth-Ogendo, 2002). Emerging policy recommendations call for greater recognition in law of such rights, the strengthening of local institutions for land administration and land management, and support for institutions and procedures for mediation and negotiation, particularly at the local level (IIED, 1999). Local institutions are vulnerable to the power plays of elites, as well as to a "politics of exclusion" (Lavigne Delville, 1999; Peters, 2002) and measures to promote transparency and downward accountability (that is, democratisation) are required (Ribot, 2002). This suggests that rights should be vested in individuals, rather than in institutions that purport to represent community members (Woodhouse 2003:1714).

This also means that central government has a key role to play in ensuring accountability, through oversight of local bodies and the application of sanctions (*ibid*:18). Some analysts emphasise the key role of ongoing processes of negotiation and conflict resolution for securing land rights, and stress the importance of state support for local institutions to mediate conflicting interests (Berry, 1993; Moore, 1998). This resonates strongly with the view that democracy in Africa requires a strong and capable state, both willing and able to empower citizens through locally accountable, representative institutions (Luckham 1998). An emancipatory version of democratisation is thus integral to the politics of communal tenure reform, both within South Africa and more widely (Cousins 2003).

The processual dimensions of policy making in relation to land rights are equally important, Given the complexity and political sensitivity of land issues, some African governments have placed severe limits on the openness of policy processes, but others (notably Mozambique and Malawi) have moved to more participatory or consultative approaches to policy development (Palmer 2000). The advantages of the latter are that they address "social legitimacy, commitment and cost all in one go" (Alden Wily, cited in Palmer 2000:274).

Policy processes around the Communal Land Rights Act reveal that rural community members are both willing and able to contribute meaningfully to public debate and parliamentary deliberations on draft laws that affect their socio-economic rights, and that civil society organisations can play a useful role in facilitating their active participation in such processes. The spaces opened by South Africa's new constitution for "bottom-up" policy making are real, and if fully utilised would probably result in more appropriate and effective policies to reduce poverty and inequality. While the judicial, legislative and parliamentary arenas do open up possibilities for successful struggles over socio-economic rights, as demonstrated clearly by the Treatment Action Campaign, another key requirement is mobilisation and organisation. Capacity to mobilise around land rights in communal areas appears to be lacking in the land sector at the moment. Another constraint is the willingness of the state to hear "the voices of the people", a willingness not demonstrated in the case of the Communal Land Rights Act. Weaknesses in both the state and in civil society are thus key deficits within South Africa's new democracy.

References

Beetham, David, 1994, "Conditions for Democratic Consolidation", *Review of African Political Economy*, Vol 21, No. 60: 157-172.

Berry, S., 1993, *No condition is permanent. The social dynamics of agrarian change in sub-Saharan Africa.* Madison: University of Wisconsin Press.

Bruce, J.W., 1993, "The Variety of Reform: A Review of the Recent Experiences with Land Reform and the Reform of Tenure, with Particular Reference to the African Experience", in: H. S. Marcussen (ed.) *Institutional Issues in Natural Resource Management*, Roskilde, Denmark: International Development Studies, Roskilde University.

Claassens, A., 2000, "South African proposals for Tenure Reform: the Draft Land Rights Bill, in: C. Toulmin and J. Quan (eds.), *Evolving land rights, policy and tenure in Africa.* London: International Institute for Environment and Development and Natural Resources Institute.

Claassens, A., 2001, *'It is not easy to challenge a chief': Lessons from Rakgwadi.* Research Report no. 9. Cape Town: Programme for Land and Agrarian Studies, University of the Western Cape.

Claassens, A., 2003, *Community Views on the Communal Land Rights Bill.* Research Report no. 15. Cape Town: Programme for Land and Agrarian Studies, University of the Western Cape.

Comaroff, Jean and Comaroff, John, 2004, "The Struggle between the Constitution and 'Things African'", *WISER Review* No. 1, Johannesburg: University of Witwatersrand.

Cousins, Ben, 2003, "The Zimbabwe crisis in its wider context: the politics of land, democracy and development in Southern Africa", in: Hammar, A., Raftopolous B., and Jensen, S., (eds.), *Unfinished Business: Rethinking Land, State and Citizenship in Zimbabwe*, Harare: Weaver Press.

Cousins, Ben, 2004a, "No Way to Communal Land Rights: Boundary Disputes Will Stall the CLR Act", *New Agenda* 16, Fourth Quarter 2004: 18-27.

Cousins, Ben, 2004b, "Grounding democracy: the politics of land in post-apartheid South Africa", paper commissioned for IDASA roundtable series, "Lessons from the Field: A Decade of Democracy", Pretoria: Institute for Democracy in South Africa.

Cross, C., 1998, "Reforming Land in South Africa: Who Owns the Land?" *Proceedings of the International conference on Land Tenure in the Developimg World*, UCT, 1998.

Friedman, Steven, 2004, "The Silent Citizen: Poverty, Participation and the Health of Our Democracy", Paper presented to a conference on "In Pursuit of Justice: Celebrating a Decade of Democracy", Foundation for Human Rights, Durban, January 25-27, 2004.

Holomisa, Patekile, 2003, "Resolving communal land rights a vital link in reform process", *Business Day*, May 21, 2003.

IIED, 1999. "Land Tenure and Resource Access in West Africa: Issues and Opportunities for the Next Twenty Five Years". London: International Institute for Environment and Development.

Kepe, T., 2001, *Waking up from the dream: The Wild Coast SDI and the pitfalls of 'fast track' development.* Research Report No 8. Cape Town: Programme for Land and Agrarian Studies, University of the Western Cape.

Lavigne Delville, P., 1999, "Harmonising formal law and customary land rights in French-speaking West Africa". IIED Issue Paper No.86 June 1999. London: International Institute for Environment and Development.

Levin, R. and Mkhabela, S., 1997, "The Chieftaincy, Land Allocation and Democracy", in: *'No More Tears': Struggles for Land in Mpumalanga, South Africa.* Trenton: Africa World Press.

Luckham R., 1998, "Are There Alternatives to Liberal Democracy?" in: Mark Robinson and Gordon White (eds.), *The Democratic Developmental State. Politics and Institutional Design*, Oxford: Oxford University Press.

Luckham, Robin, Anne Marie Goetz, Mary Kaldor, with Alison Ayers, Sunil Bastian, Emmanual Gyimah-Boadi, Shireen Hassim and Zarko Puhovski , 2000, "Democratic Institutions and Politics in Contexts of Inequality, Poverty and Conflict. A Conceptual Framework". IDS Working Paper 104. Brighton: Institute of Development Studies.

Makopi S., 2000, "Awards to provide security of tenure and comparable redress". In: B. Cousins (ed.) 2000. *At The Crossroads: Land and Agrarian Reform in South Africa Into the 21st Century.* Cape Town: Programme for Land and Agrarian Studies, University of the Western Cape and National Land Committee.

Mamdani M., 1996, *Citizen and Subject: Contemporary Africa and the Legacy of late Colonialism,* Princeton N.J: Princeton University Press.

Mbeki, Govan, 1964, *The Peasant's Revolt,* Harmondsworth: Penguin.

Meer, S., 1997. (ed.) *Women, land and authority: perspectives from South Africa.* Cape Town: David Philip.

Moore, S. F., 1998, "Changing African land tenure: Reflections on the incapacities of the state". *European Journal of Development Research,* 10(2): 33-49.

Murray, Christine, 2003, "South Africa's troubled royalty: Traditional leaders after democracy", paper presented at ?, November 2003.

Ntsebeza L., 1999, *Land tenure reform, traditional authorities and rural local government in post-apartheid South Africa*. Research Report No. 3. Cape Town: Programme for Land and Agrarian Studies, University of the Western Cape.

Okoth-Ogendo H.W.O., 2002, "The tragic African commons: A century of expropriation, suppression and subversion". Occasional Paper No. 24. Cape Town: Programme for Land and Agrarian Studies, University of the Western Cape.

Oomen, B., 2000, *Tradition on the move. Chiefs, democracy and change in rural South Africa*. Amsterdam: Netherlands Institute for Southern Africa.

Palmer, Robin, 2000, "Land Policy in Africa: Lessons from Recent Policy and Implementation Processes", in: C. Toulmin and J. Quan (eds.), *Evolving land rights, policy and tenure in Africa*. London: International Institute for Environment and Development and Natural Resources Institute.

Peters P., 1998, "The erosion of commons and the emergence of property: problems for social analysis", in Hunt R.C. and Gilman, A (eds.) *Property in economic context*. Monographs in Economic Anthropology, No 14. Lanham, New York, Oxford:University Press of America.

Peters P., 2002, "The Limits of Negotiability: Security, Equity and Class Formation in Africa's Land Systems". In: Juul K. and Lund C. (eds.): *Negotiating Property in Africa*. Portsmouth, NH: Heinemann.

Ribot, Jesse C., 2002, *African Decentralisation. Local Actors, Powers and Accountability*. Geneva: United Nations Research Institute for Social Development.

Seekings, Jeremy and Nattrass, Nicoli, 2002, "Class, Distribution and Redistribution in Post-Apartheid South Africa", *Transformation*, No. 50: 1-30.

Turner S., 1999, "Land rights and land administration in the Herschel and Maluti Districts, Eastern Cape". Occasional Paper No. 10. Cape Town: Programme for Land and Agrarian Studies, University of the Western Cape.

Turner, Steven and Ibsen, Hilda, 2000, *Land and agrarian reform in South Africa: A status report*, Research Report No. 3. Cape Town: Programme for Land and Agrarian Studies, University of the Western Cape.

van Lieres, Bettina, forthcoming, "Marginalisation and Citizenship in Post-Apartheid South Africa", in: Robins, Steven, (ed.) *Limits to Liberation. Culture, Citizenship and Governance after Apartheid*. Oxford and Cape Town: James Currey and David Philip.

Woodhouse, Philip, 2003, "African Enclosures: A Default Mode of Development", *World Development*, Vol 31, No. 10: 1705-1720.

World Bank, 2003, *Land Policy for Pro-poor Growth and Development*. Washington: World Bank.

11. Socio-Economic Rights: Cornerstone or Capstone of Democracy?

Paul M. Graham

> This Bill of Rights is a cornerstone of democracy in South Africa. It enshrines the rights of all people in our country and affirms the democratic rights of human dignity, equality and freedom.[1]

Chapter Two of the South African Constitution insists that blue, red and green rights are the cornerstone of our democracy. What else might one expect from a "rainbow nation"? The pre-eminence in which the Constitution is now held should not blind us to the controversial nature of this statement of faith nor the continuing scepticism that still attends the justiciability[2] and realisation of some of the 27 rights. In summary the socio-economic rights cluster in South Africa consists of education, food, health, land, water, social security, housing and environment rights. Comparison of achievements in the fields of education and employment suggest that this cluster may have direct bearing on the successes of the last decade – where rights are entrenched, progress is made. Where they are not, it is not.

There are at least three questions with which democrats continue to grapple. Is there a developmental pre-condition for democratic "take-off"? Are socio-economic rights a necessary foundation for sustaining democracy? Does democracy produce socio-economic development? South Africans have an a-priori bias in answering these ques-

1 Article 7 (1), Act 108 of 1996, The Constitution of the Republic of South Africa.

2 Budlender (2001), who has been closely involved with the landmark case *RSA v Grootboom*, addresses the justiciability question in regard to four levels of obligation – respecting, protecting, promoting and fulfilling the right – in an extensive paper delivered to a workshop for judges in Delhi, India in 2001.

Peris Jones and Kristian Stokke (eds.), Democratising Development, *ISBN 90 04 14821 3, pp. 271-286.*

tions. Having tasted freedom and having seen the wastage of resources and the damage to people caused by dictatorship it is hard to exchange that freedom for some form of privatized comfort or ostensibly benign authoritarianism. In this regard, it may be necessary to point out that democracy itself is entrenched as a right in the South African constitution, protected not only in the Bill of Rights but also in the protected clauses of the Preamble and Founding Provisions.

It is not necessary to spend much time on the first question. It may well still be asked by those who have a vested interest in limiting the spread of democracy, but surely the aspirations and achievements of people in East Timor, Malawi, Mozambique, Lesotho, and Somaliland – the list could continue and include Brazil, South Africa and India – must demonstrate that in the modern world, poverty is no hindrance to demands for popular self-government. As Przeworski exclaims in his study of the empirical evidence available, "Indeed, transitions to democracy are random with regard to the level of development: not a single transition to democracy can be predicted by the level of development alone" (Prseworski, Alvarez, Cheibub and Limongi 2001:168).

Saying that the struggle for democracy can emerge and even triumph in conditions of poverty and adversity is not the same as agreeing that these democracies will be sustainable. Nigeria's continuing struggle to wrench itself away from anarchy, division and violence are only too obvious. South Africa is presently facilitating the latest international efforts to breathe life into democracy in Haiti, a struggle that only this year celebrated its 200th anniversary.

Having achieved popular self-government is no guarantee of a sustainable democracy. Mattes summarises a range of recent attempts to understand what makes democracies endure:

> Social scientists have identified three key factors crucial to sustaining and consolidating democratic rule. The first fact has to do with economics. … The second has to do with political institutions. That is sustainable democracies require a professional civil service and strong viable and autonomous courts, legislatures, executives and electoral systems at national and local levels. … The third factor has to do with the attitudes of rulers and citizens. Put simply, democracies require democrats. (Mattes 2003:2)

The most thorough-going empirical analysis is that done by Przeworski and others, and although it looks only at a very limited period of history – from 1950 to 1990 – this period does provide it with rich data:

> Our central finding is the importance of economic factors in sustaining democracies. ... Indeed we have found that once a country is sufficiently wealthy, with per-capita income of more than $6 000 a year, democracy is certain to survive, come hell or high water. ... Democracies can survive even in the poorest nations if they manage to generate development, if they reduce inequality, if the international climate is propitious, and if they have parliamentary institutions. (Przeworski *et al.* 2001:177)

This latter finding leads them to conclude that poverty is a trap from which it is difficult to escape. But escape we must, if we are to sustain our initial achievements or avoid the long cycle of repression, resistance, victory and collapse. Carothers (2002) suggests that there is a large waystation between authoritarianism and democracy, a limbo of unfulfilled expectations and dashed aspirations. This limbo is too costly to countenance for South Africa, or indeed any country. As Dante said on his descent into the inferno:

> "Lost are we and are only so far punished,
> That without hope we live on in desire."[3]

However, escape is not easy. It requires insisting upon certain basic principles – and these principles were argued during the extensive constitutional debate in which South Africans participated before our founding democratic election:

> The right to be free and the right not to be hungry are both fundamental human rights to be defended and fought for as vigorously as possible. One cannot permit the existence of the one to negate or diminish the importance of the other. The fact that there needs to be a great national effort to combat hunger and homelessness is no reason for cutting back on freedom of speech or the right of access to the courts. Similarly the fact that citizens can consult their lawyers and get a court order in no way mitigates the need to provide a legal framework to combat hunger. (Sachs 1990:190)

In his series of reflections on human rights published in 1990, current Constitutional Court Judge Albie Sachs made the argument for "The Last Word – Freedom" some time before Nobel Laureate Amartya Sen published his landmark work "Development as Freedom" in which he

3 Dante Alighieri, *The Divine Comedy* – Inferno: Canto IV.

argued that "Development requires the removal of major sources of unfreedom: poverty as well as tyranny, poor economic opportunities as well as systematic social deprivation, neglect of public facilities as well as intolerance or overactivity of repressive states" (Sen 2000:3). Sen makes the case that various freedoms are not only indivisible but have a virtuous effect on one another:

> Freedoms are not only the primary ends of development, they are also among its primary means. Political freedoms (in the form of free speech and elections) help to promote economic security. Social opportunities (in the form of education and health facilities) facilitate economic participation. Economic facilities (in the form of opportunities for participation in trade and production) can help to generate personal abundance as well as public resources for social facilities. Freedoms of different kinds can strengthen one another. (Sen 2000:11)

Albie Sachs had made a similar point. "The constitution does not, of itself, immediately eliminate the immense inequalities created by past racism, but it does establish a structure of equal political rights and equal protection under the law which enables the injustices of the past to be tackled" (Sachs 1990:121). Another South African who has carried her activism into a democratic South Africa, Cheryl Carolus, said:

> I am committed to those values which are sometimes referred to as 'liberal' values' ... I am referring to freedom of speech, freedom of association and freedom of belief – first generation rights. I say this because without these talk of social and economic rights will come to naught. Workers will have food to eat and roofs over their heads one day, not primarily because a Bill of Rights states that they should, but because they have the right to get out there, organise politically and fight for those rights. Take these rights away and we will be back to square one in this country. At the same time, try and isolate these rights from second and third generation rights, from socio-economic, ecological and development rights and you have undermined the very essence of the right to freedom of speech, association and belief. They have become an empty abstraction that make sense only to the rich who already have shelter, food and the necessary material ingredients of life. (Carolus 1993, quoted in IDASA 1997)

Liv Tørres (in this volume) refers to the manner in which these rights "served as the basis for the democratic struggle against apartheid" and suggests that labour's ability to mobilise on the same rights will determine the consolidation of democracy.

Democracy unleashes the freedoms and establishes the rights which are necessary for socio-economic development and growth. It does this through establishing a virtuous circle in which "democratic debate and contestation are themselves a form of collective learning in which citizens acquire the capacity to reject what fails and to attempt something new." (Haggard and Kaufman 1995:379). Haggard and Kaufman are not overly optimistic that democratic transitions are sustainable in many parts of the world but they refuse to succumb to cynicism precisely because "the capacity to learn means that the unexpected is possible, that neither politics nor policy is simply a game of repeating what has become before. It is on this fundamental characteristic of democracy that we pin our hopes" (Haggard and Kaufman 1995:379).

The empirical evidence suggests that at the very least "looking at long term patterns of development shows that democracies are as likely to generate developmental miracles as dictatorships but dictatorships are much more likely to bring economic disasters" (Przeworski undated:2). For South Africa, it is crucial that democracy – which is our chosen regime entrenched in our Constitution – does indeed deliver development. This is no academic question – failure to meet the needs of our citizens will indeed lead to a collapse of our social project. So will political freedom lead to development?

Let us leave aside for a moment the argument of Sen that this is the wrong question and that freedom itself is a constitutive part of development. Sen's view was confirmed in the UNDP (2002) milestone report, "Deepening democracy in a fragmented world," which states that "democratic participation is a critical end of human development, not just a means of achieving it" (Malloch-Brown 2002). Asked to define democracy, Africans in general have no doubt about the "liberal" content of that definition. But South Africans particularly expect that democracy will have within its scope and power additional substantive advantages – and when these are not delivered, there is some indication that alternatives to democracy or downright retreat into private space will be sought. In the African context at least, both are dangerous.

Unfortunately, evidence that democracy leads to development is sufficiently ambiguous that those who favour more authoritarian approaches still have their say. This paper agrees with Samuel Amadi that democracy (even narrowly defined) has made a difference. "The irony is that whilst the rhetoric of Economic, Social and Cultural rights and the right to development obsessed African political commentators and nationalist leaders the need for practical realization of these rights evaded their concern. Even with arguably meagre resources available to the post-colonial states, they failed to "progressively" improve the economic welfare of the citizens. Whilst the western states that debunked the validity of ESC rights and prioritized civil and political rights ahead of ESC rights seemed to consistently better the economic welfare of the poor in their society" (Amadi 2002). Amadi makes the same point alluded to above and that Sachs takes for granted,[4] and that is that while democratic states in the western world have a current discourse which debunks socio-economic rights they have at the same time established substantial state obligations, regardless of how they presently believe these should be delivered.

The forty-year trajectory which leads Przeworski *et al.* to conclude that democracies and dictatorships have had similar economic gains, with democracies able to show better per capita performance and their insulation from famine and other catastrophes may be a study on too limited a time horizon. A longer time horizon, say from 1814, may yield other results – but there are just too many variables to make the case convincingly.

In considering whether the post 1990 "third wave of democracy" might provide some additional indications beyond those of the Przeworski 40 year period, a rough and ready comparison was made of the Human Development Index achievements of all countries that had improved their Freedom House ratings from "unfree" to "partly free" or "free" during the post 1990 period.[5] The results are inconclusive – with some indication that there are initial dividends for those countries that start from a very low developmental base. And there is some evidence that the "unfree" have a more volatile developmental trajectory. Work

4 "The right to education, to health, to nutrition, to shelter, did not easily fit into the classic scheme of individually based rights. What had previously been regarded as benevolent or charitable activities based upon moral or religious obligation, gradually became codified into law. Municipalities acquired a duty to provide clean water and collect rubbish, to build schools and hospitals. The concept of social, economic and cultural rights began to emerge and is today firmly established. ... They had one thing in common ... red rights required public institutions to be the principal agency for their realization. While blue rights compelled the state to refrain from action, red rights demanded that the state deliver benefits and services" (Sachs 1990:145).

5 Unpublished analysis by Teddy Nemeroff and Erin Brizius, volunteers from Princeton University and Stanford University respectively at IDASA in 2004.

on this is ongoing but the economic evidence for "democracy first" is growing as the recent article in *Foreign Affairs* by Siegle, Weinstein and Helperin (2004) demonstrates.

However, evidence from the Southern African region is indicative of the consensus which has emerged globally, that political imperatives such as universal suffrage and a human rights culture may be as important as economic imperatives in constraining or enhancing a county's developmental chances. The inserted chart shows the economic performance on the crude but generally accepted indicator of GDP growth for South Africa across the 1994 watershed, and the same figures for Zimbabwe across the watershed of the 1999 disputed Presidential elections. In South Africa the period from foundational elections in 1994 shows positive growth and given the adjusted rates at the end of 2004, substantial growth; in Zimbabwe the contested legitimacy of the 1999 elections mark dismal economic decline.[6] There may also be interesting parallels when considering the continuing democratic stability and prosperity in Botswana and the economic growth in Mozambique.

Figure 1: Comparative growth – S.A. and Zimbabwe

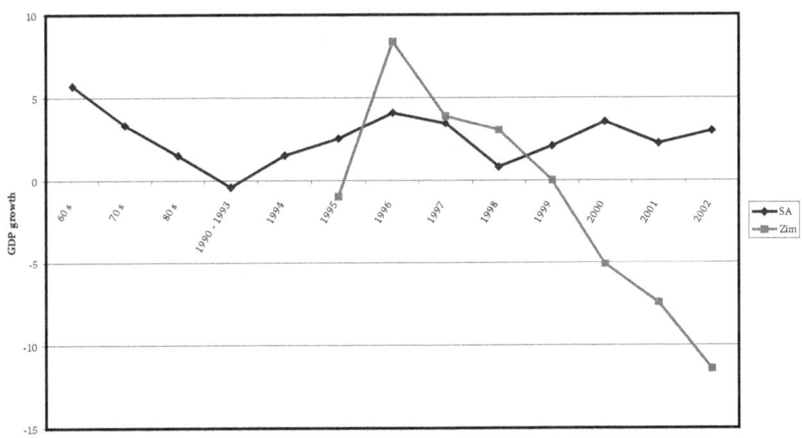

6 GDP figures have been sourced from Worldbank Circular 9/17/03, OECD African Economic Outlook 2002/03, Economist.Com, Bruggemans, Change of Pace, and the US State Department. The graph may also, of course, offer evidence of Przeworski's thesis that economic contraction is a signifier of likely state crisis.

The New Partnership for Africa's Development (NEPAD) has expressed the most recent and entirely African consensus. NEPAD has now been accepted as a programme of the African Union which has its own normative base in the Constitutive Act. Clause 79 confirms the prevailing consensus. "It is now generally acknowledged that development is impossible in the absence of true democracy, respect for human rights, peace and good governance. With the *New Partnership for Africa's Development*, Africa undertakes to respect the global standards of democracy, which core components include political pluralism, allowing for the existence of several political parties and workers' unions, fair, open, free and democratic elections periodically organised to enable the populace to choose their leaders freely."[7]

So after ten years, South Africa has chosen a democratic future; it has gambled (with some reason for hope) on democracy bringing the economic development which will sustain it. But there is one fundamental threat which remains unanswered – and this is the threat of inequality.

Unfortunately, while democracy may indeed provide a better chance for socio-economic development, it is less effective at dealing with inequality, which seems perniciously intractable. As Sen suggests, in a reflection that confirms the analysis of Przeworski "Certainly, severe inequalities are not socially attractive, and momentous inequalities can be, some would argue, downright barbaric. Furthermore, the sense of inequality may also erode social cohesion, and some types of inequalities can make it difficult to achieve even efficiency" (Sen 2000:93). While this reminds us that that inequality is not merely a matter of democratic utility, but of human pain, this paper is more concerned with the prospects for sustainable democracy in the face of inequality.

"Think of Brazil: during the past two centuries, this country was a royal colony, an independent monarchy, an oligarchic republic, a populist military dictatorship, democracy with a weak presidency, a right wing military dictatorship, and democracy with a strong presidency. Yet, to the best of our knowledge, income distribution did not budge" (Prseworski undated:19). One might equally well turn to the deep inequalities and absolute poverty in India, or the absolute and relative deprivation of African Americans in the United States of America. Haggard and Kaufmann look more closely at a whole range of unequal societies in the 1970's and 1980's and come to the conclusion that "Democracy is

7 Founding documentation for NEPAD, October 2002.

unlikely to reverse these deeply entrenched patterns of inequality [in Brazil, Mexico, Bolivia, Turkey, and Chile] quickly; indeed, democracy is in many respects inimical to radical redistribution" (Haggard and Kaufmann 1995:323). Adam Habib (in this volume) provides an interpretation of these constraints in South Africa. "Mbeki ... confronted two diametrically opposed sets of interests ..." On the one side, foreign investors and domestic business, on the other poor citizens. Haggard and Kaufmann make it clear that South Africa is by no means the only country worrying about the "golden goose". They go on to argue that economic growth may be the one thing standing between these countries and failure.

> There are simple yet compelling reasons why economic performance, and particularly economic growth, might also be important for long-term democratic stability and consolidation. Growth eases the trade-offs associated with the organization of political support, in part by permitting compensation to negatively affected groups. More generally, growth can reduce the frustrations and conflicts resulting from inequality or other social cleavages, and can thus mute the tendency to political alienation and destabilising social violence. (Haggard and Kaufmann 1995:325)

But that is not enough. "... we did find that democracy is more likely to survive in countries where income inequality is declining over time. ... People expect democracy to reduce inequality, and democracies are more likely to survive when they do so" (Przeworski *et al.* 1996:171).

Inequality is however not only a matter for the economists. It matters also in dealing with the institutional and civic requirements of sustainable democracy. Przeworski quotes John Stuart Mill, "without decent wages and universal reading, no government of public opinion is possible" and goes on to argue that "to be able to function as public persons, people must have some modicum of economic security and some capacity to understand the issues that enter into the public realm. These conditions are not automatically generated by the mere fact that people enjoy formal political rights: these rights can be exercised only if people also have the requisite material conditions" (Przeworski undated:7).

This unfortunately is often used as an argument for managed societies – on the assumption that lack of the prerequisite material conditions therefore disqualifies one from active citizenship. This assumption is not born out by our own research in the Afrobarometer where, having developed a powerful measure of lived poverty, we are able to establish levels of participation in public society on the part of the poor – a participation that rather than diminishing seems in South Africa at least to have increased as people make use of the voice that freedom has unshackled.[8] Nevertheless, if you are not fortified by a proper meal, are battling against disease, if you do not have a telephone, an adequate education, access to "town", the ability to read newspapers or own a radio, and if your presence in the chambers of power leads to you being overlooked as a result of your appearance or ignorance of the "right way" to behave or speak then both you and the democracy in which you live have been diminished.

In South Africa both public opinion and leadership consensus have agreed that democracy requires not only procedural but also substantive implications:

> But for the vote to have meaning, for the Rule of Law to have content, the vote must be the instrument for the achievement of second and third generation rights. It would be a sad victory if the people has the right to every five or so years to emerge from their forced removal hovels and second rate Group Area homesteads to go to the polls, only thereafter to return to their inferior houses, inferior education and inferior jobs. Indeed it would be a strange panoply of rights that not only ignored but excluded the right to peace and development, the right to enjoy the beauty of and benefit from the natural resources of the country, and above all, the right to be a people. (Sachs 1990:8)

However, agreeing in principle on this does not immediately lead to it happening. The papers in this volume concur with other reviews of the democratic South Africa's performance in reducing inequality and therefore increasing its chances of sustaining its democracy and ensur-

8 As the authors of the Afrobarometer Briefing Paper #4 comment in conclusion, "These findings from seven southern African countries ... suggest that the key dynamics behind the link between democracy and wealth occur at a macro level: that is, rather than poor citizens who are less democratic in thought and deed, it simply may be that poor countries are less able to afford or maintain the things vital for sustainable democracy, ranging from formal state institutions such as quality electoral machinery and a well resourced legislature, to societal institutions such as effective political parties, an independent news media and a vibrant web of civil society organisations."

ing and enshrining the rights of its citizens has been poor. In this regard, we are little different, to date, from other unequal societies.

If inequality is indeed so intractable, then it must require a special effort to reduce it. Bills of Rights are not written by the powerful, they are written by the powerless to ensure that they do not remain powerless. And so, while it remains true that the blue rights prevent the state from imposing its will on the population, red rights insist that the state also has an obligation to its citizens to ensure that they are able to participate fully in the freedoms for which we have fought. The South African constitution has been lauded for entrenching socio-economic rights, but they are not the first to do this in one form or another. The constitution of Iceland guarantees forms of health assistance and education; that of Norway the conditions for everyone to work and for self-government at work, and a healthy environment; in India – led by activist judges such as Bhagwati who had a great impact on our own drafting aspirations – the constitution's own inhibitions have not hindered judicial intervention. One might even say that such rights can be seen in even the earliest constitutional models, although their inclination was to protect the socio-economic rights of particular interest groups rather than the society as a whole.

The entrenchment of socio-economic rights in Chapter Two of the South African constitution was itself a struggle, based on arguments discussed above. But these are now entrenched. In South Africa at least this battle has been won, and this win has implications for countries and communities other than South Africa.

Like all rights, socio-economic rights have to be exercised, not merely codified. Much of the theory about rights is strangely bloodless, as though it is the preserve of lawyers and academics. Yet the codification of rights comes as a result of struggle, and their exercise requires continuing struggle. It is trite to say that rights compete and have to be balanced against one another; where socio-economic rights are concerned, this balancing becomes a matter of life or death, a contest with deep political implications and political contestation and consequence.

That is the message of this publication. In this chapter, I refer to the struggle through law, and point out some of the weaknesses in this – weaknesses which can only be remedied by a continuing struggle through mobilisation and social activism. These are discussed in other chapters. All the contributions take for granted that such struggles are contests between different interests, values and power relations. In describing a series of cases in this chapter, it is perhaps necessary to remind readers that each case has at least two sides – in some of them firmly held sides, in others merely taken for the sake of obtaining a judicial interpretation of a constitutional mandate or the filling of a policy lacuna. In South Africa socio-economic jurisprudence has evolved quite significantly.

The cases known in short hand as "Grootboom" and "TAC" are and will remain amongst the most important. In the first case, as has been drawn to our attention in a number of impromptu comments at conferences by Geoff Budlender, the relief provided by the court to a community evicted from privately owned land has not significantly improved the circumstances of that community although it has had some general policy implications. As Budlender says, "The Grootboom community are still living under highly unsatisfactory circumstances." (Budlender 2001)

In the other case, the court's insistence that Nevirapene be made available to HIV positive mothers about to give birth had immediate consequences, and formed the backdrop for further policy shifts on the general supply of anti-retroviral treatment. Budlender points to the role of social mobilisation first in voicing an issue and making use of legal remedies, and then in monitoring those remedies and assisting with them. Siri Gloppen (in this volume) describes a jurisprudential "anatomy" in which voice, court responsiveness, judges' capability, and the judgement's authority all pose challenges and problems in which at every juncture the outcome is a result of the interaction between a complex of factors. She finds no easy answers. Budlender is sceptical of judicial remedies and court appeals substituting for civic activism. This scepticism may be well placed. Advocate Wim Trengrove SC, speaking at the January 2004 conference "In Pursuit of Justice" reported on a fundamental problem in socio-economic litigation – "what if government spurns court orders?"[9]

He told the story of a series of cases in the Eastern Cape in which people resorted to the courts to get the provincial government to pay social grants. Judgements against the state were granted and in some cases were even unopposed, but these judgements were not subsequently carried out even though some were money orders. Two things stood in the way of justice – first that people may not be imprisoned for failing to satisfy a money judgement but must have their property attached; and

9 Quoted in Amato, R. "Alarming Saga of Official Delinquency", *Sunday Independent*, 1 February 2004.

secondly that the State Liability Act of 1957 indemnifies the state from having its property attached. There is some movement on this matter, with judges inclining towards using contempt of court rulings to imprison dilatory officials. These are themselves in appeal and the saga is continuing. But the story makes clear that an unwilling state faced with an adamant court could introduce instability into the democratic system and a disaffected citizenry either distrustful of government or cynical about the courts.

The roll out of treatment for AIDS sufferers might yet bring us face to face with this same phenomenon as Mark Heywood suggests in his chapter, while many poor citizens, some of whom are participating in what are now called "social movements", are already feeling they are ill served by the law and its agents despite the good intentions of the constitution.

There is, however, a very significant judgement in the Supreme Court of Appeal – not noted for its progressive nature – which has demonstrated the highly political nature of the balancing of rights, and the manner in which the courts can maintain this balance while acting in favour of the poor. This particular case provided an example also of an increasingly available civil society strategy – that of *amicus curae* or friend of the court. Judge Harms ruled that the state had infringed both on the property rights of a farmer whose land had been invaded by squatters and the rights of the squatters. The state has been ordered to pay compensation to the farmer and to find alternative land for the squatters who retain the right to occupy the land until that alternative is found. Harms relied heavily on constitutional court judgements and especially Grootboom, and makes the point that "requiring of Modderklip [the farm company in question] to bear the constitutional duty of the state with no recompense to provide land for some 40 000 people is also not acceptable."[10] The judgement has been widely welcomed in South Africa as 'solomonic'. The judgement itself summarises the balancing of interests: "Modderklip will not receive more than what it has lost, the state has already received value for what it has to pay and the immediate social problem is solved while the medium and long term problems can be solved as and when the state can afford it."[11] A heavy burden has

10 Modderfontein East Squatters, Greater Benoni City Council v Modderklip Boerdery Case Nos 187/03 and 213/03. Judgement delivered 27 May 2004, clause 41.

11 *Ibid.*

been placed on the state, which Ben Cousins and Aninka Claassens (in this volume) argue they will find it difficult to meet. And the judgement has opened up a further line of judicial advocacy for landless people in other parts of the country.

But the courts are not the only way to respect, protect, promote and fulfil socio-economic rights. If Budlender is to be followed, they should be a last resort not a short-cut. Policy, law and regulation developed in parliament as the result of social mobilization; public consultation, representative and sectoral contestation; and administrative experience such as that provided by the SA Human Rights Commission through their socio-economic protocols; the use of the guiding principles of the constitution in public education and subsequent participatory planning at municipal level; monitoring of budgets and state performance; assessment and improvement of public service capacity where will is present but ability absent; and continuing civil society advocacy where will may be absent whatever the ability are all democratic and perfectly legitimate approaches to take in ensuring that people can indeed exercise these rights. And all of them are present in South Africa today. Carolus is correct– the first generation rights must be protected so that the second and third generation rights can be realized. There are no socio-economic rights without politics; and there is no realisation of these rights without politics, understood as the engagement between people, across lines of difference, to solve problems and live together (Boyte 2004). By this we do not mean that there is no conflict of interest or social contradiction, but that these require solution – public activity by active citizens.

It is my contention that the entrenchment of socio-economic rights is essential in a democracy, whether through precedent or prescription. It is right in and of itself, it insists upon the responsibility of the state to reduce poverty and inequality, and that insistence protects the quality of public participation and institutional effectiveness. In other words, no entrenched rights, no mechanism for combatting inequality. No mechanism for combatting inequality, no way to reduce the risks of unsustainable democracy.

There is a common agenda if we want to enhance development. It is to deepen democracy in part through making use of the tools given us for this in the socio-economic and other rights entrenched, by draft or precedent, in our constitutions. Even the most impoverished (especially the most impoverished) aspire to popular self-government; having achieved this, the prospects for maintaining it are diminished if states are not held accountable for reducing inequality; and that inequality is only reduced through an ongoing struggle protected by entrenched political and socio-economic rights.

References

The Constitution of the Kingdom of Norway, 17 May 1814 and subsequent amendments.

The Constitution of the Republic of South Africa, Act 108 of 1996.

New Programme for Africa's Development (NEPAD), October 2002.

Amadi, S., *Programmatic and Conceptual Paralysis in Protecting and Promoting Economic, Social and Cultural Rights in Africa,* Socio-Economic Rights Project, University of Western Cape, 2002.

Amato, R., "Alarming Saga of Official Delinquency", *Sunday Independent,* Johannesburg, 1 February 2004.

Boyte, H.C., Constructive politics – the contributions of the Institute for Democracy in South Africa (IDASA), IDASA, Cape Town, 2004.

Bruggemans, C., *Change of Pace – South Africa's Economic Revival,* Wits University Press, Johannesburg, 2003.

Budlender, G., *Justiciability of the right to housing – the South African experience,* Paper delivered to Judges workshop, Delhi, 2001.

Carothers, T. "The end of the transition paradigm", *Journal of Democracy,* Vol 13 No. 1, January 2002.

Diamond, L. and Plattner, M.F., (eds.) *The Global Divergence of Democracies,* John Hopkins University Press, Baltimore, 2001.

Haggard, S. and Kaufman, R.R., *The Political Economy of Democratic Transitions,* Princeton University Press, Princeton, 1995.

IDASA. *Power to the people – Reflections on Democracy.* Booklet prepared for 10th anniversary, IDASA, Pretoria, 1997.

Linz, J.J. and Stepan, A., "Towards consolidated democracies", *Journal of Democracy,* Vol 7, No 2.

Mark Malloch-Brown, Foreword to *Human Development Report 2002 – Deepening Democracy in a Fragmented World.* UNDP & Oxford University Press, New York, 2002.

Mattes, R., *Healthy Democracies? The Potential Impact of AIDS on Democracy in Southern Africa,* Institute for Security Studies Paper 71, April 2003.

Michigan State University, Centre for Democratic Development & IDASA. *Democracy and Electoral Alternation: Evolving African Attitudes*, Afrobarometer Briefing Paper No. 9, April 2004.

Michigan State University, Centre for Democratic Development & IDASA. *Poverty, Poverty Measurement and democracy in Southern Africa*, Afrobarometer Briefing Paper No. 9, 2002.

Modderfontein East Squatters, Greater Benoni City Council vs Modderklip Boerdery Case Nos 187/03 and 213/03. Judgement delivered 27 May, 2004.

Przeworski, A., *Democracy and Development: What we know and what we do not.* Department of Politics, New York University. Photocopy, Undated.

Przeworski, A., Alvarez, M.E., Cheibub, J.A., and Limongi, F., "What makes democracies endure" in Diamond L. and Plattner M.F. (eds.) *The Global Divergence of Democracies*, John Hopkins University Press, Baltimore, 2001.

Ringen, S., "Where now, democracy"? *Times Literary Supplement*, 13 February 2003.

SA Human Rights Commission. *4th Annual Economic & Social Rights Report, 2000 – 2002*, SAHRC, Johannesburg, April 2003.

SA Human Rights Commission. *Socio-Economic Rights: Know your rights*, SAHRC, Johannesburg, Undated.

Sachs, A., *Protecting Human Rights in a New South Africa*, Oxford University Press, Cape Town, 1990.

Sen, A., *Development as Freedom*, Anchor Books, New York, 2000

Sen, A., "Democracy as a universal value", *Journal of Democracy*, July 1999.

Joseph T. Siegle, Michael M. Weinstein, and Morton H. Halperin. "Why Democracies Excel", from Foreign Affairs, September/October 2004.

UNDP. *Human Development Report 2002* – Deepening democracy in a fragmented world, UNDP, Oxford University Press, New York, 2002.

About the Contributors

Richard Ballard is a Research Fellow at the Centre for Civil Society and School of Development Studies, University of KwaZulu-Natal. His research interests include refugee social organisation, social movements, urban desegregation, race and identity, and urban governance. He is co-editor of a forthcoming collection on Social Movements in Post-apartheid South Africa. Recent journal articles include: "When in Rome: Claiming the Right to Define the Neighbourhood Character in Post-apartheid South Africa" (*Transformation* 2005) and "The Ant and the Grasshopper: Rationalising Exclusion and Inequality in the Post-apartheid City" (*Theoria* 2004).

Aninka Claassens is a consultant on land issues, who most recently was contracted to the Legal Resources Centre to work on the legal challenge to the Communal Land Rights Act. She has published a number of articles, research reports and book chapters, including "For whites only – land ownership in South Africa", in M. de Klerk (ed.), *A Harvest of Discontent. The Land Question in South Africa* (Idasa 1991) and "South African proposals for tenure reform: the Draft Land Rights Bill", in C. Toulmin and J. Quan (eds.), *Evolving Land Rights, Policy and Tenure in Africa.* (International Institute for Environment and Development and Natural Resources Institute 2000).

Ben Cousins is Director of the Programme for Land and Agrarian Studies, School of Government, University of the Western Cape. He has conducted research on rural social dynamics in Zimbabwe's communal areas and on South Africa's land reform process. He has published a number of articles and books, which include *People, Land and Livestock* (ed.) (University of Zimbabwe 1989); and *At the crossroads: Land and agrarian reform in South Africa into the 21*[st] *century* (ed.) (University of the Western Cape 2000).

Siri Gloppen, is a Researcher in the Department of Comparative Politics, University of Bergen and heads the "Courts in Transition" research programme at the Chr. Michelsen Institute. Her main research interest is the role of courts in political and social transformation in sub-Saharan Africa. She is the author of *South Africa: The Battle Over the Constitution* (Ashgate 1997); and co-editor of *Democratization and the Judiciary: The Accountability Function of Courts in New Democracies* (Frank Cass 2004) and *Roads to Reconciliation* (Lexington Books 2005).

Paul M. Graham is the Executive Director of the Institute for Democracy in South Africa (IDASA) which he joined in 1988 after teaching adult education and community organising at the University of Natal, Durban and Pietermaritzburg. Prior to this he was the elected General Secretary of the Methodist Church of Southern Africa's Christian Education and Youth Department.

Adam Habib is Executive Director (Democracy and Governance) of the Human Sciences Research Council, and a part-time Research Professor in the Centre for Civil Society, and the School of Development Studies, University of Natal. He has published extensively with numerous edited books, book chapters, and national and international journal articles in the areas of democratic transitions, political economy, institutional transformation, higher education reform, and state-civil society relations.

Mark Heywood is the Head of the AIDS Law Project at the Centre for Applied Legal Studies, University of the Witwatersrand. Author of numerous articles on HIV/AIDS, law and human rights, he was recently editor for *From Disaster to Development: HIV and AIDS in Southern Africa* (Development Update, Interfund). He has assisted with the drafting of important human rights documents such as the Southern African Development Community (SADC) Code on HIV/AIDS and Employment, and the United Nations International Guidelines on HIV/AIDS and Human Rights. He is also currently the National Secretary of the Treatment Action Campaign (TAC).

Nina Hunter is a Research Fellow in the School of Development Studies, University of KwaZulu-Natal, where she has undertaken research on South Africa's system of social assistance grants. Her research interests lie in the field of social policy, where she has a particular interest in informal care and social service provision. She was principal researcher on the non-legal component of the South African Social Protection and Expenditure Review, completed for the International Labour Organisation (ILO). More recently she co-led one of the qualitative components of the 2004 KwaZulu-Natal Income Dynamics Study.

Peris Jones is a Research Fellow on the South Africa Programme, Norwegian Centre for Human Rights. His research interests concern the interface between human rights and governance, with emphasis on rights-based struggles over service delivery, particularly in the context of HIV/AIDS. Recent publications include: "'A test of governance': rights-based struggles and the politics of HIV/AIDS policy in South Africa" (*Political Geography* 2005) and "When 'development' devastates: Donor discourses, access to HIV/AIDS treatment and rethinking the landscape of development" (*Third World Quarterly* 2004).

Julian May is the Head of the School of Development Studies at the University of KwaZulu-Natal. He has done extensive research on poverty and inequality in South Africa, including questions of poverty reduction policy options and systems for monitoring the impact of policy, including the social security grants. He has published over 45 papers in books and accredited journals, and produced more than 120 working papers, research reports and other publications.

Mandisa Mbali is an AIDS researcher and activist based at the Centre for Civil Society, University of KwaZulu-Natal. Her research has focused on the history of AIDS policy-making and AIDS activism in South Africa, while her AIDS activism has focused on advocacy for wider access to HIV treatment. Mbali is also a volunteer with the Treatment Action Campaign (TAC). She has published scholarly and journalistic articles dealing with gender and sexuality in the history of AIDS activism, government AIDS denialism and the emergence of the TAC.

Albie Sachs is a Justice of South Africa's Constitutional Court (since 1994). A lawyer and anti-apartheid activist, Sachs is also the author of books on various subjects, including human rights, culture, gender rights, and the environment. His most recent book is *Free Diary of Albie Sachs* (Random House South Africa 2004).

Kristian Stokke is Professor of human geography at the University of Oslo, specialising in movement politics and democratisation in South Africa and ethnic conflict and post-conflict political transformations in Sri Lanka. He has co-edited *Politicising Democracy: The New Local Politics of Democratisation* (Palgrave Macmillan 2004) and co-authored *Building Unity in Diversity: Social Movement Activism in the Western Cape Anti-Eviction Campaign* (University of KwaZulu Natal, Centre for Civil Society 2004) and "uTshani BuyaKhuluma – The Grass Speaks: The Political Space and Capacity of the South African Homeless People's Federation "(*Geoforum* 2003).

Liv Tørres is Associate Professor at the Department of Political Science, University of Oslo and senior adviser at the Research Council of Norway. She has been doing research on labour markets, trade unionism and democratisation in southern Africa for several years with publications such as *Amandla Ngewethu? The Political Role of Labour in South Africa* (University of Oslo 2000); *The Mesebetsi Labour Force Survey* (2002) and *Labour and Social Capital* (2004).

Nijhoff Law Specials

50. K. Wellens (ed.): *Resolutions and Statements of the United Nations Security Council (1946-2000).A Thematic Guide.* 2001 ISBN 90-411-1722-9
51. P. Soar (ed.): *The New International Directory of Legal Aid.* 2001 ISBN 90-411-1718-0
52. C.M. Mazzoni (ed.): *Ethics and Law in Biological Research.* 2002 ISBN 90-411-1742-3
53. I. Omar: *Emergency Powers and the Courts in India and Pakistan.* 2002 ISBN 90-411-1775-X
54. M. O'Flaherty: *Human Rights and the UN: Practice Before the Treaty Bodies.* 2002 ISBN 90-411-1788-1
55. Y. Beigbeder: *Judging Criminal Leaders. The Slow Erosion of Impunity.* 2002 ISBN 90-411-1815-2
56. Marianne van Leeuwen (ed.): *Confronting Terrorism: European Experiences, Threat Perceptions, and Policies.* 2003 ISBN 90-411-1960-4
57. Ralf Bredel: *Long-term Conflict Prevention and Industrial Development: The United Nations and its Specialized Agency, UNIDO.* 2003 ISBN 90-04-13619-3
58. Raphael Walden: *Racism and Human Rights.* 2004 ISBN 90-04-13651-7
59. Monique Leyenaar: *Political Empowerment of Women: The Netherlands and Other Countries.* 2004 ISBN 90-04-14099-9
60. Sjurður Skaale (ed.): *The Right to National Self-Determination: The Faroe Islands and Greenland.* 2004 ISBN 90 04 14207 X
61. Edward McWhinney: *The September 11 Terrorist Attacks and the Invasion of Iraq in Contemporary International Law: Opinions on the Emerging New World Order System.* 2004 ISBN 90 04 14143 X
62. B.G. Ramcharan, *The Protection Role of National Human Rights Institutions.* 2005. ISBN 90 04 14526 5.
63. Chris de Cooker, *Accountability, Investigation and Due Process in International Organizations.* 2005. ISBN 90 04 14793 4.
64. Peris S. Jones & Kristian Stokke, *Democratising Development: The Politics of Socio-Economic Rights in South Africa.* 2005. ISBN 90 04 14821 3.

For more title in this series, consult our web site: **http://www.brill.nl**

MARTINUS NIJHOFF PUBLISHERS — LEIDEN • BOSTON

www.ingramcontent.com/pod-product-compliance
Lightning Source LLC
LaVergne TN
LVHW011116300926
849160LV00008B/409